PROPHECY
at Ground Zero

From Today's
MIDEAST MADNESS
to the SECOND COMING
of CHRIST

STARBURST PUBLISHERS

P.O. Box 4123 Lancaster, PA 17604

www.starburstpublishers.com

CREDITS:
Cover design by Richmond & Williams
Illustrations by Mark Ammerman and Melissa Burkhart
Text design and composition by John Reinhardt Book Design

Unless otherwise indicated all Scripture is taken from the Holy Bible: King James Version.

Other Bible versions used are indicated by the following abbreviations:
American Standard Version of 1901 (ASV)
New American Standard (NAS)
New King James Version (NKJV)

First Printing, October 2002

ISBN 1892016737
Library of Congress Card Number: 2002107875
Printed in the United States of America

Dedicated in memory of Dr. Dave Breese, whose immense God-given talents and eloquence were surpassed only by his love for his Lord, to whom he humbly, yet so powerfully, devoted his life

Contents

SECTION THREE: SECOND COMING COUNTDOWN

Illustrations

Acknowledgments

Of all the books on prophecy with which I have been involved as general editor, this book was, I believe, delayed in its birth by God's hand. Many starts and stops seemed to plague the process as we struggled for the right combination of authors and topics. It has become evident, however, that it was the Lord's perfect timing, not a plague of any sort that delayed *Prophecy at Ground Zero* so it could come forth at this troubling yet exciting time in human history.

The first acknowledgment rightfully belongs to our Lord Jesus Christ, around whom this book revolves. I am thankful to him beyond any words, which no matter their number or high praise would never be adequate.

Second, I am deeply indebted to Angie Peters, my editorial associate and friend who is as close as a daughter, without whom I would not have attempted this special, but intricately involved project. Her superb editorial sense, fast learning, and teaching gifts kept me on course as no other person could.

My thanks to my good friend and Christian brother Dr. Daymond Duck for his considerable part in bringing this project to the publisher, for whom he has been a highly read author for many years.

My thanks to David Robie, president of Starburst Publishers for recognizing this project as worthy of inclusion in Starburst's excellent line of book offerings. His foresight and creativity is on the cutting edge in today's Christian booksellers marketplace, and I'm gratified to have our book be a part of these efforts.

My deep gratitude also to Deb Strubel, Starburst's senior editor, whose experienced guiding hand helped shape and bring the book together in fine fashion.

What can I say to express the depth of my appreciation for my friends who have contributed chapters to this endeavor?

May God reward their tremendous contributions, in so faithfully presenting the message God gave each of them for this turbulent yet exhilarating time.

As always, my love and thanks to Angie's family, Kurt, Nick, Lindsey, and Erin, who were understanding and generous in allowing Angie to devote her indispensable time and attention to this project.

To my wife Margaret, I give my love and thanks for putting up with me yet again while I wrestled in my library office with this book. Also, my love to our boys, Dr. Terry James Jr. and recent college graduate Nathan James.

Finally, my profound, undying thanks to Dr. Dave Breese, who went to be with our Lord on May 3, 2002. I never had a better friend than Dave while I struggled to put these books together over the years. His unmatched eloquence was accompanied by godly wisdom. He exuded an overflowing humor and wit that made working with him a soul-lifting experience. I wish every Christian could have known him.

Looking forward to being with Dave again is one more reason I anticipate the moment Christ says, "Come up hither!"

Introduction

BY WILLIAM T. JAMES

Let's Get Started

Television screens across America and around the world repeatedly flashed images of the huge passenger jets crashing full-throttle into the enormous buildings. Dazed people watched in awestruck disbelief while trapped victims leaped from the top floors of the World Trade Center, some holding hands with others when they jumped. The massive towers crumbled and disintegrated to flaming rubble.

It was the most heinous terrorist attack ever recorded. Almost immediately, angry, frightened people began demanding answers to the insanity now forever etched in their memories.

Many churches were filled the Sunday following the September 11, 2001, attacks in New York City and Washington, D.C. There was an instinctive sense that those murderous acts of terrorism were somehow foreordained—that the carnage known as Ground Zero and the uncertain future was, in some troubling way, linked to prophetic destiny.

TROUBLING QUESTIONS

Prophecy at Ground Zero: From Today's Mideast Madness to the Second Coming of Christ sheds light on and provides answers for the dark, troubling questions that continue to arise from the decimation of September 11, 2001.

Pundits on network and cable news shows have analyzed terrorism, the war on terrorism, and the Palestinian-Israeli conflict from every angle imaginable—except from God's angle. And that's the only one that counts!

The authors of this book have been scrupulously faithful to hold past, present, and prophesied issues and events against the brilliant light of God's prophetic truth found only in the Bible. They have provided a simple, yet forthright and thorough, presentation and analysis of each major prophetic topic covered.

Towers of Pride and Power

The 110-story towers inexplicably symbolized America's great aspirations and achievements. They stood like trophies, seemingly permanent memorial statues to this nation's fantastic accomplishments during the past century.

They gave us a sense of strength and security similar to that provided by the mighty, nuclear-tipped missiles in their launching silos that targeted our enemies during the cold war. The twin towers seemed to assure economic well-being, much like those sleek, powerful weapons of unimaginable destruction assured us that no one would be foolish enough to attack us.

The illusion of America's invulnerability to attack by foreign powers crumbled with the disintegrating buildings on September 11. No one who began his or her morning journey on the elevators inside the World Trade Towers anticipated the horrors the radical Islamic terrorists would shortly inflict.

Two Journeys

Like those in the World Trade Towers on the morning of September 11, 2001, people alive today face unknown peril. Unseen danger could strike at any moment. Against such there is most often no time to anticipate or prepare.

Just as the unsuspecting people who rode the elevators to the top floors of the towers couldn't know what they faced, most people today are unaware that they are about to undertake a journey of great consequence. This biblically prophesied truth involves two distinct peoples and two distinct journeys.

One journey will move its travelers beyond time and space

in less than a fraction of a second. These people will experience thrilling wonders throughout an eternal sphere, exponentially exceeding anything encountered by the first moon walkers. They will take a trip to heaven called the **Rapture**!

The other journey will take its travelers, a short time from now, through a series of terror-filled circumstances. Their terror will be more horrific than that suffered by the people in the twin towers. The second group's destination is the **tribulation era**, or **apocalypse**.

THE FUTURE OF TERRORISM

The movie *2001: A Space Odyssey* thrust people who watched it into a future time when machines control human beings. God's Word, which <u>cannot lie</u>, warns of entities far worse than those machine tyrants depicted in the movies. Even a million Osama bin Ladens and a billion terrorists could not wreak greater havoc upon the world. God's prophetic Word forewarns that demons, led by Satan and his ultimate dictator, the **Antichrist**, will force their victims to endure a horrific seven-year journey through hell on earth. We call that journey the apocalypse or tribulation period.

KEY TERMS

Rapture: *when believers since Pentecost are taken to heaven*

tribulation era: *seven years of great trouble*

apocalypse: *another word for the tribulation era*

Antichrist: *evil dictator who opposes and imitates Christ*

FURTHER STUDY

Jeremiah 30:7
   (tribulation era)
Titus 1:2 (cannot lie)
2 Timothy 3:1–3 (worse)

Prophecy at Ground Zero

The crumbling of the World Trade Towers, the suicide bombings, the growing threat of all-out war between Israel and her neighbors are like rings of a bull's-eye on the target of Bible prophecy about to be fulfilled. Terrorism, as insane and horrible as it is today, is foretold to get infinitely <u>worse</u>. This scourge in today's world represents a threat as great as the thermonuclear-laden missiles still directed at the population centers of earth.

Fear grows daily that Mideast terrorists are close to developing the means to deliver atomic weapons upon those they hate. Israel is the nation sitting at the center of the bull's-eye in the terrorists' murderous war strategy. Israel is Ground Zero.

1 Thessalonians 4:17 Then we who are

alive and remain shall be caught up together with them in the clouds to meet the Lord in the air; and so shall we ever be with the Lord.

The Ultimate Trip

Humankind is and has been rushing headlong down the wide, slippery slope that leads to destruction. In this end-of-the-age time frame is a narrow gateway of escape—a high road, though a narrow one, that leads to eternal life. This road of righteousness has a name above all other names: Jesus Christ.

All who call upon Jesus' name in **repentance** of sin, trusting him for salvation, are turned in a new, upward direction toward God the Father.

The true child of the living God is assured that he or she will not have to endure the coming journey of terror. Rather, the Christian will experience the ultimate trip. The journey into heaven, whether through the portal called death or through the most spectacular space launch ever called the Rapture, will be magnificent beyond all other human experiences.

The apostle Paul tells the Christian, "We shall not all sleep, but we shall all be changed, in a moment, in the twinkling of an eye" (1 Corinthians 15:51b–52a). Then Christians who are alive will be drawn up into the air to meet Jesus and spend eternity with him.

It is the prayer of each contributing author to *Prophecy at Ground Zero* that the readers of this book accept the Holy Spirit's call to Christ, the blessed hope. Prophetic signals suggest that the window of opportunity is wide open for the most stupendous space launch ever to lift off planet Earth. Don't be left behind!

KEY TERM

repentance: *turning from sin to Christ for salvation*

FURTHER STUDY

Titus 2:13 (blessed hope)

PROPHESIED MIDEAST AND WORLD PROBLEMS

End-Time Target Earth

BY WILLIAM T. JAMES

Let's Get Started

Planet Earth sits in the crosshairs of prophetic destiny. Most all signs in God's Word indicate that this might well be the final generation before Christ's Second Coming. Major signals of prophetic importance are happening around us as we sit atop the rocket of history ready to pierce the end of the age and the coming new world.

KEY TERMS

Olivet Discourse: *Jesus' message about end-time matters*

seventieth week: *last seven years before Jesus' Second Coming*

Daniel: *Old Testament prophet known for surviving the lion's den and for interpreting dreams*

FURTHER STUDY

Matthew 24, Mark 13, Luke 21 (Olivet Discourse)
Daniel 9:24–27 (seventieth week)

END-TIME TURBULENCE

Jesus Christ said in his **Olivet Discourse** that end-time events would come upon people like birth pangs. He prophesied signals that will be so obvious there could be no mistaking them. The last seven years of this age will produce trauma for mankind beyond any in recorded history. The last three and one-half of those final seven years will witness the deaths of more than half the world's population.

That era, called Daniel's **seventieth week**, was

mentioned by **Daniel** the prophet. He said it would be marked by certain characteristics involving most every aspect of human activity. Specifically, economics, culture, government, and religion will become arranged in a particular configuration.

1 Timothy 6:10 For the love of money is the root of all evil. . . .

Cultural and Economic Factors

Few would dispute that the lust for money is among the most natural of human desires, particularly in our affluent culture.

> **KEY TERMS**
>
> **comportment:** behavior; attitude
> **beast:** another term for the Antichrist

Money and power are, if not synonymous, certainly on equal footing in Western societies today. Money and power give influence to those who garner these things to themselves. While it is true that there have been men and women with both money and power who have been generous and godly in **comportment**, they are rare exceptions. Money, power, control, that is, economics, is and will be the fuel at the end of this age that energizes and gives thrust to the engines of society, government, and religion.

PROPHECY TO WATCH FOR

Ultimately, one man—the Antichrist—will grab and clutch all wealth and power in an iron-fisted grip of absolute control: "And he causeth all, both small and great, rich and poor, free and enslaved, to receive a mark in their right hand, or in their foreheads, And that no man might buy or sell, except he that had the mark, or the name of the **beast**, or the number of his name" (Revelation 13:16–17).

Daniel 9:26 And after threescore and two weeks shall Messiah be cut off, but not for himself; and the people of the prince that shall come shall destroy the city and the sanctuary, and the end of it shall be with a flood, and unto the end of the war desolations are determined.

Government

No more profound signals point to the soon return of Jesus Christ than the geopolitical realities of our day. Those realities, combined with all other prophetic signals that we are seeing, validate the angel's prophecy given to Daniel.

The prophetic flood of issues and events deluge our generation. All seem to be sweeping us toward the time of the Antichrist.

The prophet Daniel's foretelling of the Antichrist's end-time governmental structure seems to have leaped onto the pages of recent history with the forming of the **Club of Rome** in 1957. From that consortium has developed the **European Union** and, in effect, the international community—the nondescript beast of controlling authority that continues to rear its head whenever smaller, weaker nations get out of line.

World Antichrist Mindset

The United Nations seems to be the leading candidate to house the Antichrist spirit indwelling those internationalists who would be masters of the world. To be sure, anyone making such conjecture is automatically branded with the conspiracy "nut" or "kook" label. However, to be so designated when one's **eschatological** analysis is scripturally and spiritually grounded firmly in God's Word only adds credence and strength to the effort involved in trying to forewarn.

"There shall come in the last days scoffers," the apostle Peter wrote, "walking after their own lusts, And saying, 'Where is the promise of his coming?'" (2 Peter 3:3–4).

Under Lucifer's Influence

Americans watch daily, even hourly, as the power brokers of world geopolitics go about their business of enslaving us all. Most of the new world order elitists truly believe they are doing God a service. At least they think they are doing good for all humankind.

But as we become increasingly desensitized to

KEY TERMS

Club of Rome: *European countries joined in an economic pact*

European Union: *group of European nations*

eschatological: *pertaining to end-time matters*

FURTHER STUDY

Daniel 2
(governmental
structure)

spreading, intertwined governmental control, we lose the ability to discern right from wrong. Our minds, under **Luciferian** influence, accept the media lies that the pursuit of world peace must override all other **exigencies**.

God's Word warns specifically, "For when they shall say, Peace and safety; then sudden destruction cometh upon them, as travail upon a woman with child; and they shall not escape" (1 Thessalonians 5:3).

CURRENT WORLD EVENTS

Although these would-be saviors of the planet usually remain cloaked in secretive governmental, international business, and academic **enclaves**, their drive toward one-world order becomes visible through forums like the one held in September 2000.

Termed the Millennium Summit, the series of meetings that began September 6, 2000, had as its first speaker of consequence—the President of the United States. What did Bill Clinton make his clarion call to this world body of **globalists**? You guessed it! He called for unprecedented efforts to bring peace to the planet.

Preceding that world summit, the United Nations' Millennium Forum was held May 22–26, 2000, in response to UN Secretary-General Kofi Annan's summer of 1997 call for the Global People's Assembly. The meeting was subsequently renamed the Millennium Forum.

The approximately 1,350 representatives present at the meetings claimed to bring with them the majority views and wishes of their national **constituencies**, according to Gary Kah, a researcher and author who delves into the globalist agenda.

> **KEY TERMS**
>
> **Luciferian:** *devilish, satanic*
> **exigencies:** *needs, demands*
> **enclaves:** *small, secretive groups*
> **globalists:** *people who want one-world government*
> **constituencies:** *voters, citizens*

What Others are Saying:

Gary Kah: They are trying to create the impression that the people of the world want these changes that the United Nations is about to trounce upon us . . . But in reality . . . there was no true representation of the world in attendance. There comes a point that if they want to make world government a reality, they have to go public with it. . . . And I think we're right at that point where that is beginning to happen.[1]

Has the war on terrorism, resulting from the New York City and Washington, D.C. attacks, put the globalist agenda on the fast track? This is not to criticize President George W. Bush and his tremendous efforts. Clearly, something must be done to deal with the Osama bin Ladens and Saddam Husseins of the world. The swiftly moving tide of internationalist interventions into the affairs of sovereign nations, however, might quickly become the vehicle that installs the Antichrist **regime**. Rumblings from within the circles of the internationalist power elite seem to be directed more and more toward forcing Israel to come to the peace table with an enemy that wants nothing less than Israel's total destruction.

> **KEY TERMS**
>
> *regime:* administration, establishment
> *jihad:* holy war

REMEMBER THIS

The bloody terrorist suicide bombings in Jerusalem and other cities are aimed at the Jews—the nation of Israel. Despite what Palestinian Authority Chairman Yasser Arafat says to the media, he and most every Arab Islamic leader talk to their own people about **jihad** against the Jews and Israel, whom they hate.

On December 1, 2001, following four suicide bombings the night before, former Prime Minister Benjamin Netanyahu accused the Palestinian leadership of actually training children from kindergarten to be suicide bombers. If that is true, how can Israel ever come to terms of peace with such madness?

Revelation 13:15 And he hath power to give life unto the image of the beast, that the image of the beast should both speak, and cause that as many as would not worship the image of the beast should be killed.

Religion

The elite in favor of globalism tell us that mankind's magnificent self-charted odyssey cannot begin successfully until unity is achieved. We must, like the songs "Imagine" and "We Are the World," proclaim unity to build a better world.

The globalists intend to use religion as the catalyst to galvanize all peoples into one world village. Religion is the common denominator that can negate the divisions between us. They believe religious differences are the root cause of wars, especially the ancient feud between Arab Muslims and Jews. Forcing all belief systems into a single theological worldview is the answer, they believe.

John 14:6 I am the way, the truth, and the life; no man cometh unto the Father, but by me.

No Compromise

True Christianity cannot join or fuse with one or all of the world's religions. All roads do not lead to the true God. Jesus Christ is the only true God. His shed blood on the cross at Calvary is the one and only cure for the sin of fallen man and the only road to God.

Christianity blocks the pathway upon which the global elitists intend to begin mankind's odyssey into their self-realized utopia. One result of the September 2000 Millennium Summit seems to be this push toward one-world religion. Once all or most religions have been forced into the global mold, more grandiose plans are in the offing for the citizens of the world.

CURRENT WORLD EVENTS

In his book, *The New World Religion*, Gary Kah presents the text from the one-world passport. Kah quotes the portion of the passport that includes the **credo** to which the world citizen must agree and by which he must abide: "As a world citizen, I affirm my commitment to world government founded on three universal principles of one absolute value, one world and one humanity which constitutes the basis for world law. As a world citizen, I acknowledge the world government as having the right and duty to represent me and all that concerns the general good of humankind and the good of all. . . ."[2]

KEY TERM

credo: philosophy

NATIONS IN PROPHECY

Signals of where this generation stands on God's prophetic timeline can be seen in literally every direction the interested observer cares to look. The nations of prophecy—Israel, Russia, China, European Union, and Babylon—are chief among these signals.

Israel

From God's perspective, Israel is clearly the most important nation on planet Earth. Israel comes into view early in the Bible through Jacob the **patriarch** and is commissioned for specific prophetic purposes. The nation is dealt with in great depth throughout the Scriptures, particularly as human history climaxes in the Book of Revelation. Daily news accounts coming out of Israel and the Middle East often appear to be prophecy unfolding from the pages of the Bible.

No singular national entity referenced in God's Word more profoundly points to how far the world has gone toward God's judgment than does contemporary Israel. More particularly, the Mideast peace process gives the prophecy student a pinpoint issue of astounding significance to consider as we near the end of this **age of grace**.

Russia

The Russian government's controversial actions in August 2000 involving the sunken submarine *Kursk* clearly showed the world that the former Soviet Union was technologically unable to cope with such emergencies.

Since the Soviet Union's **dissolution**, most of Russia has gone ever deeper into depression, economic and otherwise. The citizens, freed to some extent from the oppressive communist controls, continue to air complaints and demand an improved way of life.

President Vladimir Putin, a proud, tough former communist with close ties to Russian military interests, was severely stung by criticisms in his perceived disinterest in the fate of the submariners

---

KEY TERMS

patriarch: *founding father in God's redemptive plan*

age of grace: *church age*

dissolution: *ending; disbanding*

FURTHER STUDY

Genesis 28:10–16 (Jacob)

trapped in their ship. The accident occurred while he was on vacation somewhere along the Black Sea coast, and he failed to return immediately to Moscow or to visit the site of the accident. Russia repeatedly refused offers of help from around the world.

Considering the pressures that were brought to bear upon Putin, who many say tends to be militant in his outlook, one wonders what circumstances could push him to thrust his nation toward aggression. Would he want to achieve victory for his military friends and spoils to prove his worth to the Russian people?

Putin and Russia recently began to put their best foot forward. They almost eagerly embraced the U.S. war on terrorism termed Operation Enduring Freedom. The Russian leader threw Russia's diplomatic arms around the United States and the other coalition partners, joining in the efforts against bin Laden, the Taliban, and Al Qaida. He allowed U.S. forces to stage military strikes from a former Soviet republic, and even gave weapons and uniforms to the forces opposing the Taliban.

KEY POINT

Despite the dissolution of the Soviet Union, Russia is still aggressive in nature.

Once the Taliban were on the run, however, the Russians rolled into Afghanistan without UN permission, and without warning.[3] The press and the State Department made little note of it because the Bush administration was busy building a coalition. The Russian bear has changed nothing but its name. Its nature remains aggressive and dangerous.

China and the Asian Nations

Despite its economic overtures to the United States and western Europe, communist China moves ever closer to complete dominance over nations east of the Euphrates River.

Recent alleged thefts and bribes by the Chinese involving some of America's most sophisticated weapons technology point to a troubling future for the world.

With China's surreptitious acquisitions of advanced weapons technology, how can America proceed in developing relations with it without trepidation? The fact that China is well on its way to becoming a world-class intercontinental ballistic missile nuclear power is legitimate cause for alarm.

China could field a land force of 200 million people today. Revelation 9:16 mentions an army of that size controlled by the kings of the East. While that great conflict is still considerably in the prophetic future, China's threat is a real and growing one.

According to some experts, China might initiate a conflict with Taiwan at any time. America, in such case, could do little to prevent China from overrunning that island. America's naval presence is almost nonexistent in the Straits separating the two enemies, and it is conjectured that nuclear force would be the only option available if China made such a move.

Reliable sources report that China has surface-to-surface missiles with a range of more than 375 miles positioned along its western coast pointed toward Taiwan. Tensions are high, and anything can happen at any time.

European Union

The economic union of Europe makes it potentially, if not in fact, the most powerful influence on earth today. At the same time, Europe is progressing on many fronts in establishing itself as the ten-toe power sphere prophesied in Daniel 2.

The revived Roman Empire will give its power and authority to the <u>beast</u>, also known as the Antichrist. That increasing power could be detected in Europe's threatening of the Kosovars in the recent Balkan conflict.

> KEY TERM
> *euro: unit of currency*
>
> FURTHER STUDY
> **Revelation 17:12–13 (beast)**

The powerful heads of Europe, aided and abetted by the Clinton Administration—proceeding under the unofficial banner termed the "international community"—intervened with NATO's forces into the sovereign affairs of another nation. Whether one agrees with one antagonist or the other in the conflict, the vicious bombings by the intervening world police force set a troubling precedent. Truly, with the introduction of the **euro** in January 2002, the European Union is developing at a torrid pace.

Jeremiah 50:9–14 For, lo, I will raise and cause to come up against Babylon an assembly of great nations from the north country: and they shall set themselves in array against her; from thence she shall be taken: their arrows shall be as of a mighty expert man; none shall return in vain. And Chaldea shall be a spoil: all that spoil her shall be satisfied, saith the Lord. Because ye were glad, because ye rejoiced, O ye destroyers of mine heritage, because ye are grown fat as the heifer at grass, and bellow as bulls; Your mother shall be sore confounded; she that bare you shall be ashamed: behold, the hindermost of the nations shall be a wilderness, a dry land, and a desert. Because of the wrath of the Lord it shall not be inhabited, but it shall be wholly desolate: every one that goeth by Babylon shall be astonished, and hiss at all her plagues. Put yourselves in array against Babylon round about: all ye that bend the bow, shoot at her, spare no arrows: for she hath sinned against the Lord.

Back to Babylon

Humankind's attention is again focusing on the area of the world where **Nimrod** was first thought to, like Lucifer, play God by establishing government totally apart from the Lord's controlling hand.

The international community, led by the United States, again looks with concern at the dictator Saddam Hussein and his mischief making. The Iraqi tyrant is not only thought to sponsor many of the most violent terrorist organizations on the planet but also is believed to have weapons of mass destruction—chemical, biological, and nuclear. He has, on many occasions, promised to use them against Israel, which he hates with satanic force. Something must be done to prevent Saddam from developing further capabilities of that terrifying sort.

KEY TERM

Nimrod: *Babylonian king; leader in the tower of Babel enterprise*

FURTHER STUDY
Genesis 10:8–10 (Nimrod)

Many prophecy watchers find it fascinating to ponder whether this volatile region is preparing for the rebuilding of a literal end-time city called "Babylon the Great." Such an entity, whether a literal city where ancient Babylon once sat (see illustration below) or a great economic system symbolized as a Babylon-type center, is prophesied in Revelation 17 and 18. The Bible says this great commercial and religious structure will be completely destroyed.

Certainly, if the ancient site is to be the location of the end-time place called Babylon in Bible prophecy, Saddam Hussein and his despotic regime must be removed.

Jeremiah 50 contains prophecy that has not been totally fulfilled, although the Gulf War of 1991 was, at the time, thought to be the possible prelude to fulfillment.

Present-day Iraq has never been rendered uninhabitable, as the prophecy in Jeremiah 50 says, so we know the prediction has not yet come to pass. Is the present gathering of coalition forces to remove Hussein possibly that force of nations prophesied to begin clearing the way so that end-time Babylon can be rebuilt?

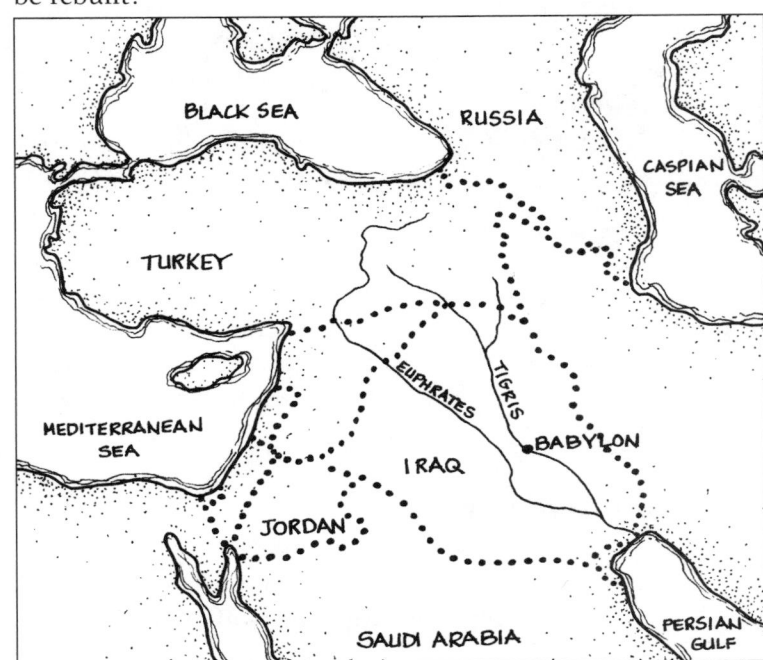

Map of Babylon

This map shows the location of the Old Testament city of Babylon by the Euphrates River. Present-day Iraq includes this ancient site.

In Satan's Bombsight

The indicators in these troubled days that are convulsing the world like the labor pains of an expectant mother point to the prophetic truth of our time. Israel and all the world is in Satan's crosshairs. This generation might well witness the prophesied launching of his last-days missiles of hatred.

Fortunately, Christians have the great promise of "that blessed hope, and the glorious appearing of the great God and our Savior, Jesus Christ" (Titus 2:13). We might be the generation that will experience a launch of another sort: the launch into the heavenlies, when Jesus calls, "Come up here" (Revelation 4:1). This launch is called the Rapture.

THE BLESSED HOPE

Some scoff at "Rapture teaching" as escapism. They mockingly imply that real saints of God must stand during the time of Tribulation and wash their robes white by that mighty deed. By so doing they will have proved themselves worthy to stand in the presence of the Lord when the **apocalyptic** smoke clears.

But God's Word tells us that the Christian alive at the end of the age should be looking for something other than for the Tribulation, the Antichrist, and all other horrors associated with that prophesied time.

> **KEY TERMS**
>
> **apocalyptic:** *related to the end times*
> **purifies:** *makes righteous*
> **wrath of God:** *God's judgment for sin*

Titus 2:13–14 Looking for that blessed hope, and the glorious appearing of the great God and our Saviour Jesus Christ; Who gave himself for us, that he might redeem us from all iniquity, and purify unto himself a peculiar people, zealous of good works.

Kept from God's Wrath

Jesus Christ is the Savior who **purifies** the Christian. It is the Lord from heaven to whom Christians must look for salvation from the **wrath of God**, which is what the Tribulation is all about. Christ <u>saves</u> us from God's wrath, which comes as a result of unforgiven sin. Only belief in and acceptance of **Christ's sacrifice** on the cross of **Calvary** can bring forgiveness and **redemption**.

Matthew 16:13–18 When Jesus came into the coasts of Caesarea Philippi, he asked his disciples, saying, Whom do men say that I the Son of man am? And they said, Some say that thou art John the Baptist: some, Elias; and others, Jeremias, or one of the prophets. He saith unto them, But whom say ye that I am? And Simon Peter answered and said, Thou art the Christ, the Son of the living God. And Jesus answered and said unto him, Blessed art thou, Simon Barjona: for flesh and blood hath not revealed it unto thee, but my Father which is in heaven. And I say also unto thee, That thou art Peter, and upon this rock I will build my church; and the gates of hell shall not prevail against it.

KEY TERMS

Christ's sacrifice: *death on the cross*

Calvary: *place where Jesus was crucified*

redemption: *God's purchase of sinners; salvation*

church age: *time from Pentecost to the Rapture*

born again: *born spiritually into God's family*

FURTHER STUDY

1 Thessalonians 5:9;
    Revelation 3:10 (saves)
John 3:3–21; 1 Peter 1:23
    (born again)

Who Is the Church?

The question "Who is the church?" is a proper one. The church, in God's eyes is not a "what," but a "who." Jesus clearly says that his church is a distinct group of people, individuals, who believe that he is the Son of the living God. These individuals that comprise the church are, and will continue to be throughout the **church age**, those he later describes as being "**born again**."

Jesus is building his church with people who fully accept God's loving sacrifice for the forgiveness of sin and the redemption of all human beings. Jesus' death on the cross, burial, and resurrection is the foundational gospel truth upon which Christ's church stands.

Dispensational Viewpoint

Prophecy at Ground Zero is presented from a dispensational viewpoint. "**Dispensation**" simply means "era" or "time frame." God's Word deals with several dispensations, such as the Creation, the Flood, the time of the patriarchs, the law (Moses' time), and so forth.

The church age is a dispensation. The church age is sometimes referred to as the "dispensation of grace" or the "age of grace." This means it is a period of time during which God redeems sinful people based upon belief in and acceptance of the death, burial, and resurrection of his only **begotten** son, Jesus Christ, for the **remission** of the deadly soul disease known as sin.

The church age began at Pentecost when Christ sent the **Holy Spirit** to live within believers. The church age will conclude when the **Rapture** takes place. The Rapture will be the stunning moment when Jesus calls all who have lived or are living during the church age to meet him above planet Earth. He will then take them to God the Father's house—heaven—to live with him forever.

Rapture Views

There are three main viewpoints on the Rapture of the church and the Tribulation (see illustrations, page 22). They can be confusing, to say the least.

Although it is okay to read and listen to what different people holding the various views of the Rapture have to say on the subject, Christians should read and study the Bible for themselves and ask the Holy Spirit to give them **discernment**.

One view holds that the church will be raptured before the Tribulation. This view is called the pre-Tribulation view. A second view says the Rapture of the church will occur following the seven years of Tribulation. This view is called post-Tribulation view.

Today, most teaching within Christianity puts forward the

KEY TERMS

dispensation: *era or time period*

begotten: *fathered*

remission: *cure of*

Holy Spirit: *third member of the Godhead*

Rapture: *believers since Pentecost taken to heaven at Christ's return*

discernment: *understanding*

FURTHER STUDY

Acts 2:1–12 (Pentecost)
1 Corinthians 15:55–58; 1
    Thessalonians 4:13–18
    (Rapture)
John 14:1–4
    (Father's house)

mid-Tribulation Rapture viewpoint. This presents the Rapture of the church taking place somewhere near the middle point of the seven-year tribulation period. This view is held mostly by those who accept the **premillennial** viewpoint.

To confuse things even further, there are other views within both the mid-Tribulation and pre-Tribulation schools of belief. Some believe in a "progressive" Rapture (the belief that several Raptures take place in stages throughout the Tribulation). Some believe the Rapture will take place prior to the Tribulation but that only Christians living holy lives will be taken. This is most often referred to as the "split Rapture" or "partial Rapture."

One other view that has gained prominence is the pre-wrath Rapture. This view proposes that the church will be removed before the second three and one-half years of the Tribulation. This view holds that Jesus referred to the last half of the Tribulation as a time of "Great Tribulation." The pre-wrath Rapture proponents believe that God's wrath doesn't begin until midway through the seven-year period of the Tribulation. They believe Christians will not be facing God's wrath, but manmade wrath, in the first half of the Tribulation.

Prophecy at Ground Zero presents the Rapture from the pre-Tribulation viewpoint. God's Word teaches that Jesus will call all believers of the church age, both living and dead, to meet him in the air prior to the beginning of the seven-year tribulation period. Thus, we will be <u>forever with</u> the Lord. We believe this truth is given by God in order that we know about the Rapture and <u>take comfort</u> from his words in these prophesied troubled times.

> **KEY TERM**
>
> ***premillennial:*** *Jesus will return and then rule one thousand years on earth*
>
> **FURTHER STUDY**
>
> 1 Thessalonians 4:16–17 (forever with)
> 1 Thessalonians 4:18 (take comfort)
> Revelation 19:11–16 (Second Coming)

Three Different Views of the Millennium

There are also three different views about when Jesus Christ will return to earth in what is called the Second Advent or Second Coming and set up his throne on earth and reign one thousand years. A millennium is one thousand years.

Christ's <u>Second Coming</u> is the moment when he will return to earth, leading his heavenly armies. He will come to put an

Rapture Theories

Pre-Tribulation Rapture

The church is raptured before the tribulation period.

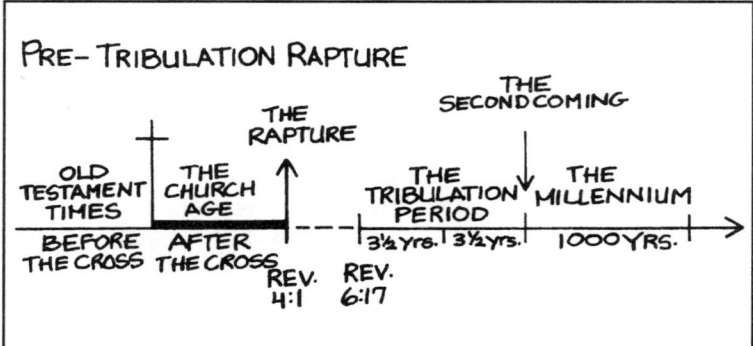

Mid-Tribulation Rapture

The church is raptured in the middle of the tribulation period.

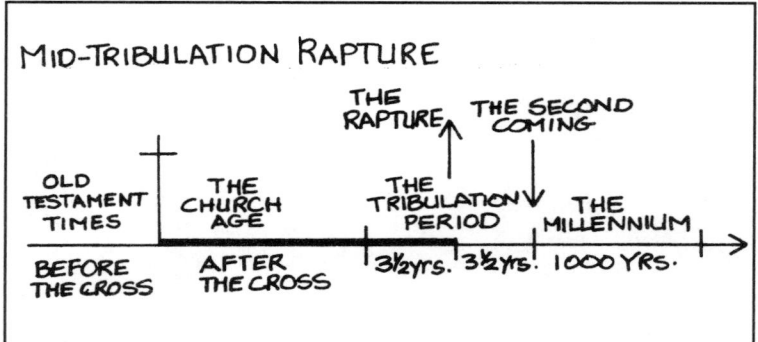

Post-Tribulation Rapture

The church is raptured after the tribulation period.

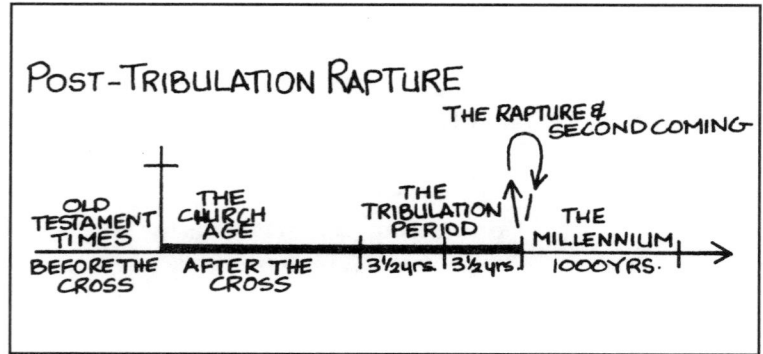

end to man's great conflict termed **Armageddon** and to establish his **millennial throne** on earth. This occurs at the end of the **Tribulation**, which is also called Daniel's seventieth week.

Each of the three theories says there is a Second Coming, but each disagrees about when it will take place. Each view agrees that believers will spend eternity with God. Here are the three main views on the Millennium and Christ's Second Coming:

1. Premillennial view proposes that Jesus will return before his one-thousand-year rule on earth.
2. Postmillennial view says that Jesus will return following a one-thousand-year period of peace on earth, which the church will produce.
3. Amillennial view says there will be no one-thousand-year reign of Christ on earth. Many people who believe this view think the Rapture and the Second Coming are one event.

Millennium Theories

Millennium Theories	Church Age	Rapture	Tribulation	Millennium
Premillennial view	Now	Before Tribulation	After Rapture	Second Coming ushers in kingdom with Jesus on throne in Jerusalem
Postmillennial view	Now and getting better	None	Not applicable	Before the Second Coming
Amillennial view	Now	Occurs with the Second Coming	Not applicable	No earthly kingdom

HEADLINE

HIGHLIGHT

Time On Line

Times Newspapers Ltd.

June 03, 2002

Terror War Must Target 60 Nations, Says Bush

By James Doran

THE United States must be prepared to take the War on Terror to up to 60 countries if weapons of mass destruction are to be kept out of terrorists' hands, President Bush said at the weekend.

His impassioned speech to 1,000 graduates of West Point Military Academy in New York State on Saturday marks a watershed in the Administration's foreign policy.

Mr. Bush said that terrorism cells in countries that make up close to one third of the globe must be actively sought and dismantled. "We must take that battle to the enemy, disrupt his plans and confront the worst threats before they emerge," he said, adding that Americans must be "ready for pre-emptive action when necessary to defend our liberty and to defend our lives."

He said: "In the world we have entered, the only path to safety is the path of action. And this nation will act." . . .

"(Containment) is not possible when unbalanced dictators with weapons of mass destruction can deliver those weapons on missiles or can provide them to terrorist allies," he said.

The criticism of foreign countries appeared to go further than any other he has made since September 11. "Some nations need military training to fight terror and we will provide it," Mr. Bush said. "Other nations oppose terror but tolerate the hatred that leads to terror and that must change." White House officials told The Washington Post that these comments were directed at Middle East allies such as Saudi Arabia and Jordan.

If the United States decides to make surprise strikes on other countries, it will mark a big change in strategy for the US military, which traditionally acts only in self-defence . . .

Mr. Bush said that America's foreign policy would have three strands. "We will defend the peace against threats from terrorists and tyrants. We will preserve the peace by building good relations among the great powers. And we will extend the peace by encouraging free and open societies on every continent."

He said that the conflict the graduates would be required to fight would differ greatly from that fought by their forefathers in Japan and Europe. "Enemies in the past needed great armies and great industrial capabilities to endanger the American people and our nation," Mr. Bush said. "The attacks of September 11 required a few hundred thousand dollars in the hands of a few dozen evil and deluded men. All of the chaos and suffering they caused came at much less than the cost of a single tank."

Abdul Rahman Yassin, one of the men accused of bombing the World Trade Centre in 1993, planned to attack New York's biggest Jewish districts, but his cohorts decided that more Jews would be killed if the Twin Towers were destroyed, according to CBS news. The station said that the bomber had told them that he was talked into the attack as revenge for "my Palestinian brothers and my brothers in Saudi Arabia."

PROPHETIC IMPACT

Although President George W. Bush is doing all he can in the war on terror, Americans are frequently told to expect terrorist attacks as bad or worse than the September 11 attack on New York and Washington, D.C.

Bible prophecy makes it clear that "evil men and seducers will grow worse and worse" (2 Timothy 3:13). Jesus declared that men's hearts will fail "them for fear, and for looking after those things which are coming on the earth" (Luke 21:26).

Fearful things are prophesied to befall this judgment-bound planet. Those horrors are for the Tribulation rather than for this church age, even though we are already experiencing near-apocalyptic atrocities. This is because Satan and his henchmen, both human and supernatural (fallen angels and demons) are stepping up their assault on God's creation called humans.

Lucifer is targeting planet Earth! One day he will deceive almost the whole world by offering a politician-superman who will guarantee peace and safety for terrified people around the globe.

These promises will soon turn to terror much greater than the current Mideast terrorists are inflicting. "For when they [humans during the Tribulation] shall say, peace and safety; then sudden destruction cometh" (1 Thessalonians 5:3).

CHAPTER WRAP-UP

- Many signs in God's Word seem to indicate that this is the final generation before Christ's Second Coming.

- Jesus prophesied that the generation alive just before his return will witness the most troubled times of earth's history. Jesus said we will recognize his coming is near because of specific events and issues.

- Prophecies indicate that money and its use for control will be the drive for a one-world governmental system. That system will come under the rule of the Antichrist.

- The prophet Daniel's foretelling of the Antichrist's end-time governmental structure seems to have begun with the forming of the Club of Rome in 1957. From that developed the European Union and the international community.

- Most of the new world order elitists think they are doing good for all humankind. They are actually carrying out Satan's conspiracy to bring the Antichrist to power.

- People today become desensitized to the constant assault on their liberty.

- The bloody terrorist suicide bombings in Jerusalem and other cities are aimed at the Jews—the nation of Israel. Most Arab Islamic leaders talk to their people about jihad against the Jews and Israel, whom they hate.

- Out of all the terrorism perpetrated by Islamic fanatics has come the cry from the media and global leaders for the coming together of all religions in tolerance and acceptance.

- While Christians are commanded to love all people, Christianity cannot share common principles with ungodly religious systems. Jesus Christ is the only true God. His shed blood is the cure for the sin of fallen man.

- Nations prophesied to be at the forefront when Christ's coming nears are now in the news on a regular basis.

- The Rapture of the church must be very near, considering all the prophetic signals appearing on the world's horizon today.

- All Christians will be called into heaven before God's wrath falls upon earth. No Christians will be left behind.

Israel at Ground Zero

Citizens of Israel: The state of Israel is in a war, a war against terrorism. This is a war that was imposed on us. It is not a war that we decided to embark upon. This is a war over our home.
—ISRAELI PRIME MINISTER ARIEL SHARON

BY ZOLA LEVITT WITH LAWRENCE FORD

Let's Get Started

For most citizens of the world, September 11, 2001, marked the beginning of the war on terrorism. The murder of over three thousand men, women, and children in New York, Washington, D.C., and Pennsylvania by Islamic radicals created in us all a new fear—the fear of the terrorist. But for the state of Israel, the war on terrorism did not begin in 2001; it started decades before at the birth of the Jewish state.

Matthew 24:9 Then they will deliver you to tribulation, and will kill you, and you will be hated by all nations . . .

ISRAEL'S AMAZING SURVIVAL

Whether attacked by Arab nations or Arab suicide bombers, Israel has defended itself like no other nation on earth in a seemingly unending struggle that continues to threaten its very existence.

How has Israel survived until now? Will the Palestinian Authority succeed in its mission to destroy the Jewish people? Do the Arab nations genuinely want peace with Israel once and for all? Has the United States turned its back on God's **chosen people**? What is the role of the church today in relation to Israel? How does Bible prophecy detail the current state of the Jewish nation as well as its eventual restoration?

Fighting for Survival

At the close of World War II, the land of Israel was finally recognized as the ancestral home of the Jewish people and eventually returned to them by the foreign powers that had conquered it. But on May 15, 1948, just one day after the state of Israel was established, this infant democracy began to fight for its survival as Egypt, Jordan, Syria, Lebanon, and Iraq crossed its borders in an attempt to push the Jewish people into the sea. The War of Independence ended some fifteen months later with the Arab armies retreating in defeat. Over six thousand Israeli lives were lost as a result. And this was just the beginning of Israel's "war on terrorism."

The Six Day War

Continued assaults by Arab terrorists across Israel's borders eventually led to the Six Day War in June 1967, in which the hostile armies of Egypt, Syria, and Jordan attacked Israel once again. At the end of six days of fighting, not only had Israel defended its borders but also had captured additional land from those nations—land that historically had been a possession of Israel for thousands of years.

The Yom Kippur War

Israel's Arab neighbors remained angry over the existence of the Jewish state. So Israel became the target of yet another unprovoked war in 1973 when it was caught off guard by an Arab attack on the Jewish high holy day, **Yom Kippur**. In the end, though, the Israeli army soundly defeated Syria and Egypt, forcing them back within twenty miles of Damascus and across the Suez Canal, respectively.

Yom Kippur is the highest Jewish holy day of the year, occurring in either September or October, depending on the year. (It occurs on the tenth of Tishri on the Jewish calendar.) Jews believe it was instituted by God according to Leviticus 23:26. It is a day set aside to "afflict the soul," to atone for the sins of the past year. On this holiday many Jews who otherwise would not observe Jewish customs will not work, will fast, and will attend synagogue services.

Hatred for God's Chosen

In March 2002 the Arabs violated yet another Jewish holy day when a suicide bomber blew himself up in a Netanya hotel on Passover. This kind of attack hearkens back to A.D. 67 when the Romans laid siege to Jerusalem at Passover, eventually sacking the city. The media made only passing reference to the fact that the attack was carried out on a Jewish religious holiday and gave the impression that no one cared. And yet, when the United States began its bombing campaign in Afghanistan in retaliation for 9/11, the media gave voice to many who were up in arms about bombing the Taliban during Ramadan, the holy season of Islam.

Despite international acknowledgment of Israel's right to exist in the land without fear of further attack, formally ratified in UN Resolution 242, Arab leaders refused to recognize that right (see for instance, the Khartoum Summit Conference, August 1967).

The prevailing attitude in the Arab world to deny Israel peace and security has continued to fuel the hatred against the chosen people, resulting now in what many believe to be a crossroad in Israel's survival.

Passover is the most commonly observed festival. According to the 1990 National Jewish Population Survey, more than 80 percent of Jews have attended a Passover.

The Passover story is found in Exodus, chapters 1–15. Passover refers to the angel of God who "passed over" the houses of the Jews who had lamb's blood over their doorposts when he was slaying the firstborn of Egypt. This event symbolizes God's salvation, based upon acceptance of God's way of forgiveness for and cleansing of sin. Passover also is in remembrance of the sacrificial offering (a lamb) that was made in the Temple on this holiday. Passover begins on the fifteenth day of the Jewish month of Nissan.

RAGING MIDEAST CONFLICT

With the expansion of Islam around the world into Europe, Asia, and even North America, today's scene of Mideast conflict takes on a global dimension as never before. The attack upon America by Muslim terrorists is only one symptom of the seriousness of Israel's struggle to survive. Arab solidarity against Israel—and those who side with her—has put the world on notice: Support the Jewish nation and run the risk of terror on your own soil.

Israel in the World's Crosshairs

As a result, Muslim extremists everywhere have begun to raise their fists against the Jewish people. Israel is clearly in the crosshairs of world ire. Israel faces condemnation on every side of the globe—from the Arabs, Europeans, Russians, Chinese, and other Asian nations. To its shame the United States, distracted by its own agenda for war and retaliation, continues to waver in its support of Israel's fight against terrorism.

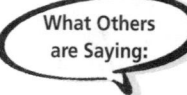

Dennis Prager: If ever Arab hatred of Israel was purely political, that time has long passed. Arab, Iranian and other Muslim literature today is as anti-Semitic as Nazi literature was. Hitler's *Mein Kampf* is a best seller in the Middle East. Articles regularly appear there describing how Jews kill non-Jewish children to use their blood in holiday foods. Jews have been expelled from nearly every Arab country. And the deliberate killing of Jews, including Jewish children, is celebrated throughout the Muslim Middle East.[1]

God Protects Israel

Of course, Israel has been hated by the Muslim world for centuries. The Arabs' drive to push the Jewish population into the sea has never succeeded—and it will not because God remains faithful to his <u>promises</u> to protect his chosen people. But the Arab world is not the sole source of hatred against Israel.

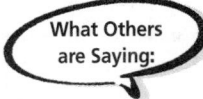
What Others are Saying:

Dennis Prager: Because Europe fears its immense Muslim population, because of its own anti-Semitism, because it is leftist, because it is dependent on Arab oil, and because America supports Israel, Europe is the primary support of those who wish another Jewish Holocaust. Europe, which has been a decaying civilization since the end of World War I, has reached a moral **nadir**—and once again at the Jews' expense.[2]

British and French Anti-Semitism

Examples of European anti-Semitism are on the rise, and sometimes from the most unlikely places. Lauded Oxford University professor Tom Paulin stated publicly that Jewish settlers in Israel "should be shot dead."[3] "I feel nothing but hatred for them," he told the Egyptian paper *Al-Ahram Weekly*. The essayist and academic empathized with the plight of the Palestinians, too, commenting, "I think attacks on [Israeli] citizens in fact boost morale." What an amazing statement from one who represents an institution of such respect!

> KEY TERM
>
> ***nadir:*** *low point*
>
> FURTHER STUDY
>
> Jeremiah 32:37–42
> (promises)

The French Interior Ministry reported that in the first two weeks of April 2002 nearly 360 anti-Semitic crimes were reported to police. Perpetrated mostly by North African Muslims, incidences ranged from anti-Jewish graffiti to the burning and desecration of Jewish synagogues and graves.[4]

Germany's Wave of Anti-Semitism

During the Israeli operation to eliminate the terror infrastructure in the Palestinian territories, Germany, one of Israel's most reliable allies in Europe, broke its silence and sharply criticized Israel's war on terror. The government held up arms deliveries to Israel as a result. Despite their memories of Holocaust guilt, the German people have now thrown their weight of condemnation around the neck of the Jewish people, with one politician calling Israel's actions a "war of extermination," words normally associated with Hitler's murder of 6 million Jews.[5]

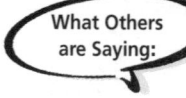

What Others are Saying:

Oriana Fallaci: I find it shameful that in Italy there should be a procession of individuals dressed as suicide bombers who spew vile abuse at Israel, hold up photographs of Israeli leaders on whose foreheads they have drawn the swastika, incite people to hate the Jews.

I find it shameful that the Catholic Church should permit a bishop, one with lodgings in the Vatican no less, a saintly man who was found in Jerusalem with an arsenal of arms and explosives hidden in the secret compartments of his sacred Mercedes, to participate in that procession and . . . thank in the name of God the suicide bombers who massacre the Jews in pizzerias and supermarkets.

I find it shameful that in France, the France of Liberty-Equality-Fraternity, they burn synagogues, terrorize Jews, profane their cemeteries. I find it shameful that the youth of Holland and Germany and Denmark flaunt the **kaffiah** just as Mussolini's avant garde used to flaunt the club and the fascist badge. I find it shameful that in nearly all the universities of Europe Palestinian students sponsor and nurture anti-Semitism.

I find it shameful that in the name of Jesus Christ (a Jew without whom they would all be unemployed), the priests of our parishes . . . flirt with the assassins of those in Jerusalem who cannot go to eat a pizza or buy some eggs without being blown up.[6]

> KEY TERM
>
> ***kaffiah:*** *or kaffiyeh, Arab headdress of square cloth held on by a cord*

Prophecy to Watch For

Could this growing hatred toward Israel signal the beginning of the European domination spelled out in the Scriptures? The formation of political, military, and economic solidarity personified in the European Union today must cause thinking Christians to consider the close proximity of end-time prophetic fulfillment pointing to the entrance of the Antichrist.

America's Growing Blindness

Misinformed Americans continue to call radio talk shows to express their disgust at the Israelis for "occupying" Palestinian land, perpetuating the Arab myth that the "Palestinians" ever possessed land anywhere. The Palestinians are not a distinguishable race; they are simply Arabs who happen to live in the territory of Israel.

CAMPAIGN OF TERROR

The war against terrorism is Israel's war; it is America's war; it is the struggle of free nations everywhere that now find themselves vulnerable to attack by religious zealots whose history and holy books command them to conquer and convert, not with peace, but with the sword. Today, their weapon of choice is the suicide bomber.

Yasser Arafat: Patriarch of Palestinian Terror

The terrorism facing Israel today has long carried the signature of one man: Yasser Arafat. Despite his teary-eyed recollections of childhood memories in Jerusalem, Arafat was actually born, raised, and educated in Cairo, Egypt.

> KEY TERM
>
> **hashish:** *drug derived from the hemp plant*

At an early age he began his life of terror, eventually orchestrating murders, airplane hijackings and bombings, including the suicide bombings of today. We must not forget that he is the person responsible for the murder of Israeli athletes in the 1972 Munich Olympic Games, for the Achilles Lauro hijacking, and for the assassination of American diplomats. One of the world's most notable living serial killers, Yasser Arafat has made his mark on the world not through his education in civil engineering, not through a genuine search for peace, but rather as an engineer of terror.

Webster's dictionary describes the etymology and history of "assassin" as "one of a secret order of Muslims that at the time of the Crusades terrorized Christians and other enemies by secret murder committed under the influence of **hashish**." Today's terrorists are promised pleasure and paradise in return for dying while killing. What better word describes Yasser Arafat and his army of suicide bombers?

False Peacemaker

Arafat, the one who has most promoted terror in the Middle East, having pledged in writing (in the Palestinian National Covenant) the annihilation of the Jewish people, is the same man the world lauds as "statesman" and "partner for peace." The announcement that Yasser Arafat would be awarded the Nobel Peace Prize in 1994 drew the ire of millions of rational citizens around the world.

> ### KEY TERMS
>
> **intifada:** *means "uprising" in Arabic; violent protests by Arabs against Israeli rule*
>
> **Zionism:** *political movement to establish a Jewish state*

Not long after Arafat unleashed the violence of the most recent **intifada**, a movement began to grow to petition the Nobel Prize committee to revoke Arafat's "peace" prize (www.revoketheprize.org). Tens of thousands began signing the petition each month. Then in April 2002, the Nobel Prize committee members finally expressed regret for awarding the peace prize to—that's right—Shimon Peres!

Deadly Brainwashing of Children

KEY POINT
_____
The world's hatred against the Jewish people is bred in the misinformed and deceived and passed down to their children.

While Israeli children spend their summers in camps to learn swimming, horseback riding and crafts, Arab children in the Palestinian territories are taught how to kill Israelis. A study of education among Palestinian children revealed how hatred against Jews is fostered at early ages. Instead of encouraging older students to draw their own conclusions from history and current events, Palestinian high school textbooks tell students how to think and feel about the Jewish state.

What Others are Saying:

Palestinian high school history book: The student will compare the foundations of Fascism and Nazism to those of **Zionism**. The student will acquire the following (learning) directives: Zionism is an aggressive, racist movement; the sense of racial superiority is the essence of Zionism, Fascism, and Nazism. The student will acquire the following values and perceptions: Understanding the dangers arising from Zionism and from racial discrimination . . . assessing the negative impact of Zionism on the Arab's revival and development. The student . . . will make the connection between Zionism and racial discrimination and will trace the connection between Zionism and terrorist movements in the modern world.[7]

THINK ABOUT IT

How can Israel expect to win its war on terrorism when every new generation of Arab children is taught to hate them? What will it take to stem this tide of hatred and terror?

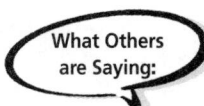

What Others are Saying:

Golda Meir: There will be peace in Israel when Arab mothers love their children more than they hate the Jews.

One Aim: Eliminate Jews

KEY POINT

No real peace is possible when those offering peace with one hand support terror with the other.

As long as Arab mothers continue to proudly strap explosive belts on their sons and daughters, the hatred and terror will not stop. It will not stop as long as Yasser Arafat can bring the television cameras into his besieged hovel to draw sympathy for "his" poor people.

Had he genuinely sought peace, Arafat would have shaken hands with Ehud Barak and accepted the most outrageously generous peace proposal to date. But he did not because he does not want peace. Yasser Arafat desires to complete one mission in his life: to remove the Jewish people from the land and "restore" all of it to the Arabs, triumphantly raising his "Palestinian" flag over Jerusalem, the city of the Jewish king, David.

Dire Forewarning

Prime Minister Sharon declared Arafat "irrelevant" and "the enemy of Israel . . . the enemy of the entire free world." Former Israeli Prime Minister Benjamin Netanyahu warned the United States that if the terror sanctioned and funded by Yasser Arafat is not dealt with swiftly and permanently, that same brand of terror would flood American streets and supermarkets and cafés.

ARAB PEACE TREATY EQUALS DEATH FOR ISRAEL

Prince Alwaleed bin Talal of Saudi Arabia tried to donate $10 million to the victims of the September 11 attacks in New York City. Then-mayor Rudolf Giuliani quickly refused the gift for good reason. The prince blamed the United States for bringing the attack upon itself (as the Arab world similarly chastises Israel about suicide bombings). Months later the prince donated his money ($27 million) to what he considered a more worthy cause—Yasser Arafat and the families of suicide bombers—during a three-day telethon that raised over $56 million for the haven of terrorists under Arafat's "authority."[8]

This same family of Saudi dictators—our "friends," President Bush calls them—announced their idea for a peace treaty to end the conflict in Israel. Their announcement was "coincidentally" made when media coverage began to remind us that fifteen of the nineteen suicide bombers who attacked the United States were Saudi citizens, that terror mastermind Osama bin Laden was Saudi Arabian (and idolized in the Arab world), and that the alliance between America and Saudi Arabia may not have been as solid as we were led to believe.

Repackaged Death to Israel

The Saudi leader's peace plan was not new. It was simply a repackaging of old ideas, formally pushing Israel back behind the pre-1967 borders into a hopeless defensive posture. The Arabs refused the UN partition in 1948. They refused it again in 2000 when Barak offered them the land. Peace is not their objective. Posturing for advantage over Israel leading to the annihilation of the Jewish people *is* their ultimate goal.

The Arab leaders who met in Beirut to ratify this plan barely survived one day of meetings before infighting and bickering dashed their hopes to salvage credibility as peace brokers in the eyes of an expectant world.

Islamic Atrocities

Weeks later in Malaysia at the summit of Islamic leaders, these followers of a "peaceful" religion refused to declare that Palestinians who blow themselves up in Jewish neighborhoods with the sole purpose of killing innocent Israelis had anything to do with terror.

These are the same "peaceful" worshipers of Allah who burned fifteen teenage girls to death in a Saudi Arabian school. For what crime? They were not wearing black robes and head scarves![9] But murdering Jewish teenagers at pizzerias and cafés is not a crime to them. Partners in peace? Ridiculous! Allies against terror? Never!

Saddam Hussein has publicly offered $25,000 to the families of suicide bombers (an attractive incentive to people who earn only about $30 per month). No wonder Palestinian young people are lining up to strap on explosives! Of course, Saddam—the one rebuilding Babylon, don't forget—is enemy number one to the United States. And therein lies America's problem with Israel.

AMERICA'S AMBIVALENT SUPPORT

The Bush Doctrine, as some have called it, states that when it comes to terrorism, "you're either with us or against us." This maxim was a necessary and strong declaration of war against bin Laden, Al Qaida, the Taliban, and any other individual, group, or nation involved in terror operations against America.

President George W. Bush showed himself a capable leader in the midst of a grave national crisis, and he pursued the enemies of our peace and security around the world, particularly in the caves of Afghanistan. He sent troops to other countries to assist "coalition partners" in their fight against terror. When it comes to Israel, however, the Bush Doctrine is conveniently forgotten.

Caving to Pressure

As a response to the Passover massacre on March 28, 2002, by a Palestinian suicide bomber, Israel initiated Operation Protective Shield. President Bush's initial supportive statements for Israel quickly gave way to Arab and international pressure until finally the young commander-in-chief scolded the aged Israeli general Ariel Sharon and said, "Enough is enough!"

Bush Rebuffed

Although President Bush naively promotes his "vision" for an eventual Palestinian state, the real issue nagging the younger Bush is Iraq. Despite Vice President Dick Cheney's tour of Arab states to drum up support for an American campaign against Saddam Hussein, he was rebuffed at each stop. The same was true with Secretary of State Colin Powell's Mideast peace drive. Failure both times.

With that failure came growing criticism from Britain and other NATO allies about going after Saddam. America's support for Israel takes turns with its condemnations of Israel on alternating days, and the bandwagon of dissent grows as one by one the nations of the world turn against God's chosen people.

ISRAEL AT GROUND ZERO

Can Israel defend itself in another war with Arab neighbors? Will it have the ability to sustain repeated blows when nation after nation drops its support of the tiny democracy?

With nearly a million citizens available for the draft, high-tech weaponry, and perhaps even a nuclear arsenal, Israel could defend itself adequately, especially against the poorly trained and sparsely equipped Arab armies that currently exist in the region. But is that enough?

One Saudi remarked that although the Israelis are better equipped, the Arabs have 200 million people. In other words, the hatred and the terror and the war will continue.

False Peace Fallout

Should Israel come to terms with the Arabs and make peace, allowing for a Palestinian state, it will have to defend itself at even greater odds than before as the Palestinians establish a more secure base of terror against them. Recent history demonstrates that the Palestinians will attack at every opportunity. The use of nuclear weapons by Israel cannot be ruled out.

On the other hand, should Israel continue to resist the false peace plans offered by its Arab neighbors, it will be seen as unforgivably uncompromising by the world. In both scenarios, global anti-Semitism will continue to rise, eventually bringing Israel to the brink of destruction.

Prophesied Peace Treaty Rumblings

What is remarkable about Israel today is the long parade of peacemakers—from Madrid to Olso to Tenet to Mitchell to Powell, and now Saudi Prince Abdullah. It only takes one seven-year peace treaty to open the door for the Antichrist and to inaugurate the Tribulation. Again, it will be a false peace, and the Antichrist will break this treaty after three and a half years and invade Israel. "For then there will be a great tribulation, such as has not occurred since the beginning of the world until now, nor ever will" (Matthew 24:21 NAS).

Amos 9:11–15 NAS "In that day I will raise up the fallen booth of David, and wall up its breaches; I will also raise up its ruins and rebuild it as in the days of old; that they may possess the remnant of Edom and all the nations who are called by My name," declares the Lord who does this. "Behold, days are coming," declares the Lord, "When the plowman will overtake the reaper and the treader of grapes him who sows seed; when the mountains will drip sweet wine and all the hills will be dissolved. Also I will restore the captivity of My people Israel, and they will rebuild the ruined cities and live in them; they will also plant vineyards and drink their wine, and make gardens and eat their fruit. I will also plant them on their land, and they will not again be rooted out from their land which I have given them," says the Lord your God.

> FURTHER STUDY
> Genesis 12:1–3 (promises)
> 2 Samuel 6; Psalm 89:3
> (to David)
> Ezekiel 37:4, 26 (foretold)

Promises Still Good

Israel is not left without hope. They are, in fact, God's chosen people. The promises God made to Abraham, Isaac, and Jacob are eternal pledges for a nation and for a land. The promise given to David guarantees a kingdom without end.

Though the nation remains blinded in part to its Messiah, Jesus Christ, God in his grace continues to lead his people back into the Promised Land, as Ezekiel foretold of the "dry bones."

KEY TERMS

remnant: *believing Jews who won't worship the Antichrist*

Jacob: *son of Isaac, son of Abraham, father of the nation Israel*

FURTHER STUDY

Zechariah 14:2
   (will increase)
1 Thessalonians 4:17
   (caught up)

Despite the Jews' unbelief in the true Messiah, God remains faithful to his promises. He will defend and preserve the **remnant** of Israel, just as he did for them in their Babylonian captivity. "For I know the plans that I have for you," declares the Lord, "plans for welfare and not for calamity, to give you a future and a hope" (Jeremiah 29:11).

America: Future Friend or Foe?

The enemies of Israel <u>will increase</u>, the Bible predicts. Today, we are seeing that take place in rapid succession throughout Europe and Asia. The Arab nations, of course, have hated Israel for centuries. Will the United States—the only nation to be founded upon *Judeo*-Christian values—join the rest of the world and turn completely against the chosen people? And could that betrayal ultimately be the demise of America and the reason this nation fades into obscurity in the end times? May God help us to remain steadfast in our commitment to Israel!

Prophetically speaking, Israel is *at* Ground Zero not because of suicide bombers but because God has placed these descendants of **Jacob** on display to the entire world. The media may not understand why they devote so much time and energy to this tiny sliver of land that straddles Asia, Europe, and Africa, but God's purposes succeed nonetheless. One day soon we shall say as Moses did: "Do not fear! Stand by and see the salvation of the Lord which He will accomplish for you today" (Exodus 14:13 NAS).

Church's Role

The church has a special interest in what happens to Israel right now. In spite of denominations and seminaries that have either forsaken (or replaced) the chosen people altogether or simply relegated Israel's importance to some faraway future time, believers must be all the more concerned about the nation from whom the Messiah came. Every Christian will one day be <u>caught up</u> in the air to meet their Jewish Savior at the Rapture, transported to the Father's house in heaven for a seven-year <u>wedding feast</u>. Believers will eventually be brought back to earth by the King of kings to rule and reign with him for one thousand years.

From where? From Israel! Think of it. A thousand years in the Promised Land with the chosen people under the righteous reign of the Jewish Messiah and King!

Is Israel important today to the Christian? You bet it is. That's why we must not only defend our sister democracy but also continue to teach and preach that Israel sits at the crossroad of biblical prophecy today, waiting to be ushered into a new era of trial and then triumph. Now more than ever the church must take the good news of salvation "to the Jew first." Who knows how many of the future <u>144,000</u> Jewish evangelists we will impact by our faithful witness to Israel today?

After a thousand years of peace and righteousness, the Lord will wipe away the old earth and heavens and create it all over again—a new heaven, a <u>new earth</u> . . . and a new Jerusalem!

Sha'alu Shalom Yerushalayim! Pray for the peace of Jerusalem.

FURTHER STUDY
Revelation 19:9
(wedding feast)
Revelation 7:4–8 (144,000)
Revelation 21:1-2
(new earth)

HEADLINE HIGHLIGHT

The Jerusalem Post Newspaper: Online News From Israel
UN Calls for "Robust" Armed Int'l Force in Territories
By Edith M. Lederer
Associated Press

UNITED NATIONS - UN Secretary-General Kofi Annan appealed Thursday for a "robust" armed international force to halt the escalating Israeli-Palestinian conflict but Israel said no and the United States said any Mideast solution must have the support of both parties.

Annan told the UN Security Council that a multinational force large enough to take "decisive action" is essential to halt the deadly cycle of attacks and reprisals by Israelis and Palestinians and restore security . . .

USATODAY.com:

Wednesday, May 15, 2002
Europe Struggles for Role in Mideast
By Robert H. Reid
Associated Press Writer

BRUSSELS, Belgium - European negotiators worked out an arrangement Thursday under which 13 of the Palestinian militants who sheltered in the Church of the Nativity, Christ's reputed birthplace, will be transferred to European countries and 26 to the Gaza Strip. . . .

It offers an example of the role which some European diplomats believe they can play in the Middle East—standing alongside the United States in promoting Western values while at the same time offering the Palestinians the option of dealing with governments not so closely identified with Israel.

It is a role for which the European Union appears well suited. The EU is Israel's biggest market and a major source of funds for Yasser Arafat. Over the last two years, the EU has given the Palestinian Authority $305 million. . . .

Many Europeans blame the Palestinian suicide bombings on Israel's military occupation and settlements policy. On the other hand, many Americans see such bombings as no different from the Sept. 11 terrorist attacks. . . .

To many Europeans, America's strong support for Israel is misguided. Several European leaders were also quick to condemn Israel for refusing to allow a UN fact-finding team to visit the Jenin refugee camp after Palestinians claimed a massacre had occurred. No evidence was found, but Swedish Foreign Minister Anna Lindh said Israel's actions strengthened suspicions "that the Israeli armed forces committed serious crimes against human rights in Jenin."

PROPHETIC IMPACT

United Nations and European demands are becoming more adamant. Israel is increasingly viewed as the major sticking point in the matter of whether there will be war or peace in the Middle East.

This is no surprise to the true student of biblical prophecy. Zechariah long ago said, under divine inspiration: "Behold, I will make Jerusalem a cup of trembling unto all the people round about, when they shall be in the siege both against Judah and against Jerusalem. And in that day will I make Jerusalem a burdensome stone for all people: all that burden themselves with it shall be cut in pieces, though all the people of the earth be gathered together against it" (Zechariah 12:2–3).

Although the prophecy above is for the tribulation period (the time of Jacob's trouble described in Jeremiah 30:7), the nations of earth are already beginning to gather around this one tiny spot that God says he, himself, will make a cause of great anxiety for the whole world.

Israel sits at Ground Zero!

CHAPTER WRAP-UP

- The world experienced widespread terror on September 11, 2001, when New York City and Washington, D.C. were attacked. But terrorism has been around for centuries. Modern Israel has lived with almost daily terror since its birth in 1948.

- Whether attacked by Arab nations or Arab suicide bombers, Israel has defended itself like no other nation in a seemingly unending struggle that continues to threaten its very existence.

- Israel was forced to defend against wars started by its Arab neighbors in 1956, 1967, and 1973. It continues to defend against constant assaults, including suicide bombers and ongoing ambushes by terrorists.

- Radical Islamics hate Israel. It is a supernatural hatred from the mind of Satan. With the expansion of Islam around the world into Europe, Asia, and North America, today's scene of Mideast conflict takes on a global dimension as never before.

- The whole international community blames Israel, primarily, for ongoing violence and threat of war in the Mideast region. At the same time violent anti-Semitism in Europe is again rearing its ugly head.

- Growing hatred toward Israel might signal the beginning of European domination spelled out in the Scriptures. The formation of political, military, and economic solidarity personified in the European Union today should cause every thinking Christian to consider the close proximity of end-time prophetic fulfillment pointing to the entrance of the Antichrist.

- The terrorism facing Israel today has long carried the signature of one man: Yasser Arafat. Arafat has made his mark on the world not through his education in civil engineering, not through a genuine search for peace, but rather as an engineer of terror.

- According to a study of education among Palestinian children, while Israeli children spend their summers in camps to learn swimming, horseback riding, and crafts, Arab children in the Palestinian territories are taught how to kill Israelis.

- Radical Arab Islamics have one goal: to completely eliminate all Jews from the Holy Land region. Their leaders have vowed to push all Jews into the Mediterranean Sea.

- Should Israel come to terms with the Arabs and make peace, allowing for a Palestinian state, it will have to defend itself at even greater odds than before as the Palestinians establish a more secure base of terror against them.

- Bible prophecy says there will be a seven-year peace treaty made between Israel and her enemies. The Antichrist will confirm, or guarantee, its implementation and continuation. It will, God's Word says, be a covenant made with death and hell. This begins the Tribulation.

- Israel is not left without hope. They are God's chosen people. The promises God made to Abraham, Isaac, and Jacob are eternal pledges for a nation and for a land. God's promise to David guarantees a kingdom without end.

Jerusalem's Earthshaking Northern Threat

BY PHILLIP GOODMAN

KEY TERMS

Temple Mount: *Mount Moriah in Jerusalem*

Dome of the Rock: *Muslim shrine on Mount Moriah*

Al Aqsa Mosque: *Muslim structure of study and worship in Jerusalem*

Great Tribulation: *three and one-half years of terrible distress prophesied in Daniel 9:24–27*

FURTHER STUDY

2 Thessalonians 2:4 (rebuilt)

Let's Get Started

The prophecies of the Bible say the Jewish Temple will be <u>rebuilt</u>. With the world the way it is today, heaven and earth will have to shake before the Temple of Israel can rise again on its sacred site. The Bible predicts precisely such an earthshaking event. It will jolt the world into allowing the restoration of the Temple.

The **Temple Mount** in Jerusalem has been occupied for the past thirteen centuries by the **Dome of the Rock** and the **Al Aqsa Mosque** of the idolatrous Islamic religion. But for a brief moment, history will stand frozen when the world sees Russia invade Israel in the latter years. That epic event will trigger a surge of political sentiment that will cry out for the Temple to rise a third time. The rebuilt Temple in Jerusalem will set the stage for mankind's final plunge into the age-ending **Great Tribulation**.

PRINCE OF ROSH

Ezekiel 38:2–9, 14, 16, 22 NKJV Thus says the Lord GOD, "Behold, I am against you, O Gog, prince of Rosh, Meshech, and Tubal. And I will turn you about, and put hooks into your jaws, and I will bring you out, and all your army . . . you will be summoned; in the latter years you will come into the land that is restored from the sword, whose inhabitants have been gathered from many nations to the mountains of Israel . . . you will go up, you will come like a storm; you will be like a cloud covering the land, you and all your troops, and many peoples with you. . . . and you will come up against My people Israel. . . . It will come about in the last days that I shall bring you against My land. . . ." Thus says the Lord GOD: "I will bring him to judgment with pestilence and bloodshed."

Poised for Fulfillment

The prophet Ezekiel wrote these words from God on a papyrus scroll around 580 B.C. It has now been twenty-six centuries since he penned that epic prophecy, yet it has never been fulfilled. Not yet. However, ours is the first generation ever to be in prime position to see the prophecy of "Gog, the land of **Magog**" (KJV) launch forth from the pages of the Bible and from the northern-most regions of the earth.

Ezekiel indicates that Gog, commonly believed to be the area of Russia, and a coalition of nations will invade Israel in the "latter years." Then God, the Creator of the heavens and the earth and the seas and all that is in them, will rise up in his anger. As "Judge of all the earth," he will destroy the massive international force that will have set its collective mind and evil heart on the destruction of the Jewish nation (Genesis 18:25). The physical descendants of **Abraham**, to whom God has given

> KEY TERMS
>
> **Magog:** *area believed to be in current Russia*
>
> **Abraham:** *father of Isaac; founding father of God's chosen people, Israel*
>
> FURTHER STUDY
> Revelation 20:7–9 (Magog)

perpetual and irrevocable <u>promises</u>, will continue to persist according to the plan of biblical prophecy—even as they do today.

THINK ABOUT IT

God's promise to Abraham was unconditional. It will never be broken. Nothing Abraham did either made or broke that covenant or agreement. God did it all.

KEY TERMS

current age: *church age or age of grace*

Mosque of Omar: *Muslim shrine covering a flat rock of religious significance*

FURTHER STUDY

Genesis 12:2–3; 13:14–17; 15:4–15 (promises)

An Intriguing Inquiry

Ezekiel's prophecy offers the prospect of an amazing scenario involving a series of events that frame the climax of human history for this **current age**. What makes this scenario credible is that it will answer one of prophecy's most perplexing questions, one that has puzzled prophecy watchers for years: How will it be possible for the Jews to rebuild the third Temple on the site now occupied by the third most holy shrine in the Muslim world, the **Mosque of Omar**, also called the Dome of the Rock?

Jerusalem's Three Temples

The Bible mentions three Temples on the same site in Jerusalem. Two of them have been built and destroyed. One remains to be built.

1. Solomon's Temple was destroyed by the Babylonians in 587 B.C.
2. Jerubabbel or Herod's Temple was destroyed in A.D. 70 by Roman legions of Titus.
3. The Tribulation Temple will be built in the future. The Antichrist will use it to reveal himself to the world.

PROPHECY TO WATCH FOR

Here is the order of prophesied end-time conditions and events regarding the building of the Temple on the site where the Dome of the Rock now sits:

1. A half century of strife and violence between Israel and Arabic nations will drive the international community to demand a peaceful solution to the Mideast problem.

2. An internationally brokered peace agreement will give Israel a false sense of security.

3. Russia will then lead a massive coalition of multinational forces to invade Israel in the wake of the "peace" agreement.

4. In defense of Israel, God will miraculously destroy the Russian allied forces.

5. The reaction across the world will include both true and false professions of faith from **Gentiles** and Jews, and recognition from the nations that Israel's God has acted.

6. Unbelievers, motivated by fear rather than faith, will "know that [God] is the Lord" (Ezekiel 38:23). With this same "knowledge" of the Lord through his fearful judgment of the Russian forces, the Antichrist will muster the world's support and demand that peace be made for Israel and that her Temple be rebuilt on its original site. Furthermore, the decimation of the Muslim nations as a result of their participation in the Russian invasion will render them impotent regarding any opposition to the rebuilding of the Temple on the site now occupied by the Dome of the Rock.

7. The **Antichrist** will then rise to his moment of destiny and proclaim the divine right of the Jews to rebuild the third Temple. He will give false acknowledgment to God's intervention on behalf of Israel. He will then strike a seven-year "peace" covenant and order the rebuilding of the Temple.

IDENTIFYING MAGOG

Though Ezekiel 38 and 39 clearly describe the coming invasion of Israel by a northern confederacy, it's important to identify these nations and find the correct chronology of events.

First, let's consider the following: Who are the people and nations who invade Israel? How do we know that the perpetrator is actually Russia? Some Bible scholars have used **etymology** to tie the terms "Rosh" (Ezekiel 38:2 NAS and NKJV) with Russia and "Meshech" and "Tubal" with Moscow and Tobolsk, two of the principal cities of modern-day Russia. But we must look elsewhere to find conclusive evidence for the identity of Ezekiel's principal invader as the modern nation of Russia.

> ### KEY TERMS
>
> **Gentiles:** all who are not Jews
>
> **Antichrist:** earth's final and most terrible dictator
>
> **etymology:** study of roots from which names come

Magog's Tracks on the Steppes of Russia

The leader of the invading force, Gog, is said in Ezekiel 38:2 to come from "the land of Magog." Biblical and secular historians tell us that Magog, the grandson of **Noah**, was scattered along with the other families away from the tower of **Babel**, which was located in present-day Iraq. Magog's descendants were represented among the various **Scythian** tribes who journeyed from the Indus Valley to the steppes of Russia. Their kinsmen can be traced to the founding of Russia. The tracks the Scythians left across the Russian expanse for 2,500 years brand that land, in the eyes of God, Ezekiel, and the facts of history as the "land of Magog."

From this land Gog will arise as the leader of the Russian state and the innovator of the master plan, preordained in the Master's prophetic plan, to mobilize hatred and nations against Israel.

THINK ABOUT IT

Satan has caused leaders throughout history to make war on the Jews, God's chosen people. Gog, like the Antichrist, will be such a leader to come forth in fulfillment of Ezekiel chapters 38 and 39.

Ezekiel 38:15 NKJV Then you will come from your place out of the far north, you and many peoples with you, all of them riding on horses, a great company and a mighty army.

The Geography of Magog

KEY POINT

Magog was alive during the building of the tower of Babel and was a great-grandson of Noah.

In biblical geography, Jerusalem is directionally at the <u>center</u> of the nations. All nations radiate outward from Jerusalem in various directions like spokes on a wheel.

The land of Magog is said in Ezekiel 38:15 to be situated to the "remote parts" (NAS) of the north. Russia is caught squarely on the needle of the compass here—the hard facts of the global grid locate Moscow directly to the far north of Jerusalem.

The rise of the Russian state to superpower status has paralleled the birth of the state of Israel, giving what appears to be conclusive evidence that Russia is the perpetrator of Ezekiel's vision of the latter-day invasion of Israel.

Isaiah 66:8–9 Who hath heard such a thing? who hath seen such things? Shall the earth be made to bring forth in one day? or shall a nation be born at once? for as soon as **Zion** travailed, she brought forth her children. Shall I bring to the birth, and not cause to bring forth? saith the Lord: shall I cause to bring forth, and shut the womb? saith thy God.

> **KEY TERMS**
>
> **Zion:** *Jerusalem, spiritual center of the Promise Land*
>
> **two levels:** *part of the prophecy is fulfilled in one time period or event and part in another time or event*
>
> **Armageddon:** *battle at the end of the world*
>
> **FURTHER STUDY**
>
> Zechariah 12:2–3 (fear of war)

Two Important Dates

The verses above seem to be a prophecy with **two levels** of fulfillment. On the first level, the rebirth of Israel took place on May 14, 1948, when modern Israel was "born" in a day. The second, more distant level refers to a remnant of believing Jews who will be saved or "born again" on the day Christ returns at **Armageddon**.

THINK ABOUT IT

Today, Jerusalem is the focus of attention for the whole world, because of the <u>fear of war</u>. Jerusalem is the most important place on earth to God, according to Zechariah 2:8. No wonder this generation is troubled over Jerusalem!

Political Characteristics

Today, Russia qualifies both politically and militarily as the country of Gog from the land of Magog. Politically, in spite of its archaic "democratic" reforms, Russia retains its tradition as a brutal and autocratic state.

CURRENT WORLD EVENTS

The Russian president-dictator Vladimir Putin has shown his true iron-hand style of rule. He has done the following:[1]

- Revived military training in schools
- Increased surveillance of citizens
- Elevated KGB personnel to key positions
- Cracked down on fledgling democratic organizations
- Divided Russia into seven new "super regions" whose handpicked leaders control eighty-nine regional governors.

Russia has lurched back toward its "police-state past."[2] Experts widely acknowledge that Putin "wants to restore a centralized Russian state whose power relies on fear."[3] He has been bringing this about by doing these things:

KEY POINT

Russia's actions will cause God to declare, "Behold, I am against thee, O Gog" (Ezekiel 38:3).

- Weakening the power of political underlings[4]
- Reining in the brief freedom the press has enjoyed since the early 1990s[5]
- Brutalizing evangelical Christians[6]
- Requiring all religious organizations to register with the state[7]
- Recertifying Russia's original atheism

A Mighty Military

KEY TERM

apocalypse: *violence just before Christ's return*

Militarily, in spite of its declared intent to cut its forces by 350,000 troops,[8] Russia retains mega-destructive capacity because she possesses more than 20,000 nuclear weapons.[9] Even if the Start III nuclear arms-reduction treaty between Russia and the United States reaches its goal of cutting Russia's stockpiles to around 2,500 warheads,[10] the remainder would be strategically spread over thirty-nine Russian districts, storing up ample destructive potential for the day of **apocalypse**.[11]

THINK ABOUT IT

Only a God whose "fury will mount up in" his anger (Ezekiel 38:18) could save today's tiny Jewish enclave in a carved-up nation, which at most can muster 1.2 million soldiers to defend the mountains of Israel.[12]

TIMING OF THE INVASION

FURTHER STUDY
Daniel 9:24–27
(Antichrist covenant)

When will the Russian invasion occur? By a process of elimination based on biblical clues, we find that the Russian invasion of Israel must occur near the beginning of the final seven-year period of our current age—that is, near the start of that period. But will it happen before or after the <u>Antichrist covenant</u> that triggers the tribulation period?

THINK ABOUT IT

If the invasion is *concurrent with or after* the seven-year covenant, then it will occur after the Rapture of the church, and Christians living now will not see it. If it occurs *before* the covenant, then a peace treaty followed by the Russian invasion could precede the Rapture and could come at any time. The evidence shows that the Russian invasion of Israel occurs *before* the seven-year peace covenant.

TWO PEACE TREATIES

Since Jerusalem is a holy city to 2 billion Christians and 14 million Jews, and since over a billion Muslims have laid illegitimate claim to it, there will continue to be such strife, violence, and international outcry over who owns Jerusalem that the situation will demand an international solution. The tension over who will control Jerusalem has reached proportions beyond human solution.

We see this by the only proposal finding common ground among the contentious parties. The *Tulsa World* reported: "The proposal to declare God the sovereign over Jerusalem shrines is tentative, but it has the potential to help defuse the most emotional dispute in the Mideast peace talks. It has won the guarded endorsement of Jerusalem's hawkish Israeli mayor and a top Palestinian official—making the first time the two sides have found any common ground on how to share the city."[13]

KEY POINT

There will be two different peace treaties regarding Jerusalem.

Bible prophecies refer to a temporary peace treaty for Israel in both Daniel 9:27 and Ezekiel 38:11, but the prophecies are not the same. First, according to the Ezekiel passage, there will be a peace treaty ostensibly in force at the time of the Russian invasion. As a result of that episodic event, a second, more ominous "peace" treaty will be put into place—the seven-year covenant mentioned in Daniel 9:27, the one implemented by the Antichrist, which will authorize the rebuilding of the Temple.

BATTLE PLANS

> **Ezekiel 38:10** NKJV Thus says the Lord God: "On that day it shall come to pass that thoughts will arise in your mind, and you will make an evil plan:"

Maps and Methods

KEY POINT

Nothing takes God by surprise.

Russia and her conspirators will probably follow the historical invasion routes of Israel's former enemies—the Assyrians in the eighth century B.C., the Babylonians in the seventh century B.C., and the Roman legions of Titus in A.D. 70. The geography of the Mideastern landscape still demands that ground forces follow the paths of least resistance and the most strategic routes.[14]

The Bible says the battle plans will be conjured up in secretive, satanic planning sessions. Only the Creator of all humankind can <u>look</u> into the minds of men. In doing so God has revealed to us, 2,800 years in advance, the actual thoughts that

FURTHER STUDY
Ezekiel 38:10–12 (look)

will well up inside the minds of these covert planners. They will contemplate their wicked schemes behind closed doors within their darkened, inner sanctums filled with war maps and communications technology.

> **Ezekiel 38:11** NKJV You will say, "I will go up against a land of unwalled villages; I will go to a peaceful people, who dwell safely, all of them dwelling without walls, and having neither bars nor gates";

A Disarming Demeanor

The "unwalled villages" mentioned above could be a literal reference to the modern unwalled cities of Israel. Or it could refer to a disarmed military. More likely, however, it describes cities that have become easy prey because of the false peace agreement fostered on Israel under international sponsorship.

Such an arrangement will mentally disarm Israel. She will be a nation of unwalled or unprotected cities. Israel will let her guard down under the false perception that peace has finally arrived. This possibility is reinforced by the fact that the Russian allied planners will boast that Israel is ripe for attack because she perceives herself "at rest" and living "securely."

A THREE-STAGE INVASION

The Russian invasion will unfold in three stages: moving forces into a staging area, using air strikes, and falling disaster for invading forces.

Stage 1

Based on the historic invasion logistics of Israel and in light of modern military capacities, stage 1 will involve the movement of forces into staging areas from which Gog will launch the invasion. The most likely staging areas from which to launch a massive attack involving ground forces coming from the remote parts of the north would be within Turkey and Syria.

Stage 2

Such diversionary tactics could open the way for stage 2—a massive air invasion "like a cloud, to cover the land" (Ezekiel 38:16 NKJV) launched from southern Russian airfields.[15] In tandem with the air strikes, troops amassed in the staging areas will surge forward in a seemingly endless caravan of armored transport vehicles, perhaps in a two-pronged invasion. Both thrusts will pin their military sights squarely on Jerusalem.

Stage 3

Stage 3 will witness the earthshaking demolition of the forces of Gog. We will come back to this a bit later in the chapter. But first, it's important to look at the objectives of the Russian invaders.

OBJECTIVES OF THE RUSSIANS

The conspirators will have in view several objectives. In order to achieve them, their ultimate goal will be the total destruction of Israel.

> **Ezekiel 38:12–13** To take a spoil, and to take a prey; to turn thine hand upon the desolate places that are now inhabited, and upon the people that are gathered out of the nations, which have gotten cattle and goods, that dwell in the midst of the land. Sheba, and Dedan, and the merchants of Tarshish, with all its young lions thereof, shall say unto thee, Art thou come to take a spoil? hast thou gathered thy company to take a prey? to carry away silver and gold, to take away cattle and goods, to take a great spoil?

To Capture Great Spoil

For the cash-poor Russians, the passage above tells us that one objective of the invaders will be to seize the riches of Israel—her natural and agricultural resources and her technology-based economic infrastructure.

A survey of Russia's recent economic decline is startling in light of Ezekiel's prophecy. In 1998, the government defaulted on its debts to the tune of $12 billion. Fifty million Russians, one-third of the population, live below the poverty line. There are looming food shortages and growing food lines. The middle class is disappearing as the rich grow richer (on pseudo-capitalism) and the poor grow poorer.

Russia's huge budget deficit has repeatedly been bailed out by the **International Monetary Fund**, while the government has had to spend millions to prop up the **ruble**. Russia was even declared to be in an economic depression in 1998, about the same time that their cash-strapped government asked NASA to pay Russia's part of the joint U.S.-Russian space station.[16]

> ### KEY TERMS
>
> **International Monetary Fund:** *organization of nations that pool money for assistance*
>
> **ruble:** *Russian currency*

> **Ezekiel 38:11–12** I will go against those [people] who are at rest . . . to turn your hand against the waste places which are now inhabited [the land of Israel], and against the people [the Jews] who are gathered from the nations . . .

To Curse the Jews

KEY TERMS

Isaac: promised son of Abraham and his wife, Sarah

Ishmael: son of Abraham and Hagar, Sarah's Egyptian maid

FURTHER STUDY

Genesis 12:3 (enmity)

Russia's oil-rich Muslim allies will have in mind two objectives deeply rooted in the spiritual darkness of Islam—the obliteration of "the people" and the possession of "the land." Each of the countries named in Ezekiel's prophecy is united around these same strategic objectives today!

A scan of Islamic-Israeli relations is sufficient to impress upon the mind of even the most casual reader of recent history the underlined enmity with which Muslim nations hold the Jewish people. The 3,800 year-long, deeply embedded animosity between **Isaac** (covenant Israel) and **Ishmael** (Arab nations), further poisoned by the thorough saturation of Near East peoples by militant Islamic fanaticism, is central to Satan's plan to curse the covenant people of God.

THE FINGER OF GOD!

KEY POINT

The hatred of the Arabs and Jews goes back to their forefathers Ishmael and Isaac.

Now, back to the third stage of the Russian invasion. Remember that the first stage involves the movement of forces into staging areas from which Gog will launch the invasion. And the second stage involves a massive air and land invasion. Finally, stage 3 will be the earthshaking demolition of the forces of Gog.

> **Ezekiel 38:18–20** "And it will come about on that day, when Gog comes against the land of Israel," declares the Lord GOD, "that My fury will mount up in My anger. And in My zeal and in My blazing wrath I declare that on that day there will surely be a great earthquake in the land of Israel. And the

> fish of the sea, the birds of the heavens, the beasts of the field, all the creeping things that creep on the earth, and all the men who are on the face of the earth will shake at My presence."

Blinding the Cleverness of People!

In the verses above we see that a series of catastrophes, the timing and severity of which will be inexplicable by natural causes, will befall the Russian-Muslim forces at the moment they are poised on the mountains of Israel to launch forth their collective wrath on Jerusalem.

Russia's overthrow will be caused by the direct intervention of God. Two facts bear this out. First, fire and brimstone and a massive earthquake will set off the chain reaction-like collapse of the Russian forces. A similar catastrophe befell **Sodom and Gomorrah** without the aid of atomic warfare. Second, the world will react by giving immediate credit to the God of Israel.

> **KEY TERM**
>
> **Sodom and Gomorrah:** two ancient cities God destroyed with fire
>
> **FURTHER STUDY**
>
> Genesis 19:24–25
> (Sodom and Gomorrah)

Another factor in Russia's defeat will be "every man's sword against his brother." This seems to indicate confusion rather than intent, which implies the inflicting of a kind of tactical blindness on the armies. There could be a manmade explanation for this confusion: holes in cyberspace and glitches in high-tech computer systems!

The Russian forces will be blinded as high-tech military radar and communications systems yield to fire, brimstone, and earthquake activity thundering forth from the finger of God!

> **Exodus 14:4** Thus I will harden Pharaoh's heart, and he will chase after them [the Hebrews]; and I will be honored through Pharaoh and all his army, and the Egyptians will know that I am the Lord.

The Lord Fights for Them

God stated the words above when he led the Hebrews through the Red Sea as they fled from Pharaoh and slavery in Egypt.

The reaction of the world to God's judgment on the Russian forces will follow the pattern of Pharaoh and the Egyptians in their reaction to the plagues of the Exodus.

Exodus 14:25 And He caused their chariot wheels to swerve, and He made them drive with difficulty; so the Egyptians said, "Let us flee from Israel, for the Lord is fighting for them against the Egyptians."

They Will Know That I Am God

KEY POINT

God, through his acts in history and his interaction with man, has always, in his omniscience, allowed both true and false believers to exist at the same time.

As the water of the Red Sea trapped the Egyptian forces, they knew the power behind nature was God, the Lord who made heaven and earth. So the situation will be with the nations when they witness the divine overthrow of Russia: "Then they shall know that I am the Lord" (Ezekiel 38:23b). Just as it was with the Egyptians, however, most people will acknowledge the fact of divine power but will not accept the Redeemer as their Lord.

During the end times the whole world will rivet its attention on the divine overthrow of the forces of Magog and will demand that the Jewish Temple be rebuilt on its sacred site. Down will come the Dome of the Rock. Up will rise 144,000 Jewish believers in Jesus Christ along with a multitude of Gentile believers.

FURTHER STUDY
Revelation 7:3–8 (144,000)

Onto the world stage will step one who appears to be the ultimate friend of Israel, the architect of the new Temple, the Antichrist. The Antichrist will order the rebuilding of the Temple but will not bow to the Creator. The world will go its merry way, but the Lord will raise up a believing remnant to preserve his holy name in the earth—and they will prepare for history's darkest hour.

The prophet Isaiah foretold the buildup to that coming time of terrible darkness. "[The Lord] will raise a banner for the nations and gather the exiles of Israel; he will assemble the scattered people of Judah from the four quarters of the earth" (Isaiah 11:12). People alive today have lived through a major part of the buildup toward the time of the Antichrist and the Tribulation!

THE THIRD TEMPLE

> **Zechariah 12:3** And it will come about in that day that I will make Jerusalem a heavy stone for all the peoples; all who lift it will be severely injured. And all the nations of the earth will be gathered against it.

Temple Site at Ground Zero

The Mideast issue has finally come down to Jerusalem, Ground Zero, as Zechariah predicted. Today, the land has already been <u>divided</u> up, apportioned, and allotted to the enemies of Israel. The burning political issue of who gets the land of Abraham is basically a done deal from the world's standpoint. The burden of all of this land transfer to the Muslims has now arrived at the doorstep of Jerusalem, and not just Jerusalem, but East Jerusalem: the biblical city; the holy city; the city of David, Jesus, and—as the baseless belief of the Muslims goes—Muhammad.

FURTHER STUDY
Daniel 11:39; Joel 3:2
(divided)

The real issue in focus is even more finely tuned. Like a sword of contention spawned in the loins of Isaac and Ishmael at the dawn of written history, the bloody blade has zeroed in on the Temple Mount. At this strategic juncture in prophetic history, the zealots are poised at the foot of the temple site, braced for the mother of all holy wars.

Atop the Temple Mount there is no Jewish Temple, only the memory of one or, more accurately, two. The original Temple built by King Solomon was destroyed in the Babylonian captivity. The second one, the one Jesus and the apostles frequented, was laid waste by the Roman legions of Titus in A.D. 70. In that same war the Jews were uprooted from the land of Israel and sifted among the nations for the next two millenniums.

The Russian defeat will set the stage for the rebuilding of the third Temple. God's prophetic time clock is ticking. The earthshaking invasion from the northern enemies of Israel could begin at any moment.

China Daily

HK edition
Wednesday, Feb. 20, 2002

MOSCOW - Russia's top arms negotiator said yesterday he expected to strike a deal on nuclear disarmament with his Washington counterpart at the start of talks here. The aim is to draft an agreement for signature at a May presidential summit. . . . Moscow has sought a legally-binding document with Washington that would put a ceiling of 1,700-2,200 warheads on the two sides' respective nuclear arsenals over the next 10 years. . . . The cuts in nuclear weapons were decided by Putin and Bush at their summit in Washington and Crawford, Texas, in November, but Washington has until recently been reluctant to formalize the agreement on paper . . .

PROPHETIC IMPACT

Nations observing the gathering Gog-Magog forces will apparently send a note of protest, accusing them of planning an invasion into the Middle East (Ezekiel 38:13–15). But these protesting nations will not take action.

The "young lions," in this passage (verse 13), have been thought by some scholars to indicate the offspring of Great Britain (the merchants of Tarshish). The United States would be among that group.

Something has caused this group of formerly powerful, nuclear arms-bearing nations to back down in this showdown in the "latter days." Russia constantly and consistently seeks arms advantage. Possibly, they will one day achieve superiority to the extent they feel capable of invading the Middle East and Israel for petroleum and other plunders of war.

CHAPTER WRAP-UP

- Bible prophecy says a third Jewish Temple will be built on the sacred Temple Mount. But Islamic religious structures now sit there. It will take an earthshaking event for a Temple to be rebuilt there.

- According to Ezekiel 38–39, that earthshaking event will be a Russian-led invasion from Israel's north. It will take place near or during the tribulation era.

- The buildup to the invasion might be already in view.
- The probable scenario is this: Violence in and around Israel will grow until it is intolerable; the world community (United Nations) will demand, then broker a supposed peace; Israel will feel secure with this plan, but it will be false security.
- When Israel feels secure, the Russian-led forces will invade from the north.
- God himself will defend Israel and destroy the attackers; many across the world will recognize God's work and will be converted through salvation.
- The Antichrist, earth's final despot, will rise to power during this time. He will, as part of a false peace plan, allow Israel to rebuild a Temple atop Mount Moriah in Jerusalem.

The Islamic Bomb

BY LARRY SPARGIMINO

Let's Get Started

"I will cast terror into the hearts of those who have disbelieved" (*The Koran*, Surah 8:12).

The men who carried out the terrorist attacks on America on September 11, 2001, were motivated by their religious beliefs. In their letters and notes they mentioned Allah, the God of Islam. They quoted from the Koran, the Muslim holy book, and were involved in a jihad, a Muslim "holy war." A few years earlier, terrorist leader Osama bin Laden had pronounced a *fatwa*—an Islamic ruling of death—to wage war on America and her allies. September 11 was the outcome.

Had these terrorists "hijacked Islam," as the media reported? Were they representing a fringe group of Islamic dissidents who have nothing to do with true Islam, or were their actions perfectly in keeping with the example of Muhammad, the founder of Islam, and the basic writings of that faith, the Koran and the Hadith? Following the tragic events of September 11, three different answers were given to this question.

> **KEY TERM**
>
> *fatwa: Muslim decree of death*

ISLAM: A PEACEFUL RELIGION

The view that Islam is a peaceful religion was immediately presented by the media. Predictably, President George W. Bush articulated this thought. It was also the opinion expressed by Yusuf Islam—the former musician Cat Stevens, who now promotes Muslim education in England.

Muslim organizations throughout North America sought to put the world at ease by denouncing the terrorist attack on America, as did the governments of Iran, Bahrain, Egypt, Lebanon, Oman, Pakistan, Palestine, Qatar, Saudi Arabia, Turkey, the United Arab Emirates, and Yemen. Shortly after this initial response, however, another view surfaced.

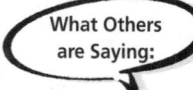

What Others are Saying:

Yusuf Islam: Today I am aghast at the horror of recent events and feel it a duty to speak out. Not only did terrorists hijack planes and destroy life; but they also hijacked the beautiful religion of Islam.[1]

ISLAM: A THREAT TO THE WORLD

The view that Islam poses a threat to the world emphasizes Islam's dark side. Novelist Salman Rushdie, against whom the late Ayatollah Khomeini issued a decree of death, stated that if September 11 isn't about Islam, why the worldwide Muslim demonstrations in support of Osama bin Laden and **Al Qaida**?[2]

British journalist Julie Burchill wrote an article highly critical of the British media for the sustained effort to present Islam—even after the Rushdie affair and during the Taliban's reign of terror—as something essentially "joyous" and "vibrant," sort of like Afro-Caribbean culture, only with fasting and fatwas.[3]

> **KEY TERM**
>
> **Al Qaida:** also spelled Al Qaeda; Islamic terrorist organization run by Osama bin Laden

In the weeks and months following September 11, news organizations began showing footage of certain groups actually rejoicing over the devastation caused by the terrorist attack. In many nations the attack was presented as a victory for Islam. Rick Bragg, writing for the *New York Times*, related that boys were running through their school compounds on September 11 with great glee. They were celebrating, stabbing the fingers on one hand into the palm of the other to simulate a plane stabbing into a building.

Palestinian authorities were working overtime to suppress images of rock-throwing youths dropping their rocks just long enough to celebrate the deaths of thousands of people in America.[4]

Militant and Destructive

The militant view of Islam says the devastation wrought on September 11 is really what Islam is all about. This is the belief of Osama bin Laden, namely, that all Muslims are to be faithful to the teachings of their religion and to destroy the infidels. They define "infidels" as anyone who is not of the Islamic faith. Its proponents believe that the ones who have hijacked Islam are those who say it is a religion of peace. While there are peace-loving Muslims, Islam is not a peace-loving religion.

MUHAMMAD'S DEADLY LEGACY

Muhammad, the founder of Islam, was born in A.D. 570 in the city of Mecca, which is located in what is now Saudi Arabia. Muslims believe that while meditating in a cave during the month of **Ramadan**, Muhammed received a vision through the angel Gabriel, who was the channel of revelation from Allah to Muhammad.

KEY TERM

Ramadan: *ninth month of the Islamic calendar and now the holiday celebrating the revelation of the Koran to Muhammad*

The revelations Muhammad received from the angel provided the content of the Koran. Other sacred writings, not part of the Koran, record Muhammad's life and deeds. These ancient writings, called the Hadith, were collected several hundred years after Muhammad's death in 632.

THINK ABOUT IT

Ramadan occurs during the ninth month of the Islamic lunar calendar, which is eleven days shorter than ours. Muslims believe this is the month in which heaven's door is open, hell's doors are closed, and Satan is bound in chains.

Beginning of Islam

Because he wanted to bring social and religious reform, Muhammad did not get along well with the leaders of Mecca and was forced to leave the area. One of the most important dates in Islam is July 16, 622, the date of the Hegira, the flight of Muhammad and his followers to Medina, a city located about 200 miles north of Mecca (see illustration below). This is the date for the beginning of the Islamic calendar, 1 **A.H.**

Because Medina lacked a strong central government, there was much strife between the tribes and a general state of lawlessness prevailed.

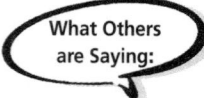

KEY TERM

A.H.: in the year of the Hegira; Muslim designation for A.D.

What Others are Saying:

George W. Braswell Jr.: For Muhammad [this] was a place to establish his religion, and for the people of Medina it was an opportunity to have a reconciling leader.[5]

Map of Islam's Beginnings

This map of present-day Saudi Arabia shows Mecca and Medina where Muhammad began the religion of Islam.

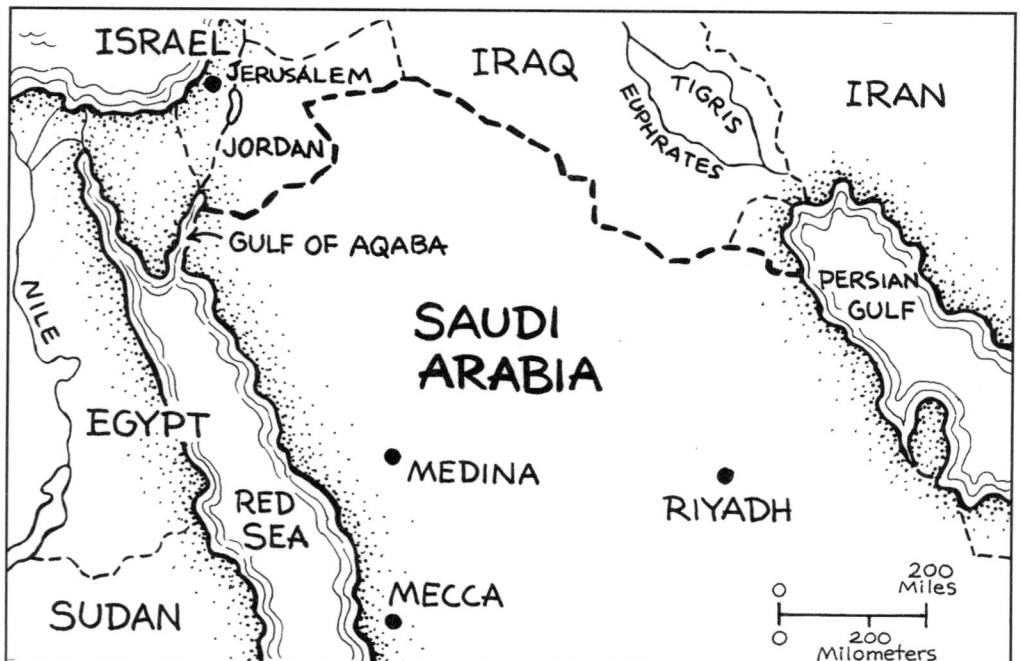

Growth of Islam

During his early years of leadership, Muhammad was persecuted by the rich merchants of Mecca and his followers were few. When his army grew in size and strength, however, he became more militant and more intolerant of Jewish and Christian opposition to his teachings.

The Koran teaches two different approaches to nonbelievers.

1. Muslims are simply to warn and teach, and to leave the doom of unbelievers to Allah.
2. Muslims are to fight in the cause of Allah (become **mujahideen**) in exchange for **absolution** of all their sins and, should they die in battle, instant residence in paradise.

What Kind of Man Was Muhammad?

• *A Man of War*—Muhammad was definitely not a man of peace. He was involved in several major battles of his day: Battle of Badr (624); Battle of Uhud (625); Battle of Trench (627), and various battles against the Jewish tribes residing on the Arabian Peninsula.

• *A Pedophile*—When Muhammad was fifty-three, he married a six-year-old girl. While some Islamic authorities claim that this was only an "engagement," all would admit that the marriage was consummated when the girl was nine.

• *A Pampered Prophet*—According to the Koran, Allah granted Muhammad certain exemptions from required duties and also gave special revelations to silence any questions about the prophet's behavior. Other passages record revelations from Allah to help the prophet deal with embarrassing situations.

For example, Muslim men are allowed to have no more than four wives (4:4), but Muhammad was allowed to take as many believing women in marriage as he desired (33:50).

> ### KEY TERMS
> **mujahideen:** *men who fight for Allah's cause*
> **absolution:** *removal of guilt*

• *A Brutal and Vindictive Individual*—The Hadith of Abu Dawud describes an incident in which a slave woman, used as a concubine by her Muslim master, paid for her criticism of Muhammad with her life.[6]

CHARACTERISTICS OF ISLAM

Islam has no concept of human **depravity**, a condition that renders our best works to be no better than <u>filthy rags</u> in God's sight.

In the day of judgment, according to Islam, the scales of justice will weigh the good and bad deeds of each person. Those who are trying to balance the scales with their good deeds can never know for sure if the scales will tip in their favor. The only way to be sure—that is, to have assurance of salvation—is by dying a martyr's death. "And if you are killed or die in the Way of Allah, forgiveness and mercy from Allah are far better than all that they amass [of worldly wealth]" (3:157).

Paradise is for martyrs: "Verily, Allah has purchased of the believers their lives and their properties that theirs shall be the Paradise. They fight in Allah's cause, so they kill and are killed. It is a promise in truth which is binding to Him" (9:111).

In Islam only the martyred are absolutely assured of salvation. In contrast, John 10:28 says all who believe in Jesus Christ as the Son of God are absolutely assured of salvation because Christ died for them on the cross.

Phony Promises of Paradise

The wave of terrorist attacks that has plagued the world for the last several years has been an attempt by members of Islam to guarantee a place for themselves in paradise. In an article in *Time* magazine entitled "Why the Bombers Keep Coming," David Van Biema explains that Islam lauds martyrdom. The traditions of Muhammad [the Hadith] state that a **shahid**'s sins will be forgiven when he sheds his first drop of blood, that he can admit seventy relatives to paradise, and that he himself will be married there to seventy-two beautiful virgins, a point emphasized by Osama bin Laden.[7]

KEY TERMS

depravity: *inborn state of sinfulness*
shahid: *martyr*

FURTHER STUDY
Isaiah 64:6 (filthy rags)

Characteristics of Paradise

According to the Koran (52:17–24), paradise will feature these things:

- Beautiful gardens
- Plenty to eat and drink
- Handsome boy servants
- Inhabitants who "recline on couches arranged in rows" and are wed to "dark-eyed **houris**"

Theocratic Aspirations

Islam does not allow its followers to restrict their faith to a few items of religious devotion related to public meetings in the mosque. Rather, it is a pervasive world- and life-view that controls and motivates its adherents at every level of behavior. Islam emphasizes national involvement rather than just personal piety.

Islamic fundamentalism is a more potent force, and a greater threat to the West, than any religious movement could ever be.[8] Faithful Muslims are therefore seeking to establish a **theocratic** kingdom on earth under the authority of Allah.

The concept of theocracy leads to a blending of religious, political, and ideological goals that produces a situation of extreme danger for the entire world—especially in view of the widespread proliferation of weapons of mass destruction. With these realities upon us, the horrors of **Armageddon** may be closer than most care to acknowledge.

> **KEY TERMS**
>
> **houris:** beautiful virgins
> **theocratic:** strongly religious in nature
> **Armageddon:** battle at the end of the world
>
> **FURTHER STUDY**
>
> Revelation 16:16
>   (Armageddon)

Teachings of the Koran Contrasted with the Bible

What the Koran Teaches	What the Bible Teaches
Polygamy	Monogamy
War and bloodshed	Peace and harmony
Revenge	Forgiveness
Fear	Hope
Insecurity	Security

PERILOUS TIMES FOR AMERICA

Many Muslims regard America as the "Great Satan." Our support of Israel and our Christian roots make us particularly odious to them. Millions of Muslims will not rest until America is either destroyed or turned into an Islamic nation.

In a column posted on November 17, 2001, Joseph Farah of WorldNetDaily.com observed that while President Bush has dismissed Al Qaida-sponsored terrorism as being supported by only a few radicals, others disagree. Farah quotes Mideast expert Daniel Pipes, who states, "Muslims on the streets of many places—Pakistan and Gaza in particular—are fervently rallying to the defense of Al-Qaida's vision of Islam. Likewise, the president's calling the terrorists 'traitors to their own faith, trying in effect, to hijack Islam' implies that other Muslims see them as apostates, which is simply wrong. Al-Qaida enjoys wide popularity."

No doubt, as the leader of a nation known for religious liberty and ethnic pluralism, President Bush cannot make an outright condemnation of Islam. He doesn't want the war on terrorism to be a religious war—something that sounds very un-American. He believes that there are moderate Muslim nations that will prove to be allies, and it would be politically and strategically unwise to alienate them.

The Koran and the Sword

The danger of a militant Islam is created by the Koran itself and cannot be passed off as the belief of only a few in limited fringe groups. The Koran says, "Those that make war against God and His Apostle and spread disorder in the land shall be put to death or crucified or have their hands and feet cut off on alternate sides, or be banished from the land" (5:34).

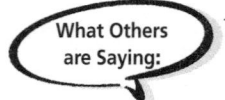

What Others are Saying:

Ravi Zacharias: However one might wish to interpret it, the sword and warfare are an intrinsic part of the Islamic faith.[9]

They Are Already Here!

Some Muslim leaders abroad and in America are raising clouds of semantic smog to confuse the issue. Appearing on talk shows and writing in local newspapers, they sound the oft-repeated litany that "Islam is a religion of peace." They have been so effective that they have even fooled some of our leaders.

The *Washington Post* reported on October 2, 2001, that President George W. Bush opened the White House and shared the platform with some questionable characters. The report related that on September 20, FBI agents went to the house of Hamza Yusuf, a well-known Muslim teacher in northern California. They wanted to question Yusuf about a speech he had given two days before the September 11 attack in which he said that the United States "stands condemned" and that "this country has great tribulation coming to it."

When agents knocked on Yusuf's door, his wife said: "He's not here. He's with the President." That very day Yusuf was at the White House, the only Muslim in a group of religious leaders invited to pray with President Bush and sing "God Bless America." Maybe he thought the words meant "God *blast* America."

THINK ABOUT IT

Despite the semantic smog, the truth is inescapable. The problem is not the so-called Israeli atrocities or American presence in the Middle East—or a thousand other silly reasons that are given and believed by the gullible.

Proverbs 14:25 reminds us, "A true witness delivereth souls, but a deceitful witness speaketh lies." Our leaders are welcoming deceitful witnesses who are speaking lies. Who knows what is being said and taught in thousands of mosques across America. Do we naively believe that fanaticism only occurs in mosques in some other country?

> **FURTHER STUDY**
> 1 Chronicles 16:13 (chosen)

Allah Hates God's Chosen People

KEY POINT

Islam is a religion that breeds hate and spawns terrorism.

According to the Koran, the Islamic god, Allah, has an unquenchable hatred for the Jews, the people God's Word calls the Lord's <u>chosen</u> people. The murderous hostility against the Jews has its roots in the Koran:

- "You will find that the most violent of all men in enmity against the faithful are the Jews" (5:82).
- "The Jews are smitten with vileness and misery and drew on themselves indignation from Allah" (2:61).
- "Wherever they are found, the Jews reek of destruction—which is their just reward" (3:112).

The Coming Showdown between Jews and Muslims

Osama bin Laden was once asked if he had bio-weapons to use against America. His response has chilling ramifications. Men are never so diligent in doing evil as when they do it in the name of their God.

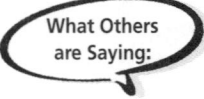

What Others are Saying:

Osama bin Laden: If I have indeed acquired these weapons then I thank God for enabling me to do so.[10]

Jessica Sterns: Terrorist groups motivated by religious concerns are becoming more common . . . religious groups are more likely than others to turn to WMD [weapons of mass destruction]. . . such weapons are especially valuable to terrorists seeking to conjure a sense of divine retribution . . . to kill large numbers of people . . . religious groups are becoming more common, and they are more violent than secular groups.[11]

An Eager Audience

Why the increase in religiously motivated terrorism? It may be due to a revival of orthodox Islam. Though Muhammad is dead, he still speaks to an eager audience. We are also moving toward a confrontation, a cataclysmic grand finale.

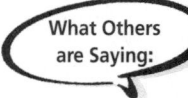

What Others are Saying:

Dr. Israr Ahmed, *Amir of the Tanzeem:* The process of revival of Islam in different parts of the world is real. A final showdown between the Muslim world and the non-Muslim world, which has been captured by the Jews, will take place soon. The Gulf War was just a rehearsal for the coming conflict . . . Muslims of the world including those in the U.S.A., prepare yourself for the coming conflict.[12]

THINK ABOUT IT

Militant Muslims are sending out plenty of signals. If anything good can come out of the tragedy of September 11, it ought to be that we take such signals seriously.

Suicide Bombers Alert

Suicide bombings in Israel are just one of the indicators of a coming showdown between Israel and the Arab world. Significantly, in 1996 only about 20 percent of the Palestinians surveyed supported suicide bombing as a way of dealing with so-called Israeli atrocities. At present, however, more than 70 percent approve.[13]

The coming showdown is now receiving financial incentives. Recent reports indicate that Saddam Hussein is donating $25,000 to every Palestinian family of a martyr who has died in the conflict with Israel. He also gives $1,000 to those who are wounded in the conflict. This state-sponsored subsidy keeps the Palestinians in a condition of chronic rage. Saudi Arabia and Kuwait have donated funds to pay the wages of 130,000 unemployed Palestinian workers. One militiaman summed it up in a Palestinian newspaper: "It *pays* to continue our uprising against Israel."[14]

ABC World News Tonight broadcast footage on April 12, 2002, of an American-style telethon being held in Saudi Arabia to raise funds for families of injured or killed Palestinian "martyrs." Banks of phones had operators standing by to accept pledges, and the cameras repeatedly panned piles of cash and jewelry pouring in from donors. One Saudi princess donated her Rolls Royce. When questioned, Saudi officials running the telethon admitted that they will make no distinction in who gets the money. It will benefit families of both suicide bombers and civilians killed by Israeli forces.

Terrorists Organizing for Apocalypse

Islamic terrorism is sponsored by various organizations, including Hamas, which not only has a military wing but also has a well-organized welfare wing. Among other activities, this wing cares for the families of suicide bombers and others who have died fighting the Israelis, making suicide bombing a macabre form of life insurance in impoverished Palestinian communities.[15]

Shockingly, Hamas's welfare wing has been collecting funds from donors in the United States. The Holy Land Foundation for Relief and Development, located in Richardson, Texas, is operated by Ghassan Elashi, a Palestinian who has been in the United States for twenty-three years. President Bush froze the group's $5 million in assets, claiming that the money was used to indoctrinate children in the West Bank and Gaza strip to grow up into suicide bombers.[16]

All of these funds will be used to aid the coming showdown. Traditional Muslim **eschatology** reveals an apocalypse involving a confrontation with Israel and those who side with her. One Hadith states: "The resurrection of the dead will not come until the Muslims will war with the Jews and the Muslims will kill them . . . the trees and the rocks will say, "O Muslim, O Abdullah, here is a Jew behind me. Come and kill him."[17]

KEY POINT

Fervor for a show-down between Muslims and Jews has been building since about 1990.

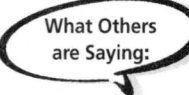

What Others are Saying:

Sheikh Abdul Aziz Oudeh, *leading figure in the Islamic jihad movement:* Now Allah is bringing the Jews back to Palestine in large groups from all over the world to their big graveyard where the promise will be realized upon them, and what was destined will be carried out.[18]

THE CHRISTIAN RESPONSE

Much of the information I have shared will raise strong feelings, but we must be careful to distinguish between the *religion* of Islam and the *people* who are Muslims. However strongly Christians may feel against the religion of Islam, we must have nothing but concern and compassion for the people who are enslaved by it—even those who may hate us and want to destroy us.

Muslims and fanatical Islamic terrorists are not the real enemy. The real enemy is the evil one who is described in the Bible as our <u>adversary</u>. Jesus said Satan "was a murderer from the beginning, and abode not in the truth" (John 8:44). Violence and false religion clearly have their origin in Satan. The evil of terrorism is a reflection of the <u>ongoing struggle</u> in the universe.

KEY TERMS

eschatology: *study of end-time events*

FURTHER STUDY

1 Peter 5:8 (adversary)
Ephesians 6:10
(ongoing struggle)

FURTHER STUDY
1 John 4:18 (perfect love)

KEY POINT

The real problem in witnessing to Muslims is not the hardness of their hearts, but the hardness of ours.

THINK ABOUT IT

Strength through Christ

We must be stronger than the enemy before we can be victorious over him. You cannot bind the strong man of Islam if you are afraid of him. But how can we rise above this fear that is so natural and innate? We can by loving the Muslim as Jesus does. The Bible says that <u>perfect love</u> casts out fear. I would have defeated my purpose in writing this chapter if it leads the reader to hate Muslims. If that happens, there will be no victory because there will be no love.

Christians are to remember at all times that Jesus Christ is their reliance and their strength. Jesus has already defeated the world and all the fearful things of the world: "These things I have spoken unto you, that in me ye might have peace. In the world ye shall have tribulation: but be of good cheer; I have overcome the world" (John 16:33).

Jesus commanded Christians to love Muslims when he said, "But I say unto you, love your enemies, bless them that curse you, do good to them that hate you, and pray for them which despitefully use you, and persecute you" (Matthew 5:44).

HEADLINE
HIGHLIGHT

World Watch Daily

Tuesday, Apr. 16, 2002

Saudi: Suicide Bombings Not Terrorism

By Donna Abu-Nasr
Associated Press Writer

RIYADH, Saudi Arabia – A Saudi official said Tuesday he told President Bush and Congress in a letter that Palestinian suicide bombers are not terrorists and are instead sacrificing "their souls for freedom."

The member of the unelected Consultative Council, which acts like a Parliament, also warned that Washington's perceived support for Israel would intensify mounting hatred toward the United States.

Ahmed al-Tuwaijri said in his letter that U.S. policy has "destroyed our dreams and the dreams of peace-lovers around the world." The 120-member council is appointed by the king and reflects government opinion.

PROPHETIC IMPACT

Upside-down thinking is a signal that the end of the age might be near. Since the 1973 *Roe* v. *Wade* decision by the Supreme Court, making abortion a legal means to murder the unborn by the millions (more than 40 million babies slaughtered in the womb to date), God seems to be turning humankind over to a **reprobate** mind. For example, many of the political liberals who advocate abortion also think capital punishment is barbaric and that harming a baby seal is unspeakable savagery.

It should come as no surprise, then, that Islamics, most of whom have never heard the truth from God's Word, call suicide bombing, even by children, conduct that is perfectly acceptable, even desirable.

Prophecy says in 2 Timothy 3 that just before Christ returns people will be fierce. Certainly, the world has not endured a more violent time than today.

CHAPTER WRAP-UP

- The September 11, 2001, attack on America came from Islamic terrorists who based their justification for the murders on the Muslim holy book, the Koran.

- The media continue to portray Islam as a peaceful religion. Another view, based upon the thousands of murders inflicted in the name of Allah, says that Islam is a religion that often promotes violence and death.

- Muhammad founded Islam. He said his religious ideas were based upon a vision from Allah. He was considered the last prophet in a long line of prophets that included Moses and Jesus. He is considered by Islam to be the greatest of the prophets.

- Muhammad was, in fact, a brutal militant who forced people to convert to his religion or die.

- Islam is a religion of works. Judgment, Muslims believe, will be based upon how many "good" works they have done in the name of Allah, versus how many "bad" works they have done.

- Terrorism from the radical Islamic world is a frightening thing, but faith in Jesus Christ overcomes all fear. God has given us a spirit of power and love and a sound mind. John 16:33 says Jesus brings peace, because he has overcome the world and its terrors.

- Jesus also commands Christians to love their enemies, including those who are lost in false, deadly religions.

KEY TERMS

reprobate: *sin-perverted thinking*

The New Roman World Order

BY ARNO FROESE

Let's Get Started

Economic union of Europe makes it potentially—if not in fact—the most powerful bloc of geopolitical influence on earth today. The institution of the European single currency unit called the euro on January 1, 2002, might well push the European Union (EU) toward becoming the heart of the revived Roman Empire prophesied to appear at the end of the age.

Europe is progressing on many fronts in establishing itself as the power sphere described in Daniel 2. Ultimately, the new Roman world order will give its power and authority to the **beast**. It will, among other things, include a deadly religious mix.

A worldwide religious system put together by Satan himself is coming as part of the new Roman order. This super-religious system, with the **False Prophet** at its head, will force everyone on earth to worship the beast or risk being murdered!

> **KEY TERMS**
>
> **beast:** Antichrist
> **False Prophet:** second beast; cohort of the Antichrist
>
> **FURTHER STUDY**
> Revelation 13:11–18; 17:12–13 (beast)

THE GREAT PRETENDER

The <u>devil</u> is the great pretender or imitator of God. He has, from the beginning of his dealings with humankind, been in the process of establishing his own world order. As part of his deadly plan, he intends to create his own religious system. That religious system, the false church, is being built globally. Bible prophecy declares that it is destined to become increasingly visible and more powerful throughout the world.

REMEMBER THIS

The devil's competition with God is also humanity's biggest problem! To hinder the world from coming to Christ for salvation, the devil has become the world's greatest deceiver and most dangerous impersonator. Who is Satan out to deceive? The world! Who is included in the world? Generally, Scripture refers to the "world" as all things not belonging to the church or Israel.

THE MISTRESS OF THE BEAST

> **Revelation 17:5** And upon her forehead was a name written, MYSTERY, BABYLON THE GREAT, THE MOTHER OF HARLOTS AND ABOMINATIONS OF THE EARTH.

Mystery Babylon

Who is this Mystery Babylon? She is referred to as both a woman and a city. She is a religious system, intricately intertwined with a powerful governmental system. God's Word likens Mystery Babylon to a drunken harlot or prostitute. She is not only guilty of **fornication** with all the kings (or rich rulers) of the world but also guilty of murdering God's own saints!

She is Antichrist's mistress, who represents everything that is hideously sinful and unclean. This contrasts starkly with Christ's virginal bride, the church, who is everything pure because of the Lord's shed blood, which has washed her to a state of perfection.

Keys to Identifying Mystery Babylon

Here are some ways we can identify this city.

1. The woman is clearly identified as a city with the capacity for world rule (Revelation 17:18).
2. The blood of the martyrs of Jesus must have been shed there (Revelation 17:6). John was puzzled by this vision. The angel, in Revelation 17:7, asked him, "Wherefore didst thou marvel?" and, without waiting for an answer, the heavenly messenger continued, "I will tell thee the mystery of the woman. . . ." God's messenger wanted there to be no doubt in John's mind, or in ours, that this is a religious system of unparalleled horror, symbolized in all of its gory details by the figure of a murderous, blood-thirsty harlot that would put Jezebel to shame.
3. The city must have been built on seven hills (Revelation 17:9). This is a topographical sign that will lead us to the identity of this city and its global spirit.
4. The city must have been a world-class economic center (Revelation 18:3).

KEY POINT

Mystery Babylon symbolizes the end-time religious system and is portrayed as Antichrist's mistress.

Out of the Running

Some cities today meet some of the criteria for being the city identified as Mystery Babylon, but the Bible tells us that this mysterious woman will perfectly fit all of the characteristics.

Moscow and Jerusalem claim to be built on seven hills. Moscow can't be Mystery Babylon because the blood of the martyrs of Jesus was not shed there during the time of the apostles. In fact, Moscow didn't even exist during Jesus' time.

The blood of the martyrs, it is true, was shed in Jerusalem, and seven hills can be counted in and around that city.

Since the city must have been a world-class economic center, Jerusalem cannot be a potential candidate. Although Jerusalem has been a religious center and to some extent a political center, it has never been a tremendous economic center.

FURTHER STUDY
1 Kings 18:4; 21:25; 2 Kings 9:22 (Jezebel)

> **Revelation 17:9** And here is the mind which hath wisdom. The seven heads are seven mountains, on which the woman sitteth.

Earth's End-Time Capital

The only city qualified to be headquarters of world leadership, according to the clues given in the Bible, is Rome. Rome doesn't merely represent a geographical city; it also symbolizes the epitome of European culture and modern world civilization.

Europe is the only continent to have reached the entire globe and permanently influenced virtually every nation with its ancient Roman law.

Europe effectively conquered the rest of the world, established time zones, and instituted all the weights and measures we commonly use today. Europe—specifically ancient Rome—provided the foundation for government and today's laws.

Most of the nations as we know them are the result of European colonial powers. European explorers and their sending countries not only influenced boundaries on every continent but also named virtually every country. This is particularly evident in the Middle East today. The borders of Lebanon, Syria, Jordan, Saudi Arabia, and Egypt, just to mention a few, were drawn and established by French and British colonial powers.

Europe's common denominator is the ancient Roman Empire. It is almost impossible to deny that the entire world is subject to the influence of European civilization. For example, without European languages, most countries would not be able to communicate with one another.

The establishment of civilization on the American continent (north and south) is also the result of European colonization. Residents of North and South America almost exclusively speak European languages. Spanish is the most frequently spoken, followed closely by English, Portuguese, and French.

> **Revelation 18:3** . . . and the merchants of the earth are waxed rich through the abundance of her delicacies . . .

Peace and Prosperity

History reveals that wherever the Roman Empire has extended its influence, prosperity and peace have followed. We must take specific notice that in the verse above the Bible is referring to the entire world and not just Rome or Europe.

While democracy was born in Greece, Rome was the first to implement the system of government "by the people and for the people." Marketing freedom made not only Rome but also all the nations that dealt with her rich indeed.

SPIRITUAL FORNICATION

> **Revelation 18:3** . . . the kings of the earth have committed fornication with her . . .

Sexual Sins

God speaks condemning words to the end-time political, commercial, and religious systems that will make up the Antichrist's kingdom. These are as repugnant to the Lord as sexual immorality, and he minces no words in equating their activities with fornication! There are three types of spiritual, or figurative, fornication: political, religious, and economic.

Political Fornication

Fornication is an immoral union between two people who are not married. The word is used in Revelation 18:3 to describe the mixing of religion and politics. Rome meets this criteria because in her midst is the **Vatican**, a religious organization that is also a politically recognized entity with membership in the United Nations. That mixture constitutes political and religious fornication.

KEY TERM

Vatican: *world headquarters of the Roman Catholic Church, in Rome*

THINK ABOUT IT

In the Old Testament it was forbidden for a political leader such as a king to take on the office of a priest. Saul, the first king of Israel, lost his kingdom and ultimately his life due to political fornication. "And Saul said, Bring hither a burnt offering to me, and peace offerings. And he offered the burnt offering. . . . And Samuel said to Saul, Thou hast done foolishly: thou hast not kept the commandment of the Lord thy God, which he commanded thee: for now would the Lord have established thy kingdom upon Israel for ever" (1 Samuel 13:9, 13).

Religious Fornication

The pope is a well-known religious figure and one of the most powerful politicians in the world. Although he doesn't have any legal political authority, he has great power to sway multitudes. When the pope speaks, the entire world listens.

It is interesting to note that many politicians, particularly those from the Western world, don't seem to be considered "in" unless they have been granted an audience with the pope in Rome. In fact, even though America is an overwhelmingly Protestant country, our presidents go to Rome for that very reason.

THINK ABOUT IT

Today, religion in general is being put on a lamp stand in all the nations of the world—regardless of their particular faith. Most of us underestimate the power of religion when it is combined with politics. This is particularly true since the fall of Soviet communism, which represented **atheism**. The communists rejected religion and religion rejected them!

Economic Fornication

The ancient Roman culture on which the world is based has allowed the world to prosper to an unprecedented extent. Today's automobiles are far superior to their predecessors. The average American home is 50 percent larger than in the early 1900s. What the average worker can afford today—including dishwashers, refrigerators, washing machines, heating units, air conditioners, and microwave ovens—would have been only a dream for even the most affluent in the early 1900s. Money has become our god.

> KEY TERM
>
> **atheism:** *belief that God doesn't exist*

MYSTERY BABYLON BURNS

Revelation 18:9–10 And the kings of the earth, who have committed fornication and lived deliciously with her, shall bewail her, and lament for her, when they shall see the smoke of her burning. Standing afar off for the fear of her torment, saying, Alas, alas that great city Babylon, that mighty city! for in one hour is thy judgment come.

Where There's Smoke

All of the glorious religious, political, and economic success will ultimately end. Babylon will be destroyed. When Mystery Babylon burns, sailors aboard ships in the Mediterranean Sea will see the smoke rise. That will mark the end of the new world order.

Just as the <u>Babylon</u> of old was completely destroyed, so the city of Rome will experience the same <u>devastation</u>.

REMEMBER THIS

The end of European independence was sealed during World Wars I and II. Europe had had enough; it desired peace and prosperity—not through confrontation but by integration. After all, every nation wants peace and prosperity. The problem is that each nation claims to have the solution. The solution always winds up being a power struggle.

KEY TERM

ecumenical movement: the urge toward uniting all religions

FURTHER STUDY

Revelation 17–18 (Babylon)
Revelation 18:23–24 (devastation)

THE REVIVED ROMAN EMPIRE

The modern-era "peace process"—economic integration on an ever-widening scale—is not exclusive to Europe, but is also taking place in the Americas. Today, the spirit of ancient Babylon and Mystery Babylon is manifested politically through the avenue of democracy, economically via free trade, and religiously by means of the **ecumenical movement**. Despite the fact that some nations' economies are still in disarray and out of the developing global economic loop, the fundamentals of European civilization and Roman laws will ultimately prevail.

Based on our understanding of the prophetic Word of God, Rome's triumph is an absolute must. All nations cannot be deceived unless they all jump on the same bandwagon. Politically speaking, democracy is the only feasible form of government under which people can express their agreement openly. Freedom of religion is another important item in this prophesied end-time system because Mystery Babylon is a mixture of politics, economy, *and* religion.

REMEMBER THIS

The revived Roman Empire, new world order, global society, one-world earth, or whatever it may be called, is not something for which we are waiting. It is here today and is demonstrating power around the globe.

Foundations for the New Roman Order

To better understand what Mystery Babylon and the new Roman world order of prophecy are all about, let us look at the historical roots of this growing monster.

Although Europe was in disarray after World War II, it quickly and successfully rebuilt its economy. By 1954, Western Europe could already talk about an "economic miracle"; however, that revealed a problem. While the world had united against Germany during the war, each country was now on its own, operating independently surrounded by impregnable economic walls. Each nation had tariff and trade barriers that made it difficult, if not impossible, to carry on commerce with other nations.

Fuel for Fulfilling Prophecy

On May 9, 1950, Robert Schuman, France's foreign minister contacted West German Chancellor Konrad Adenauer with a proposal to merge the German and French steel and coal production on an international basis but not under intergovernmental authority. Adenauer responded that very evening. By May 1952, the ratification of six nations of the European coal and steel community was completed.

Organizing the New Roman Order

The success of economic unification was undeniable. This led to another negotiation for further integration. In March 1957, the Treaties of Rome were signed, establishing the European Economic Community (EEC) and the European Atomic Energy Commission. In 1962, a common agriculture policy followed.

Europe Reunites!

Agricultural integration set the stage for the Brussels Treaty of 1965, often referred to as the Second Treaty of Rome. During that negotiation, all previous treaties were merged into one and identified in a fourfold structure: commission, council, parliament, and court. Finally, in 1973, the United Kingdom was admitted as a member, accompanied by Ireland and Denmark. Greece was added in 1981, and Spain and Portugal joined in 1986. In December 1991, the EEC approved the Treaty of Maastricht, the third foundational treaty.

On January 1, 1995, Austria, Finland, and Sweden were accepted into the Union. Norway and Switzerland have also been approved, but nationals in both countries have declined the invitation.

The following eleven countries have applied for membership: Bulgaria, Cyprus, Czech Republic, Estonia, Hungary, Latvia, Lithuania, Poland, Romania, Slovakia, Slovania. Turkey has applied for membership since 1967 and has been refused by the EU.

Following the logical idea that a single market requires a single currency, the Maastricht Treaty established a three-stage (1991, 1994, 1997) creation of the European Monetary Union. The single European currency unit—the euro—was born January 1, 2002.

The success of unity is apparent. Less-developed economies of member countries have increased significantly.

THINK ABOUT IT

The power of unity is obvious and infectious. The EU needs a united foreign policy to look after its economic interests. As of June 3, 1999, the Council of Foreign Ministers developed a plan based on a common defense policy independent of NATO.

AWAITING THE COMING LEADER

Since no other system on the horizon is strong enough to challenge Europe, it is reasonable to assume that when Scripture talks about the end-time power structure, it speaks primarily about Europe. This is not a surprise because Europe (Rome) ruled when Jesus was born, and it must be in power when he returns. All that is required is one charismatic leader.

Daniel 8:25 And through his policy also he shall cause craft to prosper in his hand; and he shall magnify himself in his heart, and by peace shall destroy many: he shall also stand up against the Prince of princes; but he shall be broken without hand.

Coming World Leader

Although the European community functions relatively well, it is missing one vital element that is mentioned in the Bible: a leader. Daniel gave us details about this coming world leader who would be the decisive personality not only within the European Union but also worldwide. This man will lead the world's prosperity policy, subsequently fulfilling the Revelation 18:3 prophecy concerning merchants becoming rich.

Numerous false assumptions have been made about the Antichrist's identity. It is wrong to attempt to identify certain countries or groups of political and economic associations and label them as the empire of the Antichrist. That is precisely what Satan wants people to do. Pointing an accusing finger at others is a sure way to become spiritually blind. It really doesn't matter who rules. All people of the world fall into the category of unbelieving Gentile, Jew, or Christian.

Daniel 11:21–23 And in his estate shall stand up a vile person, to whom they shall not give the honour of the kingdom: but he shall come in peaceably, and obtain the kingdom by flatteries. And with the arms of a flood shall they be overthrown from before him, and shall be broken; yea, also the prince of the covenant. And after the league made with him he shall work deceitfully: for he shall come up, and shall become strong with a small people.

False Prince of Peace

KEY POINT

The false prince of peace will come into power peaceably and deceitfully, but not forcefully.

How will the leader mentioned in Daniel come into power? Notice the words that describe his entrance: "peaceably"; obtaining "the kingdom by flatteries"; "deceitfully." Aren't these fitting words to describe today's politician? To generate votes and be elected into office, candidates for political positions in our world democratic system often use flattery and act deceitfully. Candidates who tell the truth don't win their party's nomination in America and aren't considered for election. Imagine a candidate who told his constituents that taxes must be doubled in order to pay our national debt! Such a person would become an automatic loser.

THUNDERING TOWARD TRIBULATION!

1 Thessalonians 5:3 . . . when they shall say, Peace and safety; then sudden destruction cometh upon them, as travail upon a woman with child; and they shall not escape.

Sudden Destruction

KEY POINT

Our mission as Christians isn't to fight globalism; it is to proclaim Christ.

Europe, the root of world civilization, democracy, law, free trade, and freedom of religion, is becoming unified with such mind-boggling speed that the bulk of the world's population, even the Europeans, do not realize that we have entered the last stages of the end times. World peace will be achieved along with unprecedented prosperity, creating a global society with justice and liberty for all people. The environment will be protected and wealth shared to such a degree that it will prove the world has finally entered the kingdom of peace.

Just when things appear to be most peaceful, the world will be most deceived. Its destruction will come suddenly like labor pains come upon a woman, and there will be no escape. The world will enter the tribulation period, also known as Daniel's seventy weeks.

As Christians, we place ourselves in extreme danger when we allow our lives to be soiled with the success and glory of this world. We are in the world, but not to be of the world. We are normal people, but our goals are to involve a different agenda. We are heaven bound, not earthbound. Our responsibility and our calling lie in proclaiming truth. Jesus said that he is the way, the truth, and the life.

We have not been commanded to fight against globalism, the new world order, or the power structure of Antichrist. Our job as Christians is to tell all people everywhere that there is only <u>one name</u> under heaven given among men, whereby we must be saved.

FURTHER STUDY
Acts 4:12 (one name)

Nevada Sun

February 27, 2002

Saudi Prince Pushes Mideast Peace Plan

HEADLINE
HIGHLIGHT

JIDDAH, Saudi Arabia (AP) - Crown Prince Abdullah said he will press the Arab League to back a Saudi land-for-peace offer to end the Arab-Israeli conflict, a top EU official said Wednesday.

Abdullah, Saudi Arabia's acting leader since King Fahd suffered a stroke in 1995, had a sixty-minute meeting Wednesday with European Union foreign policy chief Javier Solana in this Red Sea port city.

Solana was the first Western envoy to discuss Abdullah's proposal which calls for Israel to withdraw from Arab territory it occupied in the 1967 Mideast war, including the West Bank, Gaza and East Jerusalem, in return for the Arab world's recognition.

The proposals have been welcomed by the Palestinians and several Arab countries, and the United States has called it a "note of hope,"

> though stopped short of considering it a
> breakthrough. Ariel Sharon told Solana earlier he
> wanted to know more about the plan, according to
> the EU envoy.

PROPHETIC IMPACT

Europe's influence on the Israeli-Palestinian peace process becomes stronger with each passing week. Even the American government sometimes seems cowed by this burgeoning new power. At present, America and the European Union seem to be on equal footing in heading up the so-called international community (another name for the new world order). We can look for America's power to decline, however, while Europe's gathers momentum.

CHAPTER WRAP-UP

- Satan wants to compete with God and to take over the very throne of the living God. Part of the devil's plan is to establish his own throne on planet Earth.
- The European Union is gaining power as a world force. The euro, the new currency unit that provides economic unity, could soon make Europe the most powerful economic geopolitical bloc on earth. Europe could be developing into the heart of the revived Roman Empire prophesied by Daniel.
- According to Bible prophecy, there will be a one-world religion or religious system, which will be a part of the last world empire and headed by the Antichrist. The False Prophet of Revelation 13 will ultimately cause all to worship the Antichrist or be killed. This false religious system of the Tribulation is symbolized in Revelation 17 as a harlot who rides the beast. She is called Mystery Babylon.
- During the Tribulation the whole world will come under the rule of the revived Roman Empire. This world system ruled by Antichrist will be destroyed according to Revelation 18 in fulfillment of Daniel 2.

The Evil Day

Wherefore take unto you the whole armour of God, that ye may be able to withstand in the evil day, and having done all, to stand.
—EPHESIANS 6:13

BY JOSEPH R. CHAMBERS

Let's Get Started

The heart of humankind has not changed. Every generation has seen a repeat of the same mistakes, rebellions, and stubbornness. God has always had a plan, and his plan will be fulfilled. Humans also have plans; however, their plans are not their own but their unseen master's plan. Humankind's plan is always opposite of the Father's plan. All we really have to do, besides believing the whole Word of God, is to look at the past and read the future. Every action of our God has moved at a preplanned pace toward a definite future. Each past expression of his redemption is like foundation stones preparing the glorious tomorrow.

Amos 6:3–8 Ye that put far away the evil day, and cause the seat of violence to come near . . . Therefore now shall they go captive with the first that go captive . . . therefore will I deliver up the city with all that is therein.

EVIL DAY DAWNS

The world's inhabitants resist God's future. The direction of human nature, which is guided by the flesh and Satan's schemes, is going in one direction while God's desires for humankind are in another direction. The flesh desires to be satisfied and Satan's world order is more than ready to offer what appears to be "living it up."

The church usually joins the world and becomes a part of its plans and schemes. One only has to visit the archaeological sites in the Sumer Valley of Iraq to see the great religious towers of Noah's day to understand that the world and most religions are always headed in the same direction. That direction is the "evil day" spoken of by Amos the prophet and written about by the apostle Paul in Ephesians. Already, we see the horizon of that dawning evil day.

Ecclesiastes 1:9 There is no new thing under the sun.

BACK TO THE FUTURE

FURTHER STUDY
Hebrews 13:8 (not change)

The past is truly a picture of the future. Our God does <u>not change</u>. Even humankind does not change its basic nature: "Can the Ethiopian change his skin, or the leopard his spots? then may ye also do good, that are accustomed to do evil" (Jeremiah 13:23).

TWO PICTURES OF REBELLION

The Bible gives us many incredible pictures of past generations acting out their rebellion until the Creator's holiness was offended to the point of judgment. Our God is perfect in all aspects of his nature, and his judgment cannot pass the line of his appointed wrath.

Two past generations provide perfect pictures of the present: Noah's world and Sodom and Gomorrah. These two civilizations serve as striking examples of unfettered human wickedness that attracted God's attention.

1. "But as the days of **Noe** were, so shall also the coming of the Son of man be" (Matthew 24:37). Jesus made that clear statement in his Olivet Discourse.
2. "Even as Sodom and Gomorrah, and the cities about them in like manner, giving themselves over to **fornication**, and going after strange flesh, are set forth for an example, suffering the vengeance of eternal fire" (Jude 1:7).

REMEMBER THIS

The point of judgment occurs when humankind loses all sense of guilt and restraint and the Spirit of God ceases to give grace. God's grace was identified in Scripture before the Flood came and destroyed the world: "And the Lord said, My spirit shall not always strive with man, for that he also is flesh: yet his days shall be an hundred and twenty years" (Genesis 6:3). God will never judge any generation until grace has been ultimately spurned.

Genesis 6:2, 4–5 That the sons of God saw the daughters of men that they were fair; and they took them wives of all which they chose. . . . There were giants in the earth in those days; and also after that, when the sons of God came in unto the daughters of men, and they bare children to them, the same became mighty men which were of old, men of renown. And God saw that the wickedness of man was great in the earth, and that every imagination of the thoughts of his heart was only evil continually.

> **KEY TERMS**
>
> **Noe:** *Noah*
> **fornication:** *sex between unmarried persons*

The Days of Noah

Genesis describes three facts about the depth of sin that characterized Noah's generation.

1. *The loss of all morals.* The laws of righteousness and any sense of the nature that God created in humans were ut-

terly lost. People's lives had become unbridled from lack of restraint, and they totally gave in to the vileness of their sinful nature. Men gazed in lust upon the opposite sex and found great pleasure in sexual pursuits. Delight in one's own lifelong companion had been lost. Sex was not intimacy but prowess. Nothing describes a society on the edge of losing all grace more powerfully than sexual perversion.

2. *The invasion of evil spirits at the invitation of the people.* As humankind lost its moral consciousness and fear of God, it quickly began to welcome the opposing spiritual realm. The daughters of men became intimate with fallen angels. Nothing is more impossible to maintain than a spiritual vacuum. If the true God is not honored, the idiot god, Satan, and his fallen angels will be.

   The women of the liberal church who are involved in the worship of Sophia present a perfect example of an invitation to intimacy with demons. If Jesus tarries, the coming wave of immorality and false spirituality will clearly be manifest. Bestiality, sadomasochism, and many other forms of sexual perversion are on the same level as consorting with demons or fallen angels. Sexual immorality leads to spiritual idolatry.

3. *The loss of all consciousness of humankind's God-likeness.* Humans were created to reason and think on a level second only to God. Adam gave every creature that the Father created a name based on the characteristics that were inbred in that creature. Naming the animals was an overwhelming task easily performed by the first man. Adam and Eve could visit with God in the evening of each day and discuss truth that only the Creator could have breathed into them.

   From that lofty place, humankind fell to an unbelievable depth. Created to have dominion over God's world and to have intimate communion with the Holy One, now humankind's only thoughts are of sex, pleasure, vileness, and self.

KEY POINT

Adam and Eve were created in God's image and could fellowship one-on-one with God, knowing his truth.

Genesis 8:21 And the Lord smelled a sweet savour; and the Lord said in his heart, I will not again curse the ground any more for man's sake; for the imagination of man's heart is evil from his youth; neither will I again smite any more every thing living, as I have done.

Judgment of Noah's Day

The sights and sounds of such a depraved multitude caused God to regret that he had made people. The judgment of Noah's day was horrible beyond description. Even the plants, trees, and animals suffered because of people's sinfulness. Apparently, even God was overwhelmed by the acts of his justice. He promised never again to judge the world in the same manner.

> FURTHER STUDY
> Genesis 6:6 (regret)

Genesis 18:20–21 And the Lord said, Because the cry of Sodom and Gomorrah is great, and because their sin is very grievous; I will go down now, and see whether they have done altogether according to the cry of it, which is come unto me; and if not, I will know.

The Days of Sodom and Gomorrah

The judgment of Noah's civilization was a worldwide event that took the lives of all humans but eight. Sodom and Gomorrah represented a localized community of a few large towns and a few thousand people. Apparently, the residents of Sodom and Gomorrah either forgot about the Flood or they snubbed their noses at the face of God. In either case the sin of moral depravity was at the heart of their rebellion.

The cry of evil, the tumult of godless confusion, had risen like a cloud out of these wicked cities, and its stench had entered the nostrils of God. In the words above, God told Abraham that he was going to destroy the cities.

Can you understand the depth of what God said to Abraham, our father of faith? There is a point at which the stench of sin

KEY TERMS

pre-incarnate son: *Christ before his physical birth*

Lot: *Abraham's nephew who lived in Sodom*

blaspheme: *to profane or injure God's name*

undefiled: *untouched by sin*

unchaste: *impure, lacking moral boundaries*

FURTHER STUDY

Genesis 19:1–7 (acted out)
Genesis 19:24–25
(destroyed)

REMEMBER THIS

ascends to God, and justice—righteous judgment—must take place. Our God does not act until he offers his last expression of mercy.

Before he destroyed the cities, God sent his **pre-incarnate son** and two angels to visit Abraham. While the angels proceeded to Sodom, the Lord and Abraham discussed mercy. When the angels entered Sodom, they discovered the source of the stench. They had no more than entered the home of **Lot** when the perverted men of the city <u>acted out</u> their cravings for evil satisfaction. The Sodomites recognized the visitors as holy, untouched flesh, which they wanted to exploit.

The ultimate act of demon possession is to defile the righteous. Satan and his unholy angels are never more animated than when they can defile the holy and **blaspheme** the Creator. These men's sodomy had passed the point at which flesh was their craving; they wanted to blaspheme that which was pure and **undefiled**.

Jude 1:7 Even as Sodom and Gomorrah, and the cities about them in like manner, giving themselves over to fornication, and going after strange flesh, are set forth for an example, suffering the vengeance of eternal fire.

KEY POINT

A righteous, just God has no choice but to treat every generation by the standard he has set forth in Scripture.

Judgment of Sodom and Gomorrah

God <u>destroyed</u> Sodom and Gomorrah because of their wickedness. God's judgment of these cities is an example of where grace ends and judgment follows. The words "giving themselves over to fornication" are translated from one Greek word, *ekporneuo*. Its definition in the *New Strong's Complete Dictionary of Bible Words* accurately describes this generation: "to be utterly **unchaste**."

The men of Sodom did not have pornographic magazines, television sex, or internet connections. Can you imagine the level of depravity the people of Sodom would have discovered if they had our modern technology?

You do not need to imagine because our generation has already experienced it. Pedophilia or sex with children reflects exactly what was occurring in Sodom and Gomorrah. Instead of being contained in a few cities as in that day, pedophilia has now become a worldwide scourge that our God will not ignore. The past has become the present!

TODAY'S EVIL RIVALS OLD

KEY POINT

God's cup of wrath is approaching the brim.

The sin of our present world is close to exceeding the sin of Noah's age and Sodom and Gomorrah. The imagination of our generation has produced the technology to send wave after wave of depravity into every nook and cranny of the globe. Homosexuals and lesbians have become part of the most potent force of societal change known to human history. Humanists have created the legal organizations to force the high court systems to support their wildest imaginations.

We are on a fast track to a literal hell on earth, and only the intervention of the Creator will stop the total destruction of both the earth and all human existence.

The Catholic Church in America has been rocked by sex scandals involving priests and altar boys. In addition, during April 2002 the U.S. Supreme Court struck down an attempt by Congress to ban computer-generated images of sex with children, reasoning that since no real children are involved it is not pedophilia and does no harm to minors. Virtual child pornography is now protected under free speech laws.

James 5:7–11 Be patient therefore, brethren, unto the coming of the Lord. Behold, the husbandman waiteth for the precious fruit of the earth, and hath long patience for it, until he receive the early and latter rain. Be ye also patient; stablish your hearts:

for the coming of the Lord draweth nigh. Grudge not one against another, brethren, lest ye be condemned: behold, the judge standeth before the door. Take, my brethren, the prophets, who have spoken in the name of the Lord, for an example of suffering affliction, and of patience. Behold, we count them happy which endure. Ye have heard of the patience of Job, and have seen the end of the Lord; that the Lord is very pitiful, and of tender mercy.

Patience in God's Judgment

Believers need to be patient. Our God never acts compulsively. "For ever, O Lord, thy word is settled in heaven" (Psalm 119:89). All his ways are pure and eternal, and he will never lie. The words of our God have assured us that grace and mercy will be extended until the last thread of hope is broken. James, the brother of Jude, wrote the words of judgment above to describe the heart of God to us.

Mercy in God's Judgment

KEY POINT

"Rainbow in the storm" means mercy in the midst of judgment.

Only one thing deters the coming of the Lord. He waits "for the precious fruit of the earth" to come to know him as savior (James 5:7). Mercy is still available for a limited period. Even in the coming judgment, God promises a harvest after the Great Tribulation has begun and after it ends. Even in judgment there is mercy. This truth is one of the great results of our Creator's words to Noah after the Flood destroyed all human life, except his family.

LESSONS FROM OLD

Genesis 7:1 And the Lord said unto Noah, Come thou and all thy house into the ark; for thee have I seen righteous before me in this generation.

Biblical Type of the Ark

We can profit from recognizing lessons from God's judgment of former generations. The ark is a great **type** of the Rapture. Noah found grace in the eyes of the Lord, and the Father instructed him to prepare an ark out of a specific wood. Living in the midst of sins so vile that even the heart of God was repulsed, Noah prepared his ark and preached the gospel of grace as he knew it. When the ark was finished in God's planned time schedule, the grace of God was finished also.

> **KEY TERMS**
>
> **type:** *symbol of something*
> **bride of Christ:** *believers in Jesus Christ as savior*

God spoke to Noah from within the ark. The Creator did not say, "Go into the ark." He said, "Come thou and all thy house into the ark."

The ark was a "chamber" or a "covering" from the storm. When Noah and his whole entourage were safe inside, "God shut the door" (Genesis 7:16). Noah was safe above the storm, but returned to land when the storm was finished. This paints a beautiful picture of the future.

Our Father has prepared a "chamber" where the **bride of Christ** will be safe during the coming Great Tribulation. When the moment of grace for this wicked world is finished, the trumpet will sound, and we will move into that prepared place. After the seven years are finished, we will return to the earth, as did Noah and his family, to continue God's plan for his earth.

> **Genesis 19:22a** Haste thee, escape thither; for I cannot do any thing till thou be come thither.

Biblical Type of Escape from Sodom

The angel spoke to Lot and said the words above. The warning enabled Lot and his daughters to escape the judgment. Lot's escape from Sodom and Gomorrah was also a type, although an imperfect one, of the Rapture. The judgment in Sodom and Gomorrah could not begin until Lot was out of the city. Likewise, God's judgment of unbelievers will not occur until believers are safely taken out of the world.

REMEMBER THIS

God never judges the righteous with the wicked. Sodom and Gomorrah serve as an example of this and a picture of the future. When God judges the wicked, he will rescue his children as he rescued Lot. We can trust God to take care of us.

EVIL DEFIANCE

KEY POINT

Nothing surprises God.

The past is a picture of the future. God is eternal; he doesn't change. Sin is defiance against the holiness of God, so sin expresses the same nature and acts in each generation.

The Bible is an **infallible** book that has recorded the past as well as the future. It is of little consequence to God to perfectly declare the future because the future is no different from the past. It is all the perfect expression of his eternal nature. Nothing and no one can surprise the God of all creation!

> **KEY TERM**
>
> **infallible:** *perfect without mistake*

This generation seems on the very edge of the "evil day." When we watch the news and see the terrible things around us, we sometimes think that *today* is the "evil day."

REMEMBER THIS

If you are a child of God, have joy in your heart. The Lord promises a new day. The perfect peace in the unstained Garden of Eden is to be replayed for eternity!

HEADLINE HIGHLIGHT

National Review Online

April 26, 2002

Saudi Telethon Host Calls for Enslaving Jewish Women

From the Saudi Information Service

WASHINGTON DC - The Saudi Information Agency has obtained a tape by prominent government official cleric Shaikh Saad Al-Buraik calling for enslaving Jewish women. The tape is called "a Monkey Desecrates Mosque," and was delivered in a Riyadh government mosque. The monkey refers to Jews.

Al-Buraik, a Wahhabi cleric, is closely tied to Prince AbdulAziz Ben Fahd, the king's youngest son, and member of the Saudi delegation accompanying Crown Prince Abdullah on his current visit. . . .

The following are excerpts of the tape:

On the situation in the Palestinian areas, he said:

> Oh Believer, it's a wish, as much as it is pains, but we have hopes that the situation in Palestine will explode. . . . No one dies before their day. Is it too dear to us that among our honorable beloved die as martyrs? Their death dates were written before their birth. That they die as martyrs. "Say even if were at your home, those who will die will walk to their death."
>
> Which is a better choice, to die on your bed, or to die perseverant, fighting, not retreating. Which is better to suffer long before death many days, or taste death quickly?
>
> Which is better to suffer a slow death, or die as a martyr on your way to heaven. A death that you will be forgiven on the first drop of your blood. . . .

On Jews and Christians, he said:

> People should know that Jews are backed by the Christians, and the battle that we are going through is not with Jews only, but also with those who believe that Allah is a third in a Trinity, and those who said that Jesus is the son of Allah, and Allah is Jesus, the son of Mary.

About America, he said:

> I am against America until this life ends, until the Day of Judgment. . . . My hatred of America, if part of it was contained in the universe, it would collapse. . . . She is the root of all evils, and wickedness on earth . . .

About Jewish women as slaves, he said:

> Muslim Brothers in Palestine, do not have any mercy neither compassion on the Jews, their blood, their money, their flesh. Their women are yours to take, legitimately. God made them yours. Why don't you enslave their women? Why don't you wage jihad? Why don't you pillage them?

PROPHETIC IMPACT

Paul the apostle wrote in his epistle to Timothy: "This know also, that in the last days perilous times shall come . . . For men shall be . . . trucebreakers, false accusers, incontinent [undisciplined and/or addicted], fierce, despisers of those that are good, Traitors, heady, highminded, lovers of pleasures more than lovers of God . . . having a form of godliness, but denying the power thereof. . . ." (2 Timothy 3:1–4).

Paul seems to be describing our times. Our State Department has declared Prince Abdullah and his oil-rich nation to be our friends. The deeds flowing from Saudi, however, gush under more pressure than the black gold of the region.

Truly, this is an evil day. We don't have to look to other nations to find dangers and debaucheries on the right hand and on the left. Much of American culture today fits Paul's words as precisely as do our traitorous friends in the Middle East.

CHAPTER WRAP-UP

- The heart of humankind has not changed. Every generation repeats the same mistakes, rebellions, and stubbornness.

- The direction of human nature, which is guided by the flesh and Satan's schemes, is in disobedience to God.

- Past generations acted out their rebellion until the Creator's holiness was offended to the point of judgment.

- The Flood of Noah's day and the destruction of Sodom and Gomorrah are examples of the results of evil.

- Jesus predicted that the time just before he comes again would be like the days of evil during Sodom and Gomorrah.

- Viciousness, greed, and sexual perversion are traits the Bible says will constitute the "evil day" at the end of the age.

- God promises that his son, Jesus, will return to earth and end evil. Believers need to be patient, recognizing that God delays judgment because he is patient and merciful.

- We can look to the ark and Lot's escape as pictures of the Rapture and our escape.

LAST-DAYS LAUNCHING PAD

CHAPTER 7

A World Lost in Space

BY DAVE BREESE

CHAPTER HIGHLIGHTS

- Human's Key to God's Plan
- Incredible Prophecies Yet Future
- History's Most Exciting Time

Let's Get Started

Earth was just a small planet, circling an unspectacular star on the outer edge of one of the billions of galaxies in God's creation. To the great amazement of most of heaven, God chose that improbable planet to be the final battlefield for the war that had raged so long in heaven.

There had been a terrible revolt. **Lucifer**, the highest-ranked creation of God, had made an attempt to tear God from his throne. A third of heaven's angels had been deceived by Lucifer and joined in his doomed <u>rebellion</u> against God. So Lucifer became **Satan** and was cast out of heaven to that little world lost in space—a place called earth.

> **KEY TERMS**
>
> **Lucifer:** *highest-ranking angel*
>
> **Satan:** *devil, Lucifer's name after he was cast out of heaven*
>
> **FURTHER STUDY**
>
> Revelation 12:7–9 (rebellion)

Revelation 12:7–9 And there was war in heaven; Michael and his angels fought against the dragon, and the dragon fought and his angels, And prevailed not, neither was their place found any more in heaven. And the great dragon was cast out, that old serpent, called the Devil, and Satan, who deceiveth the whole world; he was cast out into the earth, and his angels were cast out with him.

HUMANS KEY TO GOD'S PLAN

Planet Earth was very special to God, because on it he created unique beings called humans. Humans were unlike anything else in God's creation for they carried within them the image of God. They were creatures of great eternal destiny!

God wanted people to exercise free will and to choose to follow God, and by so doing prove the power of the grace of God. In the end, the saga of humankind will come to a dramatic climax that will forever put to rest Satan's rebellion.

Throughout history Satan has been the enemy of humans, tempting them to sin against God and attempting to steal their eternal destiny by thwarting the plan of God. He seduced Adam and Eve into eating the forbidden fruit, promising it would make them like God. In essence, he was passing on his own delusion and the sin of rebellion—for he, too, wanted to be like God. Ever since Adam and Eve sinned, earth was a world *lost* in space!

FURTHER STUDY
Genesis 3:1–7
  (Adam and Eve)
Romans 5:12 (fallen)

People Lost in Sin

So what did it mean to be lost? That lost condition, and participation in the great rebellion against God, robbed humans of so much! Every individual, rather than being born into the family of God, entered this life as a child of fallen people.

Human culture, which could have blossomed to heights we can only imagine, was decimated by sin and corruption. The home, which should have been a bastion of love and harmony, was infiltrated by confusion, conflict, and infidelity. Even religion, which should have brought people closer to God, degenerated into a collection of entities that built religious empires upon lies. Religion became false religion as it subjugated its people and stood in the way of their bright eternal destiny. Finally, even the places that professed the name of God became festering pockets of resistance to the will of God.

Christ's Redeeming Sacrifice

But God had the answer to the rebellion; he did not allow the world to remain lost. He had always known the price of **redemption**. God was prepared to pay that price to redeem people and abolish sin and the rebellion of Satan from the universe. The only begotten Son of God, Jesus Christ, took the <u>form</u> of a man and proved for all eternity the love and grace of God. Jesus <u>died</u> in the place of sinful humans, so that anyone, by choosing to believe on him as savior, could have everlasting life. It was an exotically tender and loving plan, so much so that the Bible tells us even "the angels desire to look into" it (1 Peter 1:12).

Jews Chosen by God

The heavenly Father also chose a nation to represent his truth to the world, a nation from which the Messiah, his Son, would come. That nation was Israel, and it was of Jewish descent that God brought Jesus Christ into the world as God-Man.

KEY TERMS

redemption: *God's purchase of lost people*

sedition: *insurrection, rebellion*

FURTHER STUDY

Romans 5:17 (form)
Philippians 4:8 (died)
Matthew 27:35–37 (hung)
2 Corinthians 5:21 (placed)
Romans 8:1 (paid)
Matthew 28:4–5 (rose)
Luke 24:51 (returned)
Acts 2:1–4 (empowered)

Jesus Christ gave his life on Calvary's cross that we might live. As he <u>hung</u> there suspended between heaven and earth, God reached out into every lost heart, every despairing spirit, every sinful soul, and <u>placed</u> that awful package of human sin on Jesus—the one who knew no sin. With his sacrificial death, the sin-debt was forever <u>paid</u>.

Death Conquered

Death could not keep its prey. Jesus <u>rose</u> from the dead in triumph over the grave, bringing proof that he had conquered death and sin once and for all. When Christ <u>returned</u> to heaven, he left behind an organism called the church, the body of Christ. <u>Empowered</u> by the Holy Spirit of God, the church continued to spread the message of the gospel of the grace of God. The world had the opportunity to learn again about the love of God and the **sedition** of the devil!

Prophetic Word Gives Hope

Ah, the rich tapestry which is God's plan! So there would be no room for misunderstanding, God inspired faithful men of old to write his plan in a book. That book, the Bible, contains <u>everything</u> humans need to know to live victoriously in this life and to make a triumphant entrance into the next. To prove that these are not mere words, God wove a thread of prophecy throughout the Bible that continues to prove to men the utter truth of the Word of God. It is, in essence, history written in advance.

FURTHER STUDY
2 Peter 1:3 (everything)
1 Thessalonians 4:15–18 (Rapture)

Within the marvelous framework of Bible prophecy lie the stories of faith, intrigue, hope, and sin that have made society what it is today. God's prophetic Word precisely foretold the rise and fall of the world's great empires—Babylon, Media-Persia, Greece, and Rome—the tactics of war that would be used, and more. There were hundreds of prophecies of the coming Messiah, each of which was precisely fulfilled by Jesus Christ. There are also hundreds of additional prophecies that foretell his Second Coming and give great hope to this lost world today. Why? Because history will confirm that Bible prophecy has never been in error.

INCREDIBLE PROPHECIES YET FUTURE

KEY POINT

Since the Bible has been so perfectly precise in the past, we have every reason to believe that it will continue to be so in the days to come.

Today, this lonely, seemingly insignificant world lost in space has come to an amazing crossroad. Some of the most provocative prophecies in the Bible remain yet to be fulfilled, and what those prophecies will mean to our world is incredible!

Among the most exciting prophecies (and the next major prophecy to be fulfilled) is the <u>Rapture</u> of the church. The promise of the coming Rapture means a generation of Christians will not experience death. Rather, these believers will suddenly and without warning be changed into supernatural beings that are able to inhabit and inherit all that heaven has for them.

Revelation 3:10 Because thou hast kept the word of my patience, I also will keep thee from the hour of temptation, which will come upon all the world, to try them that dwell upon the earth.

No Wrath for Believers

Some people suggest that Christians must go through the **Tribulation** in order to make their robes white and clean, but Scripture does not support this teaching. For example, in Revelation 3, Jesus promised the church at Philadelphia, which was the faithful church of the last days, that he would save them from the "hour of temptation."

Again, and again, the Bible assures us, "God hath not appointed us to wrath" (1 Thessalonians 5:9). So the Rapture of the church is an event that could happen at any time—even today!

Left to Their Own Vices

High on the list of coming events is the rise of the **Antichrist**. The Bible foretells the coming of an evil world ruler who will be the incarnation of Satan. His evil machinations will lead the world into a seven-year period of death and destruction called the Tribulation—the last half of which will be so terrible that the Bible calls it the Great Tribulation.

Since the **fall** in the Garden of Eden, humankind has pursued the lie of the devil that they can make it on their own without God. The Tribulation will be that time when God finally says, "All right, have it your way. See what you can do on your own."

The myth of autonomous humankind has so clouded people's minds that they will actually believe they can create a human utopia without God. Instead of peace, people will bring about a time so horrible that the Bible says, "And except those days should be shortened, there should no flesh be saved" (Matthew 24:22). Because of that dreadful malady called sin, the world lost in space will deteriorate to the point that it faces certain and total destruction.

KEY TERMS

Tribulation: *seven-year period of death and destruction*

Antichrist: *earth's last and most terrible dictator*

fall: *original sin of humankind in Garden of Eden*

FURTHER STUDY

Revelation 13:18
 (world ruler)

Genesis 3:6–8 (fall)

> **Revelation 19:11–14** And I saw heaven opened and behold a white horse; and he that sat upon him was called Faithful and True, and in righteousness he doth judge and make war. His eyes were like a flame of fire, and on his head were many crowns; and he had a name written, that no man knew, but he himself. And he was clothed with a vesture dipped in blood; and his name is called The Word of God. And the armies that were in heaven followed him upon white horses, clothed in fine linen, white and clean.

Christ's Glorious, Triumphant Return

During the Tribulation, the world will see the advent of the **four horsemen** of the apocalypse and the remainder of the **seven seals, seven trumpets**, and **seven bowl** judgments of God (see illustration, page 111). In that brief span, over half the people of the world will die. And that number would grow to include all life on planet Earth were it not for the glorious return of Jesus Christ.

Christ will return, riding from heaven on a white horse with his saints. Enoch also foresaw this marvelous event, and his prophecy is echoed by Jude: "Behold, the Lord cometh with ten thousands of His saints" (Jude 14).

You and I, as **born-again** children of God, will be in that cavalry charge from heaven. We will return to earth with Christ to put to rest the diabolical regime of the Antichrist. We will be in the number that saves Israel from the onslaught of the minions of the Antichrist, and we will stand by the side of Jesus as Satan is <u>chained</u> and cast into the bottomless pit for a thousand years.

Christ Restores Planet Earth

The **millennial <u>reign</u>** of Christ will break upon the world like water on the desert, and the world will flourish and bloom in peace. Only then will the world discover the joy it could have known had it chosen to accept Christ at his **first coming**.

KEY TERMS

four horsemen: *God's judgments symbolized by four riders*

seven seals: *scroll of God's judgments opened by Christ*

seven trumpets: *seven judgments in sealed scroll*

seven bowl: *last seven judgments of last sealed scroll*

born-again: *redeemed by Christ's sacrifice on the cross*

millennial reign: *Jesus' one-thousand-year rule on earth*

first coming: *Christ's birth in Bethlehem*

FURTHER STUDY

Revelation 6
(four horsemen)
Revelation 20:1–3 (chained)
Revelation 20:4 (reign)

Chart of God's Judgments

Seven Seal Judgments Revelation 6	Seven Trumpet Judgments Revelation 8–9	Seven Bowl Judgments Revelation 12:12; 16
1st seal: Antichrist appears	1st trumpet: One-third earth burned	1st bowl: Sores
2nd seal: Wars	2nd trumpet: One-third sea polluted	2nd bowl: All seas polluted
3rd seal: Economic collapse and famine	3rd trumpet: One-third freshwater polluted	3rd bowl: All freshwater polluted
4th seal: Death	4th trumpet: One-third sunlight dimmed	4th bowl: All sunlight scorches
5th seal: Martyrdom	5th trumpet: People tortured (woe)	5th bowl: Darkness everywhere
6th seal: Earthquakes	6th trumpet: People killed (woe)	6th bowl: Euphrates dried up
7th seal: Seven trumpet judgments (Rev. 8–9)	7th trumpet: Satan and the Seven bowl judgments (woe) [Rev. 12:12; 16]	7th bowl: Mass destruction

HISTORY'S MOST EXCITING TIME

What a marvelous plan has been laid before us! God has chosen to display his love to an entire universe, on planet Earth—a world lost in space.

Today, the student of Bible prophecy enjoys one of the most wonderful privileges ever known. There are signposts—identifying markers—that indicate how close we are to the end of the age. Those signs have become increasingly exciting!

> **KEY TERM**
>
> **Diaspora:** *scattering of Jews worldwide after the Babylonian exile*

In our lifetimes we have seen the fulfillment of many prophecies. Israel, once dispersed through over a hundred nations of the world, has been regathered, just as God prophesied hundreds of years before the **Diaspora**—the scattering that took place not long after the crucifixion and resurrection of Jesus Christ.

From the time of Christ to 1950, the sum of human knowledge had increased approximately sixteen fold. Since 1950, the total sum of human knowledge has increased over a thousand fold, in exact fulfillment of Daniel's prophecy: "Many shall run to and fro, and knowledge shall be increased" (Daniel 12:4). Only one generation in the history of the world has seen such an explosion of knowledge, and that generation is ours!

---

1 Thessalonians 4:17 Then we which are alive and remain shall be caught up together with them in the clouds, to meet the Lord in the air: and so shall we ever be with the Lord.

Christians' Magnificent Destiny

Jesus is coming back, and we could be the generation that sees his return.

The Bible paints a picture of the political face of the end-time world in terms of nations, alliances, conspiracies, and more. Today, the world is aligning itself so perfectly for the fulfillment of that end-time scenario that if the Lord doesn't return soon, he will have to recycle world events to bring them back to approximately where they are today, so that he may then return.

Humans are creatures of great eternal destiny, especially those who come to Christ and become children of God. As Christians, we are joint-heirs with Christ, inheritors of the universe: "Therefore, let no man glory in men. For all things are yours, Whether Paul, or Apollos, or Cephas, or the world, or life, or death, or things present, or things to come; all are yours, And ye are Christ's; and Christ is God's" (1 Corinthians 3:21–23). In Romans, Paul put it this way: "He that spared not his own Son, but delivered him up for us all, how shall he not with him also freely give us all things?" (Romans 8:32).

KEY POINT

Humans were created for a purpose. Each day we should live to bring credit to Christ.

We are here on Battlefield Earth, a small planet circling an unspectacular star in one of the billions of galaxies God created. Just a simple world lost in space, but it is the center of the attention of the universe. When the stories of our lives are written, they will be seen by all of heaven. Will they be sagas of heroic accomplishments for the Savior? I pray that for each of us, the answer will be a resounding, "Yes!"

THINK ABOUT IT

How shall we live in a world like this? We are to live in the knowledge that we are soldiers in a great army. Jesus said, "Occupy till I come" (Luke 19:13). We fight in the battle for the universe. At stake are the souls of many. Let us greet each day with the question, "What can I do today that will make me a credit to Christ and a threat to the devil?"

HEADLINE HIGHLIGHT

ENews- Koinonia House Online
April 9, 2002
American Psychological Association Admits Mistake about Pedophilia but Family Research Council Is Wrong to Be Exuberant
Staff writer

The American Psychological Association has admitted it made a mistake when it published a study which indicated that pedophilia can have a positive influence on a child.

However, J. Edward Pawlick, the Publisher of Massachusetts News says that the Family Research Council in Washington is incorrect in getting excited about the change of heart. It was only the tremendous public pressure from radio talk show host Dr. Laura and others, such as House Majority Whip Tom DeLay which caused the organization to relent, according to most sources . . . [a rally on May 20 against Pawlick protested] that his article was "hate mail" in that it discussed pedophilia and warned that "child molestation is being normalized." . . .

The professional association of psychiatrists, also known as the APA (American Psychiatrists Association) has sent a signal that it too will support the "normalization" of sex with children. They quietly changed their diagnostic manual a few years back so that a person no longer has a "disorder" simply because he molests children. To be diagnosed as "disordered," the psychiatrists must look to the psyche of the adult. If the adult does not feel anxious about the relationship with the child or if he is not impaired in his work or social relationships, then he has no "disorder."

PROPHETIC IMPACT

Many people, even Christians, believe this world is getting better and better. They are convinced that humans will solve their own problems. Human nature is not depraved, but is noble and almost godlike.

Jesus said, however, that at the time of his return to this fallen planet the state of the world would be like it was in the <u>days of Lot</u>. During those days the cities of Sodom and Gomorrah were filled with every sort of sexual perversion.

> **FURTHER STUDY**
> Luke 17:28 (days of Lot)

The growing incidences and acceptance of pedophilia fits Jesus' description of the end-time generation. Can there be a more vile, depraved activity than that practiced by pedophiles? Yet, our highest court gave its stamp of approval to those who graphically display the perversion that leads to unspeakable assaults on children. Surely Christ's return cannot be far off.

CHAPTER WRAP-UP

- God chose planet Earth, a tiny sphere among billions, on which to play out his story of love and redemption.

- God's plan was and is the answer to Lucifer's rebellion in heaven in which he wanted to be like God.

- There was great war in heaven. Michael and God's faithful angelic forces defeated Lucifer and his rebel angels. Lucifer and his evil followers were cast out of heaven.

- Satan desired to destroy humans by bringing sin upon all of God's earthly creation. All of Adam's offspring are born into sin because of Adam's original sin of disobedience.

- God sent Jesus Christ to pay for people's sin and to redeem them from their eternally lost position. Through Christ all people can be saved and live forever with God.

- Jesus is coming again, and this generation could be the one to witness his return.

Earth's Population Police

BY J. R. CHURCH

Let's Get Started

Earth's population is increasing. The only answer to the coming problem of overpopulation, say the **globalists**, is to gain control of the whole world and to unite toward a common goal of dominance through reproductive and social engineering. Globalists desire to bring everything into compliance with their design for a <u>one-world order</u>—an order that Christians know will eventually be ruled by the Antichrist.

EARTH'S PEOPLE PREDICAMENT

> **KEY TERM**
>
> **globalists:** *those who seek political influence and control over the world*
>
> **FURTHER STUDY**
> Revelation 13; 7:12–13
> (one-world order)

With every tick of the clock, 5 people are born and 2 people die. That is a net gain of 3 new people every second. That's 18 every minute; 10,800 every hour; 259,200 every day; 1,814,400 every week; and 7,826,400 every month. These are staggering statistics. Earth's population has doubled in the past forty years. On October 12, 1999, the U.S. government reported that the population had reached 6 billion.[1]

That's a lot of people, but some say that they could all fit inside Texas. Maybe so, but not what I call comfortably! Unfortunately, to fit the earth's population into Texas, thirty-five people would have to live on every acre of land. There would be no room for shopping malls, ranches, farms, wilderness, or freeways. Currently, in the average middle-class American residential neighborhood, four homes can be built on one acre or twenty homes in an average five-acre city block. If every person on the globe lived in the state of Texas, nine people would be living in every house. In anybody's book, that's a little crowded.

The exponential population increase is only now beginning to alarm us. If the present rate of growth continues, by 2040, there could be as many as 12 billion people on the planet! By 2080, our children could be living in a world with 24 billion neighbors. If the growth continues, by 2120, earth will be crowded with 48 billion mouths to feed. We cannot be sure, however, that it will take another forty years for the population to double again. It may take only thirty years—or even twenty-five. Earth's population is growing like compound interest.

The Population Bomb

In 1968, a professor of biology at Stanford University, Dr. Paul Ehrlich, published the book *The Population Bomb* in which he suggested that the world's population would reach 6 billion by the year 2000. The U.S. government now claims that human-kind has reached that critical point.

Ehrlich wrote from the viewpoint of a political liberal—a socialist in the classic sense of the term. For that reason, we conservatives tend to scoff at his findings. We would like to think that his alarming conclusion about world population growth is just another socialist ploy. We'd like to think he was trying to scare us into accepting a proposal for world govern-ment. Although he may have exaggerated in some areas, his basic premise is staggering. Is humankind really becoming its own worst enemy?

We may not be worried that the next few generations will require so much space that they replace all forests and farm-lands, but Ehrlich could be correct in his assumption that fu-ture generations will not be able to enjoy our present standard

KEY POINT

Even conservative population estimates are alarming.

of living. Will there be 48 billion people on earth in 2120? The United Nations Council on Population Growth states that it is determined to limit the population to only 12 billion in 120 years. Does such an effort really matter? Even 12 billion is an unacceptable number!

Whatever our political or religious views may be, if the present population growth continues unabated, in another hundred years there simply will be too many people scrambling for too little food, clothing, and shelter.

ABORTION SOLUTION

The excessive population growth gives the one-world order builders an excuse to use harsh methods. Earth seems headed for catastrophic overpopulation. As world government develops into a full-fledged nightmare, birth control is becoming the number one priority. The <u>sanctity</u> of human life has been replaced with an acceptance of abortion.

KEY TERM

Judeo-Christian ethic:
God's moral truth

FURTHER STUDY
Genesis 1:27 (sanctity)

To agree with such an immoral practice, one has to be convinced that there is no God. The conscience has to be fooled into thinking that a human is only an animal to be controlled like cattle. To prepare society for such a mindset, abortion has to be legalized while moral restraints are lifted. At the same time, the sanctity of marriage and a belief in moral values must be condemned. A program of hatred for the **Judeo-Christian ethic** must be enacted.

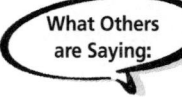

THINK ABOUT IT

Are we not already at a place where morals are arbitrary, where marriage is outdated, and where Christians are hated? Do we not now live in the most perverted society since Sodom and Gomorrah?

What Others are Saying:

Dr. Paul Ehrlich: Both government and industry in Japan supported the program of population control. Its dramatic halving of the birth rate was achieved originally through the sanctioning of abortion. Abortion is a highly effective weapon in the armory of population control.[2]

Abortion as a Weapon

Dr. Paul Ehrlich released a report lauding Japan's so-called successful experiment with abortion. The report caught the imagination of liberal politicians in Washington who wanted to promote this new weapon of abortion. Robert Packwood and Paul McCloskey led the campaign to curb America's birthrate.

Efforts were launched as early as 1970 to make abortion legal through U.S. legislation. As we now know, these attempts were not successful. But the liberal agenda was not deterred. A think tank was appointed to set a course for America's plunge into the unthinkable abyss of infanticide.

Ehrlich, along with other leaders of the globalist perspective, saw the March 1970 two-year Commission on Population Growth and the American Future with John D. Rockefeller as chairman as a good beginning for bringing the powerful resources of the United States into the battle against world population growth.

However, abortion in the United States alone would not solve Ehrlich's problem. He was determined to push his agenda on a global scale. Ehrlich lamented, "Increased U.S. funds have also been given to programs sponsored by international agencies such as the U.N. and the World Bank. . . . Next to nothing is being done toward real population control in the U.S. or on a world scale."[3]

Ehrlich's campaign attracted the attention of certain notable liberal politicians: "Beginning with Senators Ernest Gruening and Joseph Clark in the middle 1960s, there has been a small group of dedicated people in Congress who have been trying to get the government to move on these matters. More recently, the ball has been carried by Senators Joseph Tydings and Robert Packwood, and Representatives Paul McCloskey, George Bush, and James Scheuer. A few other senators and congressmen have indicated concern for the population problem."[4]

Supreme Court Circumvents Congress and the Constitution

When Congress could not muster the votes to allow the killing of innocent unborn children, the liberal members of the Supreme Court were convinced that they should make an endrun around the Constitution. Their opportunity to legalize abortion came during the infamous *Roe* v. *Wade* trial. It is more than a mere coincidence that such a trial should even enter the U.S. court system, let alone be heard by the Supreme Court during a time when liberal politicians were pushing the abortion agenda.

From the early 1970s, many anti-abortion groups have tried without success to stop the massive killings. Congress has been unwilling to listen to reasonable people who argue for the sanctity of life. Even the Reagan administration gave little more than lip service at pro-life rallies.

The killings continue unto this day. Twice in recent years both the Republican-controlled House and Senate sent bills to President Bill Clinton to curb so-called partial birth abortions, and both times Clinton vetoed them.

REMEMBER THIS

Since 1973 in America alone there have been an average of 40 abortions each day, 1,500 a month, and 1.5 million each year, for a total of 42 million abortions to date. Yet the population explosion continues unabated.

THINK ABOUT IT

Abortion advocates worked from a single perspective—there is no God; humankind is alone on the planet; someone must plan for the future. The wealthy ruling elite must keep the world's population under control for their own financial benefit. Their goal is to enslave the populace and keep us thinned out, lest we consume too much of the world's resources.

THE GREED FOR GAIN

Planet Earth's population must be controlled at all costs so that greed can work its dark magic for the privileged few who stand to gain the most from the new world order they seek to install. Fewer people make for a more manageable servant class.

Humankind's natural <u>desire</u> for wealth long ago became an unruly game. Capitalism calls it "competition." Every nation is a player—trying to outdo all others in a quest for riches and political power. The ultimate goal is to **subjugate** people and confiscate their wealth.

> **KEY TERM**
>
> **subjugate:** *conquer, bring under control*
>
> **FURTHER STUDY**
> 1 Timothy 6:10 (desire)

In the early years of human history a city-state would lust after the gold or natural resources of a neighbor. If they could not trade the nearby nation out of it, they would form an army and take it by force. Don't be deceived by the rhetoric set forth in the history books about wanting to spread culture, language, or religion to foreign shores. Greed always was the root cause, and war, the inevitable result.

The War Scroll

One-world builders also need to control earth's population so that their dictatorial version of order can be installed and maintained. But God's prophetic Word says that all of man's efforts to institute world order apart from God will lead to the <u>ultimate conflict</u>.

The only hope for peace in a world devoid of deity is for humankind to form a global government endowed with the power to eliminate competition. Communism was an experiment for eliminating competition in society, but it did not work. The only thing left to do is to provide for a controlled economy where only those loyal to the ruling regime will be allowed to buy or sell. The unwilling would simply be starved out. That is the only logical conclusion why the predicted **mark of the beast** will be developed. It should not be long in coming.

WORLD HUNGER

In 1973, *U.S. News and World Report* suggested that the human race had entered a new era—"the era of famine." That year, millions died of hunger or of some related disease in Africa and the Far East. Every five seconds, four people die of hunger, most of them children, and twenty-five more are born.

In *The Population Bomb*, Paul Ehrlich said, "If our current rape of the watersheds, our population growth and our water use trends continue, in 1984 the United States will quite literally be dying of thirst."[5]

Well, 1984 came and went—more than a decade and a half ago—and no one in the United States is yet dying of thirst.

What I do see, however, is that Ehrlich's argument has gained merit among those who do not believe in the existence of God. According to the liberal agenda, all of the farmland currently under the plow can feed only 6 to 7 billion people adequately. According to Ehrlich, within the next forty years, the world should be experiencing serious famine with untold millions dying of starvation.

The Save the Earth Manual

Time magazine (May 2000) produced a special edition called *How to Save the Earth* in celebration of Earth Day 2000. Sixteen articles scattered throughout its one hundred pages gave an exhaustive view of the United Nations report on the potential catastrophes presently facing all nations.

The United Nations has completed a study of earth's ecosystems and reports that they are strained to the limit. Human pollution of coastal areas is destroying the marine habitat. The fishing industry is now 40 percent larger than the oceans can sustain. Warming waters are causing coral reefs to die. Fertilizers, sewage, and other **effluents** are killing lakes and poisoning rivers. Half the world's wetlands have been drained, destroying habitats. So much water has been taken from rivers like the Colorado, Yellow, and Ganges that they sometimes dry up before reaching the sea.

> **KEY TERM**
>
> **effluents:** *discharged waste material*

Chemicals used on farmlands kill helpful creatures, taint groundwater, and create dead zones in the oceans. Improper farming methods are causing soil degradation and loss of nutrients. The United States has lost almost all of its original grasslands. Soil erosion is reducing the ability of the ecosystem to support livestock. Earth's forests are disappearing, especially the rain forests of South America.

According to the U.N. project *Pilot Analysis of Global Ecosystems* (PAGE), drastic measures must be taken on a global scale to save the planet. It is clear that the United Nations intends to establish a single world government for the purpose of dealing with all of these crises.

False Prophet Almost Gets It Right

In 1970, Ehrlich wrote, "The battle to feed all of humanity is over. In the 1970s and 1980s hundreds of millions of people will starve to death in spite of any crash programs embarked upon now."

According to Ehrlich, sometime in 1958, the stork passed the plow: "People are recognizing that we cannot forever continue to multiply and subdue the Earth without losing our standard of life and the natural beauty that must be part of it. . . . These are the years of decision—the decision of men to stay the flood of man."[6]

One-world dreamer Ehrlich almost stumbled into making an accurate prediction about earth's future, regarding great ecological problems. His timing was wrong. God's timing won't be! Regardless of one's religious views and whether or not Christ returns soon, it is certain that someday the human race will face incredible apocalyptic forces similar to those described by the four horsemen in the Book of Revelation! Communism has already demonstrated its failure to improve society. Socialism will also fail. Even capitalism cannot solve the problem. A free market cannot bring utopia. In the end, all will fail.

KEY POINT

Government cannot solve all humankind's problems.

HOW LONG DO WE HAVE?

We have just about reached the limits of our planet. Earth is running dangerously low on our supply of oil, chromium, gold, and other strategic minerals needed for industry. What will happen when they're gone?

If we slow down to zero population growth, however, can we sustain 6 billion people? If the United Nations is successful in saving all forests and farmlands, can we sustain the present world population? Well, let's stretch that question out a bit. Can we sustain 6 billion people for another thousand years? Two thousand years? Three thousand years? Four thousand years? Obviously not. We cannot sustain the population with dwindling natural resources.

FURTHER STUDY
Revelation 6:7–8
(ecological problems)
Revelation 6:2, 4–5, 8
(four horsemen)

Earth's Unsolvable Problem

Today, 40 percent of the world's population is under fifteen years of age. Over half the world goes to sleep hungry every night. There is simply not enough food. Can the problem be solved? Let me answer that question with a question. Do you see it being solved? The answer is no, and it can only get worse.

KEY POINT

Humanity cannot continue on its course indefinitely.

One might cite the 30,000 deaths due to mudslides in Venezuela in December 1999 as proof that nature will solve the overpopulation problem from time to time. Think again. Three people are added to the human race every second, 180 people every minute, 10,800 every hour. The deaths in Venezuela took out only a three-hour growth in the world's population. What will take care of the rest of one day's 259,200 people added to this continuing population bomb?

REMEMBER THIS

The concept that humanity evolved by chance rather than intelligent design provides no future! If there is no God, we are all doomed. Without the Creator, humankind is limited in what it can do to provide food, clothing, and shelter for the years ahead. If Jesus does not return as he promised, the human race will eventually destroy itself.

Humankind at the Turning Point

In 1974, another book took up the drumbeat for world government. It was entitled *Mankind at the Turning Point: The Second Report to the Club of Rome* by Mihajlo Mesarqvic and Eduard Pestel. Its authors mounted a strong argument for complete control of commerce around the world. In the opening pages of the book, they laid out the difficulties that face people:

KEY POINT

This planet was not designed to sustain human life, as we know it, forever.

"Several critical problem areas have been investigated, in particular the world food shortage, energy crises, population growth, and disparity in economic development. Two gaps, steadily widening, appear to be at the heart of mankind's present crises: the gap between man and nature, and the gap between 'North' and 'South,' rich and poor. Both gaps must be narrowed if world-shattering catastrophes are to be avoided; but they can be narrowed only if global 'unity' and Earth's 'finiteness' are explicitly recognized."[7]

"North" refers to nations north of the equator and "South" refers to those nations located south of the equator. Nations in the Northern Hemisphere are richer, by far, than nations in the south.

Mesarqvic and Pestel went on to mention an interesting dichotomy: population controls on the one hand and longevity efforts on the other. "Few would quarrel with the position that the global population cannot and should not be permitted to grow unchecked forever. That the population must level off sometime, i.e., that population growth should stop, is the view gaining universal acceptance. On the other hand, none would argue against the growth in medical services leading to increased life expectancy and declining mortality rates; but this leads to increase rather than decline in population."[8]

Without being explicit, this group suggested that severe measures must be imposed in order to curb population growth. Mesarqvic and Pestel implied that only a one-world government had the power to keep resources and people under control. They postulated that food shortages were inevitable and that without a one-world government all hope was lost.

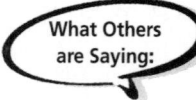

What Others are Saying:

Mihajlo Mesarqvic and Eduard Pestel: By the year 2000 the demand for food in South Asia will be about 30 percent greater than the supply—an alarming but conceivably manageable gap. With advanced planning, the gap could be reduced as low as 10 percent. However, if the same projections are extended another twenty-five years, the deficit rises to over 100 percent—clearly a catastrophic disparity.

The analyses in this book extend over a period of fifty years. If, during this coming half-century, a viable world system emerges, an organic growth pattern will have been established for mankind to follow thereafter. If a viable system does not develop, projections for the decades thereafter may be academic.[9]

Ten Kingdoms Prophesied

Mesarqvic and Pestel even suggested that the world be divided into ten political-economic regions for the purpose of controlling all food production and distribution. Their "global solution" was actually quite similar to those predicted in the Bible. The prophet Daniel wrote that during the last attempt at world domination, ungodly men would establish a global government with ten divisions. This attempt would fail with the arrival of the eternal **Ancient of Days** and be followed by a final, divinely established utopia ruled by his saints.

Daniel 7:24–28 And the ten horns out of this kingdom are ten kings that shall arise: and another shall rise after them; and he shall be diverse from the first, and he shall subdue three kings. And he shall speak great words against the most High, and shall wear out the saints of the most High, and think to change times and laws: and they shall be given into his hand until a time and times and the dividing of time. But the judgment shall sit, and they shall take away his dominion, to consume and to destroy it unto the end. And the kingdom and dominion, and the greatness of the kingdom under the whole heaven, shall be given to the people of the saints of the most High, whose kingdom is an everlasting kingdom, and all dominions shall serve and obey him. Hitherto is the end of the matter. As for me Daniel, my **cogitations** much troubled me, and my **countenance** changed in me: but I kept the matter in my heart.

> ### KEY TERMS
> ***Ancient of Days:*** *another name for God*
> ***cogitations:*** *thoughts*
> ***countenance:*** *facial expression*

Enemies of Christ

Not only did Daniel predict the current world situation but also he went on to say that God will judge those wicked slave masters and give their kingdom to the saints. Is it any wonder, then, that Christians are being targeted for ridicule and persecution around the world today? Liberal social planners are bent on establishing a new world order without God.

These people are not driven by a noble desire to save the world. Nor do they fully understand the greed that permeates their boardrooms. They are controlled by a diabolical intelligence that extends all the way back to the Garden of Eden.

REMEMBER THIS

Those who champion a one-world system are dupes of the old dragon, Satan. They are pawns in his game of enslavement. They are clueless as to why they reject biblical theology. To put it bluntly, "they know not what they do" (Luke 9:55; 23:34). May God forgive them!

THE ANTICHRIST "SOLUTION"

KEY POINT

The world's population is being groomed to accept a single benevolent "fix-it" man.

The world is looking for a single man to solve its problems. Modern politicians realize that nations must work together for the common good. Though they do not believe in the existence of a Creator, they long for someone who is able to unite all nations and offer political solutions that would please all warring factions.

Even Israel has long admitted that they are looking for a mere human messiah. They hold no such grandiose expectations that their promised savior will be anything other than human. The concept that Israel's messiah should be deity is not seriously considered. But a mere human could produce only a short-lived utopia. It would not be long until some nation, thinking it was being shortchanged, would challenge a human ruler's power. Let's face it. Wars can only continue and get worse.

If utopia were achieved under the auspices of the United Nations, it could not last long. It would only be a matter of time until an evil ruler would manipulate his way to power and drag his generation into chaos. Consider history and the effects of Hitler's and Stalin's rules.

Failed Attempts

Can we solve our problems with social planning? Does communism offer a solution? How about capitalism? Is abortion the answer?

Take any of those attempts at curbing population growth and follow them into the future. All of them will ultimately fail. Several years ago China instituted a "one child only" policy, making it a crime to have more than one child per couple. Some industrialized countries—especially Europe and America—have limited their population growth to doubling every seventy years, whereas, underdeveloped countries continue to double as much as every thirty-five years. Aside from faith in God, in the very near future, the world will reach the point where no further growth can be tolerated.

If there is no God, an exploding population is unacceptable. Eventually, humankind could be forced to accept a single world dictator offering terrifying solutions. Genocide may be distasteful, but acceptable, in a world without faith. In addition to hunger and disease, crime and war will be the norm rather than the exception.

A prime example of overpopulation can be seen in Mexico City. With over 25 million people, the city has become a breeding ground for robbery, burglary, rape, and murder. No one is safe. Mexico City is just a preview of what the entire world could be like in another century.

Supreme Problem Solver

If there is a God, then the problem of overpopulation and dwindling resources becomes solvable. The biblical prediction that God will stop the process of human procreation at the appropriate time is a far superior alternative. God has promised an "end of the world"—not an extinction of the planet but a change in the development of the human species. At the Second Coming of Christ, man's long-anticipated <u>utopia</u> will be achieved. The next thousand years with Jesus on the throne offers a far better hope than the present liberal agenda.

> FURTHER STUDY
> Revelation 21:1–4 (utopia)

HEADLINE HIGHLIGHT

CNN.com

April 18, 2002

JOHANNESBURG, South Africa (Reuters) - South Africa has said it is confident that the United States would not torpedo a global action plan for environmentally sustainable development to be adopted at a U.N. summit in Johannesburg.

Environmental groups have voiced concern that the United States and oil exporting nations will try to scale down the World Summit on Sustainable Development's action plan because of fears about the impact it could have on business and profits.

But South African Environment and Tourism Minister Valli Moosa in an interview with Reuters late on Monday dismissed such concerns as premature. . . .

Moosa said the conference, which South Africa is co-hosting under the auspices of his ministry and is a follow-up to the 1992 Earth Summit in Rio de Janeiro, would focus on measurable targets and concrete programmes for reducing poverty while minimizing the impact of development on the environment. . . .

"Following on the United Nations Millennium Declaration, we will try to find concrete proposals to meet its goal of reducing by half the proportion of people whose income is less than one dollar a day by 2015," Moosa said.

The summit, to be held from August 26 to September 4 in Johannesburg, is expected to be attended by more than 60,000 delegates, environmental activists, business leaders, and over 100 heads of state.

PROPHETIC IMPACT

Today's one-world builders express their supposed great and growing concern for the less fortunate peoples of our planet. They have the answers, they say, to earth's over-crowding. These globalists intend to bring the world into a state of "sustainable development." They mean by this that they will control the population's procreation activities so that the number of people will remain below what they perceive as a dangerous level.

What they do not say is that their plans include the elimination of millions through abortion, godless Planned Parenthood practices, and sterilization, and by legitimizing euthanasia and promoting homosexuality.

The ongoing Earth Summits might serve as early planning sessions for the system of absolute control the Antichrist will one day seek to inflict upon all the people of the world.

CHAPTER WRAP-UP

- Planet Earth gains 7,826,400 people every month in population growth. Experts believe that at the present rate, there will be 12 billion people on the planet by the year 2040. This is twice today's population.

- The number of people added to the planet multiplies at a phenomenal rate. Experts fear there will be more than 48 billion people on the planet by the year 2120, if growth remains at its present rate.

- Globalists, who do not believe in a God who cares for people, are determined to control the population through forced abortion and euthanasia.

- To accept their methods is to believe there is no God and that we are alone in the universe and must plan for our own survival.

- Greed is the real reason the one-world builders desire to control population. They need a manageable-size population so they can control the masses.

- The one-world builders will give their power and authority to the Antichrist (Revelation 17:12–13).

- Jesus will solve the presently unsolvable population problem. He will return to rule and reign on earth. Population growth and its problems, along with all other crises of the human condition, will melt into the past. Christ will bring heaven to planet Earth!

End-of-the-Age Economics

BY DAYMOND R. DUCK

Let's Get Started

It is impossible to predict what the economy will do from day to day, but the Bible gives a clear picture of what to expect after the Rapture, and it is not the kind of forecast that will put a smile on the face of most investors. It is clear that there will be an unequal distribution of the world's wealth. Extreme wealth will coexist with extreme poverty, and there will be little or no middle class. The gap between rich and poor will be much like that in the biblical story of the rich man and Lazarus.

> **Luke 16:19–21** There was a certain rich man, which was clothed in purple and fine linen, and fared sumptuously every day: And there was a certain beggar named Lazarus, which was laid at his gate, full of sores, And desiring to be fed with the crumbs which fell from the rich man's table: moreover the dogs came and licked his sores.

THE COMING DICHOTOMY

The rich man had the finest clothes on the market, and the poor man wore dirty rags. The rich man had the best food money could buy, and the poor man begged for crumbs from the rich man's table. The rich man probably received excellent medical care, and the poor man received only the help of the dogs.

> **KEY TERM**
>
> *dichotomy:* division
>
> **FURTHER STUDY**
> Matthew 24:6 (wars)

This **dichotomy** is the way it will be after the Rapture. The privileged few will have all the pleasant things, and the great multitudes will struggle just to survive. The privileged few will eat, drink, and be merry. The great multitudes will hunger, thirst, and weep. There are many things we don't know about the economy during the Tribulation, but we do know it will be worse than anything the world has ever seen.

Isaiah 4:1 In that day seven women shall take hold of one man, saying, We will eat our own bread, and wear our own apparel: only let us be called by thy name, to take away our reproach.

A Female Workforce

The "wars and rumors of wars" predicted by Jesus will decimate the male population. Women will be lonely, and many will be desperate to get married and have children. Many will gladly share the same husband and work long hours to provide their own food and clothing.

Careers outside the home are a choice many women make today. They won't have that choice after the Rapture; working will be a necessity. With each succeeding war more and more men will be called into the military. Many will be sent to a foreign land, and they will never return. Women will be forced to fill the jobs, even the dirty, hard jobs. And they probably won't have benefits such as vacations, overtime pay, and health care.

Abortion is a choice many women make today. Some don't want their children. But it will be different after every child on earth is raptured. Imagine what it will be like when God removes all the children who have not reached the **age of accountability**.

Heartbroken mothers will want their **reproach** taken away. Grieving women will want to marry and start a family, but there will not be enough men for a traditional family. Lust will be a way of life for some females. Others will want to do right but will not be able to find husbands. Children will be a prized possession once again.

> **Luke 16:22** It came to pass, that the beggar died, and was carried by the angels into Abraham's bosom: the rich man also died, and was buried.

Dead and Unburied

It is wrong to attribute words to the Scriptures that are not there, but it seems reasonable to believe that in the above passage Jesus gave an indication of the great gulf between the rich and the poor at the end of the age. Notice that nothing is said about the beggar being buried. He had no funeral, no money, and no estate. It seems likely that he did not even receive a decent burial. But it was not so with the rich man. Jesus said he "was buried."

Why is this important? Because the prophet Jeremiah speaks of a future time when the <u>dead</u> will be strewn like garbage from one end of the earth to the other. They will probably be on foreign soil, and no one there will weep over them. No one will gather the bodies for burial. Nor will anyone fill the body bags and ship them home. While government leaders and corporate executives sit selfishly in luxury, piles of bodies will lie rotting on the ground.

> **KEY TERMS**
>
> **age of accountability:** *point at which children are able to accept or reject Christ*
> **reproach:** *childlessness; disgrace*
>
> **FURTHER STUDY**
> Jeremiah 25:29–33 (dead)

Bankrupt and Hungry

KEY POINT

Covetousness, greed, want, ignorance, and unbelief will underlie Russia's sudden demise while the promises of God, his faithfulness and power, will underlie Israel's great victory.

The rich man and Lazarus were at opposite ends of the financial scale, and that is the way it will be with some nations at the end of this age. Things will change, but Israel will close out this age like the rich man: a nation blessed with gold, silver, cattle, and goods. Russia will close out this age like the poor man: a nation desperate for money and food.

That is where the similarity with the story of Lazarus ends. Russia's leader will think Israel is <u>defenseless</u>, an easy prey, and that his great army can seize whatever his heart desires. He will be drawn to Israel's wealth like a moth is drawn to the light of a fire. Flames kill moths, and fire from God will destroy Russia's troops on the mountains of Israel.

Fearful Fate for Israel's Foes

Approximately 2,500 years ago the prophet Ezekiel predicted the coming economic conditions both in Israel and in a place called Rosh. Scholars have concluded that Rosh was in the area of present-day Russia. Russia's economic woes will entice her to seek relief through warfare. Israel's great treasures will make her the target. Russia will further impoverish herself by building up her military. And Israel will enjoy her wealth for a few more months.

FURTHER STUDY
Ezekiel 38 (defenseless)
Ezekiel 39:11 (great smell)

This war by Russia will not be the same costly battle referred to earlier when the dead will be scattered like garbage upon the earth. In that battle, the dead will not be buried. In this battle, the dead will lie on the ground for as long as seven months and there will be a <u>great smell</u> in the land, but Israel will eventually get around to burying them.

Daniel 11:39 Thus shall he [the Antichrist] do in the most strong holds with a strange god [Satan], whom he shall acknowledge and increase with glory: and he shall cause them [his friends] to rule over many, and shall divide the land for gain.

Corruption in High Places

With Satan's help, the power-crazed Antichrist will establish a one-world government during the tribulation period. Multitudes will find the Antichrist appealing when he announces a plan to redistribute the world's wealth. They will gleefully authorize him to eliminate personal property rights.

These beguiled dreamers will probably think he will seize the land of the rich and divide it among the poor, but he will not care about the poor. He will seize all the property he can and use it to buy political support from the rich and powerful. His unscrupulous friends will quickly take charge of this stolen property and set out to help him rule the world under the guidance of Satan.

CURRENT WORLD EVENTS

During the tribulation period, property rights will mean no more than they mean in Zimbabwe today. Consider what is happening there right now. A recent Associated Press report says: "In a massive land seizure, Zimbabwe's government has confirmed plans to take more than 60 percent of all the country's white-owned farming land without paying for it and redistribute it to 500,000 poor black families."[1]

REMEMBER THIS

All property actually belongs to God. He is sovereign and has the right to place stewards over it as he chooses. No individual has the right to seize what God has allowed others to honestly possess. But property rights will be worthless during the tribulation period. The well-to-do people will oppress the poor, knock them down, grind them in the dirt, and steal everything they have.

DOWN ON THE FARM

Joel 1:16–20 Is not the meat cut off before our eyes, yea, joy and gladness from the house of our God? The seed is rotten under their clods, the garners are laid desolate, the barns are broken down; for the corn is withered. How do the beasts groan! the herds of cattle are perplexed, because they have no pasture; yea, the flocks of sheep are made desolate. O Lord, to thee will I cry: for the fire hath devoured the pastures of the wilderness, and the flame hath burned all the trees of the field. The beasts of the field cry also unto thee: for the rivers of waters are dried up, and the fire hath devoured the pastures of the wilderness.

Farming Industry

In the above passage, the prophet Joel is talking about the **day of the Lord**. Lack of adequate and timely rainfall will cause the farming economy to collapse. Joel lists the following events that will happen during the tribulation period:

- Severe famine
- Food disappearing from pantries and store shelves
- No rejoicing over God's blessings in the places of worship
- Seed rotting in the ground
- Granaries becoming unnecessary because there will be no crops
- Barns becoming dilapidated
- Young plants withering in the field
- Animals suffering for lack of pasture and water
- Trees burning up
- Rivers drying up

Many farmers have serious economic problems today, but current problems are minor compared to those of the future. The clouds will not move, the rain will not fall, and the ground will not produce. Tractors will be parked, and farmers will lay off hired hands to shave costs and protect assets. Many will be forced to sell animals, land, and equipment, but buyers will be scarce. Unemployment will rise in farming-related industries. Times will be hard in every farming community.

Problems will accelerate as the drought worsens and takes its toll on crops and animals. It will

KEY TERM

day of the Lord: *another name for tribulation period*

become harder and harder to eke out a living. For many, it will be impossible. Many will look to the government for help, but the Antichrist will absorb their assets and distribute them among his friends. Hard times will spill over into the nonfarm economy. Services, construction, retail trade, tourism, and every other segment of the economy will take a dive.

REMEMBER THIS

When the Old Testament Jews became complacent about spiritual matters, God was patient. For a very long time he tolerated those who ignored him. He sent many prophets to warn them.

PROPHECY TO WATCH FOR

God sends the rain and causes the crops to grow. In the past when God's people failed to thank him for his goodness and to obey him, he dried up their pools, emptied their cisterns, stripped their fields, and cleared off their plates in a call for them to turn to him. God is good, and the world could probably avoid the collapse of its farm economy if it would recognize God as the source of all food and prosperity. To our discredit many ignore God and blame him when times are bad. This drought will be triggered by man's own spiritual dryness.

RESULTS OF WAR

Throughout history nations have had rules to govern the behavior of their leaders and troops during war. Multitudes have violated these rules, however, and many have been punished for breaking them. Treaties will be ignored during the tribulation period, and the treatment of human beings will be anything but humane.

What Others are Saying:

Robert J. Pranger: Since the late 1800's, most nations have signed international treaties establishing rules of warfare. These rules deal with fair treatment of war prisoners, outlawing of gas and germ warfare, and humane treatment of civilians in areas that are occupied by military forces.[2]

> **Zechariah 14:1–2** Behold, the day of the Lord cometh, and thy spoil shall be divided in the midst of thee. For I will gather all nations against Jerusalem to battle; and the city shall be taken, and the houses rifled, and the women ravished; and half of the city shall go forth into captivity, and the residue of the people shall not be cut off from the city.

Israel Ravaged

Israel will not escape every army that comes against her. Near the end of the tribulation period, God will summon the Antichrist and his world army to fight against tiny Jerusalem. The Holy City will be captured, the houses plundered, and the women forcibly violated. This is a horrifying picture of massive theft and brutal rape by a world army. It will be done with the permission of the Antichrist, and he will reward the perpetrators by letting them divide the spoil. Israel's great wealth will motivate others to take what they want from it.

> **Matthew 25:34–36** Then shall the King say unto them on his right hand, Come, ye blessed of my Father, inherit the kingdom prepared for you from the foundation of the world: For I was an hungered, and ye gave me meat: I was thirsty, and ye gave me drink: I was a stranger, and ye took me in: Naked, and ye clothed me: I was sick, and ye visited me: I was in prison, and ye came unto me.

Many Will Suffer

In the above passage, Jesus said something that is often applied to Christians and their daily lives. But Jesus was actually talking about his Second Coming and what he will do about the treatment of his people during the tribulation period. Six things can be gleaned from these verses about the tribulation period economy. Many of God's people will

- go hungry,
- be thirsty,
- go without proper clothing,
- go without proper medical care,
- flee their homes and neighborhoods, and
- be cast into prison.

The entire text also shows that many people will help those in need even though they are poor and even though doing so will place them in great danger. Despite the horrid events, concern for the needy will be one of the great stories of the tribulation period.

THE ROOT OF ALL EVIL

2 Timothy 3:1–2a This know also, that in the last days perilous times shall come. For men shall be lovers of their own selves, covetous . . .

Treachery for Treasure

The apostle Paul revealed an economic sign in 2 Timothy 3. The word "covetous" is translated "lovers of money" in many versions of the Bible. This means that during the latter part of the church age and on through the tribulation period many selfish people will dedicate themselves to the acquisition of wealth. Times will be perilous for the honest person because the wealthy will use deceit and trickery to amass their fortunes. The problem will not be how much money these people have, but how they acquire it. Honest people will have to be leery of who they do business with and to what they commit themselves.

What Others are Saying:

Dr. Oliver B. Greene: When we study riches in the light of the Word of God we learn that the person who makes gold his god is poor indeed. When money is the objective of life, that life becomes a slave to money.[3]

Nothing is wrong with trying to succeed financially, but those who strive to succeed at any cost are dangerous. They never have enough, and the more they get the more dangerous they become.

Bloody Greed

The rich will demonstrate anger and bias toward Christians and Jews. The Antichrist will waive and modify laws to benefit his supporters, will give tariff and tax exemptions to those who overlook his dark side, and will use his sweeping powers to override laws and customs his globalist pals don't like.

When his friends have to choose between doing right or wrong, they will strive to please their satanic commander and be rewarded economically. They will deny believers the right to buy and sell, release believers from their jobs, foreclose on their property, and so forth. Until the Antichrist starts killing them, God's people will wind up in jail or sitting by the wayside begging, weeping, and wailing.

MORE HORRIBLE THAN THE GREAT DEPRESSION

Revelation 6:5–6 And when he had opened the third seal, I heard the third beast say, Come and see. And I beheld, and lo a black horse; and he that sat on him had a pair of balances in his hand. And I heard a voice in the midst of the four beasts say, A measure of wheat for a penny, and three measures of barley for a penny; and see thou hurt not the oil and the wine.

Starvation and Suffering

Economic disaster and famine walk in the shadows of war. In the passage above, black is the symbol of grief and mourning. The balances are a symbol of economic collapse. People will suffer when food becomes so scarce it has to be weighed. Their food stores will be gone, and they will leave the table hungry.

Money will be worthless, and multitudes will be unable to purchase bare necessities. A quart of wheat will cost as much as one person earns in a day. Barley will be cheaper, but it will not be sufficient to feed everyone. At first, people will go from three meals a day to two meals a day. Then they will drop to one meal a day.

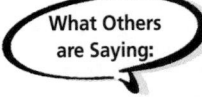

What Others are Saying:

Billy Graham: Millions will die of hunger and millions more will suffer malnutrition. With malnutrition comes disease, mental and emotional deterioration, despair and death. The black horse and its rider are God's warning of the human suffering that lies ahead if we refuse to obey His commandments, humble ourselves before heaven, and pray for forgiveness and renewal.[4]

Revelation 6:8 And I looked, and behold a pale horse: and his name that sat on him was Death, and Hell followed with him. And power was given unto them over the fourth part of the earth, to kill with sword, and with hunger, and with death, and with the beasts of the earth.

Great Loss of Life

There is more to the prophecy in Revelation 6:5–6 than economic collapse and famine. John heard a voice say, "hurt not the oil and wine." These were luxury items in the ancient world. At the same time millions are starving to death, a privileged few will be living in luxury. There will be a lack of food and an abundance of alcohol. People will be starving to death and celebrating with liquor at the same time. Russia is getting a foretaste of this today. This poverty-stricken nation sometimes pays its hungry citizens with bottles of vodka.

Just how bad this will be is indicated by the rider on the pale horse named Death and his faithful follower named Hell who appear in Revelation 6:8. Death will claim the bodies, and hell will claim the souls and spirits of one-fourth of the earth's population. This one-fourth will be taken from the unbelievers of the world. That is why they will go to hell. That is the worst thing, but the economic consequences of losing one-fourth of the population are mind-boggling.

Revelation 6:12 And I beheld when he had opened the sixth seal, and, lo, there was a great earthquake; and the sun became black as sackcloth of hair, and the moon became as blood;

Terror and Hopelessness

> FURTHER STUDY
>
> Revelation 13:16
> (bondmen)
> Revelation 8:7 (fire)
> Revelation 8:8–9
> (burning mountain)

When Jesus opens the sixth seal described in Revelation 6:12, there will be a great upheaval of nature, a devastating earthquake, and what appears to be one or more nuclear explosions. These events will cause terror and hopelessness. Terrified multitudes will abandon everything they possess in search of a hiding place. Four catastrophes of slavery, chaos, drugs, and drought will further devastate the one-world economy.

1 *Slavery.* In Revelation 6:15–16, John calls some of these frightened people bondmen, or slaves. Slavery will become common during the tribulation period. Some slaves will probably receive decent food, shelter, and clothing, but others will be forced to work long hours and suffer great persecution. Anything that took place in ancient times will probably reappear during the tribulation period.

2 *Chaos.* No one can fathom the economic consequences or the depth of destruction known as the four "judgments of one-third" mentioned in Revelation 8. Nothing like this has ever happened, and nothing like this will ever happen again. The grace of God is the only thing that will limit the devastation.

- Fire will rage out of control over a vast area. There will be no way to get help to such a large area and to so many people in time to make a significant difference.
- Something that looks like a large burning mountain will be cast into the sea. This could be a meteor, comet, missile, or something of that nature. This giant blazing thing will pollute one-third of the sea, cause the death of one-third of the sea creatures, and destroy one-third of the ships on the sea.

- A <u>fallen star</u> will contaminate one-third of the earth's water supplies. Badly polluted water will flow into one-third of the communities, towns, and cities on earth. People will quickly know their water supply has been poisoned, but extreme thirst will set in before the majority can do anything about it. Adults will have about three days to find a supply of drinkable water before they die. Infants and the sick will have less time. People will migrate, fight, and kill for water. Animals will drop dead with thirst. The problem will be so massive there will be little anyone can do.
- The <u>light</u> of the sun, moon, and stars will be reduced by one-third. The weather, plants, animals, and all life in general will be affected. These problems may come about because of a nuclear winter. Famine, people freezing to death, and the spread of disease will make this an ecological nightmare. The economy will be so terribly affected no one can predict the real impact.

REMEMBER THIS

When the Bible says one-third of the earth will burn, who knows where that one-third will be? When it says one-third of the freshwater will be polluted who knows where that tainted water will be?

3 *Drugs and Pornography.* People will try to escape from reality. John listed <u>six sins</u> that will be prominent during the tribulation period: Satan worship, idolatry, murder, sorceries, fornication, and theft. The Greek word for "sorceries" is *pharmakeion.* The English word is "pharmacy," and it refers to drugs. The Greek word for "fornication" is *porneia*, from which we get the word "pornography." While many are struggling with unemployment, poverty, and famine, others will be squandering large sums of money on drugs and pornography in an attempt to numb their pain. The moral breakdown of society will make theft a major problem, but famine, malnutrition, and starvation will make it worse.

FURTHER STUDY
Revelation 8:10–11
(fallen star)
Revelation 8:12 (light)
Revelation 9:20–21 (six sins)

> **Revelation 11:6** These have power to shut heaven, that it rain not in the days of their prophecy: and have power over waters to turn them to blood, and to smite the earth with all plagues, as often as they will.

4 *Drought, Blood, and Plagues.* During the tribulation period, God will send two men to oppose the Antichrist. John said, "They shall prophesy a thousand two hundred and threescore days . . ." (Revelation 11:3). In addition, they will have supernatural power from God to prevent rain.

Imagine what three and one-half years without rain will do to the economy. The coming famine will be far more severe than anyone can conceive, and even when the rain does fall again, the economy will not quickly recover. Imagine what will happen to businesses that depend upon water in their manufacturing processes. Imagine the quality of life when people cannot take a bath or wash their clothes. The entire cleaning industry will dry up along with the rains. Imagine the competition for food and water, and what some people will charge for it. Nothing anyone owns will be worth as much as a loaf of bread and a glass of pure water.

THE ULTIMATE ECONOMIC BOYCOTT

Economic boycotts are rarely as effective as their promoters would like us to think. The United States boycott against Cuba, the Arab boycott against Israel, and the United Nations boycott against Iraq are examples. No one can doubt that these boycotts caused a great amount of hardship and suffering, but no one can rightly claim they accomplished all of their goals.

In the near future the most effective boycott in the history of humankind will go into effect. When the False Prophet institutes the mark of the beast, perhaps as a way to ration water and food, the result will be an economic boycott against individuals instead of nations or groups of nations.

> **Revelation 13:15–16** And he causeth all, both small and great, rich and poor, free and bond, to receive a mark in their right hand, or in their foreheads: And that no man might buy or sell, save he that had the mark, or the name of the beast, or the number of his name.

Technologies to Control People

The mark will be the False Prophet's way of trying to force everyone on earth to support world government and one-world worship of the Antichrist. He will require all people, regardless of status in life, to put the mark of the Antichrist or his name or the number of his name in their right hand or on their forehead. Complying will be like purchasing a license to buy and sell. Those who agree to do this will be granted the right to purchase goods, materials, and services, but those who don't agree to do this will be denied that right. Control over necessities such as food, water, electricity, and medical care will amount to control over people.

In order for this satanic scheme to work, the False Prophet will need a way to track all buying and selling. This is where the high-tech industry comes into play. Global Positioning Satellites (GPS), computers, scanners, and the internet have made it possible to wire all banks, manufacturers, and stores into one global network. They have also enabled people to collect and store information about buying and selling, and then to concentrate that information and place it into the hands of one or two individuals in a matter of seconds. This isn't imaginary. It's the real world.

Some United Nations authorities are already calling for food and water to be used as weapons to bring people into line with global thinking. Those with the power to deny people the necessities of life can force them to submit to their will.

A universal numbering system capable of tracking people from cradle to grave is being pushed by the United Nations. A few countries have already complied, and others are slowly coming along. Injectable, tamper-proof tracking microchips powered by the movement of human muscles are now being implanted in animals and humans. Individualized body tattoos are being tested. Voice, hand, and eye scanners are being used for security purposes. Supercomputers that can monitor 2 million telephone calls per hour are eavesdropping on today's conversations.

Numbers and Marks System Foretold

Almost two thousand years ago, Scripture said the day would come when a world government would track all buying and selling. The equipment to do this is being purchased and installed worldwide right now. The day when one person can monitor all buying and selling is now on the prophetic radar screen.

The Rapture of the church will soon take place. When the dust from our heavenly thrust settles, the Antichrist and False Prophet will be on the scene. As far as most of us are concerned, eye hath not seen nor ear heard of the amazing advances in technology that will be available to these two wicked people.

If, as some say, knowledge doubles every two years, then ten years from now people will know more than thirty times as much as we know today. We are experiencing exponential growth in technology, quantum leaps are being made every year, and few people can visualize the far-reaching developments that are only months away. Instead of being tools to control crime and violence, these things will be used to control God's people.

WHAT ABOUT AMERICA?

Many people want to know what will happen to the United States during the tribulation period, but the answer to this question is pure speculation. America has led the world in developing the technology the Antichrist and the False Prophet will use to force the mark of the beast on people. Washington has used the wealth of our nation to strengthen the United Nations and the World Bank, and to force weaker nations to sign NAFTA, GATT, and other treaties that remove their sovereignty. We have forced Israel to accept a <u>division</u> of their God-given land, a mistake the Bible says will drag the world into the Battle of Armageddon.

THE CHURCH OF THE APOCALYPSE

When the <u>Rapture</u> of the true church takes place, all unsaved church members will be left behind. The False Prophet will incorporate these pretenders into the one-world <u>religious</u> system he controls. The Bible calls this global religious system the "Mother of Harlots" (Revelation 17:5). It will pride itself on being **ecumenical** and inclusive. The only doctrines to be excluded will be those from the Bible, and the only people to be excluded will be Jews and anyone who accepts Christ after the Rapture. This corrupt system will take in any false religion that wants to join, and it will tolerate any false doctrine the evil hearts of wicked men conjure up.

Revelation 17:3b–6b I saw a woman sit upon a scarlet coloured beast, full of names of blasphemy, having seven heads and ten horns. And the woman was arrayed in purple and scarlet colour, and decked with gold and precious stones and pearls, having a golden cup in her hand full of abominations and filthiness of her fornication: And upon her forehead was a name written, MYSTERY, BABYLON THE GREAT, THE MOTHER OF HARLOTS AND ABOMINATIONS OF THE EARTH. And I saw the woman drunken with the blood of the saints, and with the blood of the martyrs of Jesus.

KEY TERMS

ecumenical: *all inclusive*
blasphemer: *one who profanes God's holy name*

FURTHER STUDY

Joel 3:2 (division)
1 Corinthians 15:51–55; 1
    Thessalonians 4:15–18
    (Rapture)
Revelation 13:8, 12; 17:1–16

Bloodthirsty Partners

This scarlet beast is the bloodthirsty Antichrist. He will be a first-class **blasphemer** and will strongly support the one-world religion when he first begins to reign. The two will be such good friends it will be difficult to tell them apart. When one speaks it will be difficult to know which one has spoken. This global religion will be clothed in purple—the official color of kings and queens. It will be adorned with gold, precious stones, and pearls—signs of great wealth. It will drink from a golden cup filled with abominable things, false doctrines, demonic spirits, and so forth.

FURTHER STUDY
Genesis 11 (Babylon)
Revelation 17:16–17
(destroy)

God calls it the "Mother of Harlots" because it is the source of all false religions. It originated in <u>Babylon</u> during Old Testament times. Notice how it will treat God's true people: It will be drunk "with the blood of the saints, and with the blood of the martyrs of Jesus." This doesn't say much for ecumenism and inclusiveness, but we want to focus on economic matters.

Phony Christianity

After the true church is raptured, all of its great earthly wealth and that of the believers who were raptured will be in the hands of make-believe Christians. These adulterers will quickly join the false one-world religious system and turn the church's vast resources over to it. This money and property will not be used to help the poor. It will be used to merge church and state and to assist the Antichrist in his rise to global domination. He will use his power to kill, not love, all who oppose his false doctrines.

PROPHECY TO WATCH FOR

If you think ethnic cleansing is evil, wait until you see religious cleansing. The effort of the Antichrist and his false religious system to purge the earth of true believers will be horrid.

The Harlot's Execution

KEY POINT

The false church's great wealth will temporarily wind up in the hands of the one-world government and will be used to do evil.

You have heard the saying "What goes around comes around." At the middle of the tribulation period there will be a falling out between the Antichrist and this false religious system. The world's politicians will develop an intense hatred for this so-called global ethic. God will inspire them to <u>destroy</u> this one-world religion. They will do it, and pick its fat-covered bones clean.

THE NEW WALL STREET

The world is not only moving toward one-world government and one-world religion but also toward a one-world economy. This global economy will be an economy of the rich, by the rich, and for the rich. The new Wall Street during the tribulation period will be the rebuilt city of Babylon. An incredible amount of wealth will soon start flowing in and out of that despicable place. John said, "The merchants of the earth are waxed rich through the abundance of her delicacies" (Revelation 18:3b).

The global economy will be good to some, but it won't last. Tears will flow down the cheeks of the wealthy when that great city burns to the ground in one hour. They won't weep over the poor beggars who are starving to death, but they will <u>weep</u> over their mountain of wealth when it turns into a molehill of ashes.

> FURTHER STUDY
> Revelation 18:11–13 (weep)

How can Babylon grow so fast? Saddam Hussein has already spent hundreds of millions of dollars to rebuild part of it. It seems likely the Antichrist will take over the project, provide unlimited funding, send in thousands of workers from nations all over the world, offer incentives for global corporations to relocate there, fine-tune laws to please them, and do everything he can to turn that place into a one-stop shopping center. The real estate, construction, service, and high-tech industries will love it.

The Bible and Money

The Bible has much to say about economic matters. Here are a few of its teachings:

- Riches come from God.
- God expects us to use our riches wisely.
- God will judge us for misusing our riches.
- Riches make it difficult for a person to be saved.
- It is far better to be rich toward God than to have earthly riches.

One reason for the tribulation period is to <u>humble</u> the wealthy. This world would be a much better place if people wouldn't ignore God's teachings. But since they do, the judgments of God will soon fall.

> **Revelation 13:10** He that leadeth into captivity shall go into captivity: he that killeth with the sword must be killed with the sword.

Sin Brings Judgment

Now let's look at the way God deals with unrepentant sinners. Examine the contrasts in this list of happenings during the tribulation period:

- People will reject the Bread of Life (Jesus), so God will send famine.
- People will reject the Prince of Peace (Jesus), so God will send war.
- People will reject the Christ, so God will send the Antichrist.
- People will reject the True Prophet (Jesus), so God will send the False Prophet.
- People will reject the Living Water (Holy Spirit), so God will send thirst.
- People will reject the seal of the Holy Spirit, so God will allow the mark of the beast.
- People will impoverish believers, so God will send poverty upon the unbelievers.
- The false church will kill believers, so God will let the false church be destroyed.

In Old Testament times this was called "an eye for an eye and a tooth for a tooth" (Leviticus 24:17–22).

No one has to face judgment, though. The way to avoid the tribulation period is to turn to Christ.

FURTHER STUDY
1 Chronicles 29:12; Proverbs
10:2; Amos 5:11; Luke
18:24 (humble)

HEADLINE
HIGHLIGHT

𝔉inancial 𝔖ense 𝔒nline
April 12, 2002
National Debt
Storm Watch Update from Jim Puplava

As the graph of total American debt illustrates, America has now become the largest debtor nation in the world—a trend that is not sustainable. No nation can borrow its way to prosperity in **perpetuity**. From our government and corporations to its citizens, debt permeates every sector of the American economy. . . .

As memories of the depression and post-war hardships faded, a new generation of Americans took to the credit markets like a duck to water.

The thrift-conscious, buy-with-cash culture has disappeared. The revolution in the credit markets, the wave of technological change in the financial industry, and the plethora of financial products and means for borrowing money has been embedded in the American way of life. The willingness with which debt is assumed is one of the more dominant aspects of the American economy. From the **ubiquitousness** of credit cards, home mortgages, home equity loans to margin debt and installment debt, credit has **securitized** and mortgaged the entire asset base of the U.S. economy. We have become our own worst enemy and day after day, we sink deeper in debt.

KEY TERMS

perpetuity: *eternity*
ubiquitousness: *widespread use*
securitized: *pledged*

FURTHER STUDY

1 Timothy 6:10 (root)
Proverbs 6:16–17 (pride)

PROPHETIC IMPACT

Love of money (and the material luxuries it can buy) is the <u>root</u> of all evil. While nothing is wrong with money itself, because it is merely a means of exchange, human nature tends to make a god of it. Money too often is used to buy materialistic objects of worship that bring forth <u>pride</u>, which is one of the things God hates.

Americans, in particular, have been blessed with material things. In some cases, however, people have made of God's blessings, a curse. Lust for buying bigger, better, more beautiful cars, homes, wardrobes, and obtaining larger lines of credit has resulted in our culture being saturated with greed. Many now worship at the altar of mammon (money).

Revelation 18 tells of the destruction of commercial Babylon, the corrupt economic system that will be worldwide by the end of the Tribulation. We can see that system developing rapidly in America and the world. Computer technologies, combined with credit seduction offered by the titans of finance, might soon bring humans to the point the prophet John described in Revelation 13. It will be an economic straitjacket that will control the buying and selling of most every human being on the planet.

People will be forced to agree to take the Antichrist's number and mark, or face starvation or death by other means. Ultimately, taking the mark will mean the individual agrees to worship the beast (the Antichrist).

The only way to escape eternal separation from God in hell, at death, or to avoid this most horrible time of history, is to accept Christ today.

CHAPTER WRAP-UP

- There is already a wide disparity between the haves and have-nots in this world, but the disparity will get much worse.
- The female workforce will increase profoundly, because the males will be fighting and dying in the horrific wars.
- The bodies of those dying and dead through famine, pestilence, and war will pile up around the world.
- Farming and related industries will collapse due to wars and drought.
- Terror and hopelessness as well as slavery, chaos, drugs, and drought will replace consumer confidence.
- Technology will be used to track all buying and selling. Finally, money will be in the form of marks and numbers on hands or foreheads. Accepting the mark means the person agrees to worship the Antichrist. Without the mark people will not be able to buy or sell anything.
- The love of money is the root of all evil, the Bible says. God will punish those who make money their god.

Last-Time Technology

BY LARRY SPARGIMINO

Let's Get Started

Biblical prophecy leads us to believe that there is coming a worldwide domination by a single entity. He will, through technology, usher in a period of unbelievable oppression and hardship far worse than has ever been experienced by humankind. Though there have been periods of oppression and persecution in the past and present—the Assyrian, Babylonian, and Roman invasions of Israel, the Holocaust, the **pogroms** of Russia, the slaughter of Christians and other religious groups in various parts of the world—this future time of oppression will be far worse. Why? Technology will make it easier for spying and surveillance and for the elimination of those who dissent. There literally will be no place to hide.

> KEY TERM
>
> *pogroms: organized massacre*

GREAT SCIENTIFIC BREAKTHROUGHS

Daniel 12:4b . . . Even to the time of the end: many shall run to and fro, and knowledge shall be increased.

Revelation 13:16 And he causeth all, both small and great, rich and poor, free and bond, to receive a mark in their right hand, or in their foreheads.

Science and the Bible

The two Scriptures above speak of knowledge and technology and are, therefore, vitally important. Daniel says knowledge will increase during the last days. Revelation says a mark will be placed on everyone. This identifying mark will be universally required for all transactions. The fact that "knowledge shall be increased" informs us that the technology will be available to implement the use of this identifying mark on a universal scale. An important question, therefore, must be asked: Is knowledge increasing?

Knowledge Increases

Scientific breakthroughs in the twentieth century alone were staggering. "In 1900," writes Barbara Palmer, Science Notebook editor of the *Daily Oklahoman*, "Gregor Mendel's 19th century work on heredity was just being dusted off by scientists; by 1997, the world's first artificial chromosome was created. The Wright brothers made the first flight of a powered air-craft in 1903—in 1999 some of us were putting down deposits for the first commercial sub-orbital space flights."[1] Almost all science was developed in the last one hundred years, and the pace of development is growing exponentially.

EurekAlert is a website created by the American Association for the Advancement of Sciences [www.eurekalert.org]. It announced, for example, on July 5, 2000, that a fifty-one-year-old patient had coronary bypass surgery at a Pittsburgh hospital while he was wide-awake.

It was also announced on the same day that scientists at Cornell University had genetically engineered a potato vaccine that triggered human immunity to the Norwalk virus, a food-borne illness, which infects 23 million people in the United

States every year. The vaccine will be licensed for general use. Mom can now take the kids to lunch and by eating fries from a certain kind of potato get them inoculated against the Norwalk virus as well.

Sophisticated Surveillance Technology

Not all of these developments are benign, however. New developments in surveillance and tracking technologies have sinister implications. At present, surveillance technologies have reached a high level of sophistication, though tracking and monitoring technologies have been slow in overcoming some of the major obstacles to effectively track large numbers of individuals. Some of the limitations of tracking devices have been their unwieldy size, the frequency of maintenance requirements, problems with power supplies, and activation difficulties.

The limitations have now been overcome as devices have been perfected. On December 15, 1999, Applied Digital Solutions (ADS) announced that it had acquired patent rights to a miniature digital transceiver, named "Digital Angel," which can be used for the monitoring and tracking of people, but which suffers from none of the above-mentioned technical limitations.

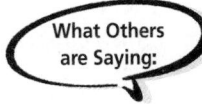

What Others are Saying:

ADS press release: The implantable transceiver sends and receives data and can be continuously tracked by GPS [Global Positioning Satellite] technology. The transceiver's power supply and activation system are unlike anything ever created. When implanted within a body, the device is powered electromagnetically through the movement of muscles, and it can be activated either by the "wearer" or by the monitoring facility. A novel sensation feedback feature will even allow the wearer to control the device to some degree. The "smart" device is also small enough to be hidden inconspicuously on or within valuable personal belongings and priceless works of art.[2]

Human Implantation Now Possible

It is now possible to implant a tracking device in a human being. The ADS device is small enough to make such an implant feasible. It does not require any huge battery pack for a power source, is virtually maintenance-free, and can be easily activated by the monitoring facility. These features make it ideal for locating children and others who may either wander off due to mental incapacitation or who have been abducted. However, the current level of technology is such that it can be used on humans for any purpose—even for search-and-destroy purposes.

There are so many valid uses for the latest advances that technology creates its own vacuum by which we are enticed to use it—even though we may be aware of the possibilities for its abuse, leading to our own enslavement. It is difficult to know when to embrace or reject certain advances in technology.

Orwell's Fiction, Today's Fact

George Orwell's novel *1984*, written more than half a century ago, was meant to serve as a wake-up call to the possibility of abuse of technology for evil purposes. As reported in the *Washington Times* on June 15, 1999, an Orwell scholar counted 137 predictions of the "total surveillance future" envisioned in *1984*, and announced that more than 100 have already become reality. For example, in the Orwell novel three great superpowers—North America, Europe, and China—rule the world. In each of these countries, the central government enforces strict conformity with the wishes of the ruling political party by monitoring every thought and action of the people through the use of surveillance technologies.

The *Times* article quotes one author who has studied Orwell in detail: "The more I read from the list, and the more snooping I observe into personal affairs, and how the government even wants to read our e-mail, the more I see '1984' as an accurate revelation about the future."

Smart card technology is making advances. The *Navy Supply Corps Newsletter* for January and February 2000 featured an interesting article by George Ganak, Project Officer, Smart Card Technologies, Naval Supply Systems Command. According to the article, Ganak has majored in "information management and organizational behavior," and is "helping to establish the infrastructure to support Smart Technologies."

Ganak writes that the latest innovation is the multipurpose smart card. There are many single-purpose smart cards—cards for ATMs installed on naval ships at sea, food service accounting, and so on. Multipurpose cards are a new development, but one that the Department of Defense is pursuing. They want one card that allows soldiers to do everything from getting soft drinks from vending machines to accessing personnel files.

War Technology

Advances in technology will also be used on the battlefield. General Wesley Clark, who served as the NATO Supreme Allied Commander in Europe from 1997 to May 2000, has witnessed the "improvement" of military campaigns. Even in comparison to the weapons of World War II, which for the time were quite advanced and lethal, modern weapons are far more effective in destroying property and human lives.

Humankind now realizes it has the ability not only to destroy enemies but also to destroy the planet. A global police force, a global military, and global government are all being offered as the only solution to avoid a war that could bring an end to life as we know it.

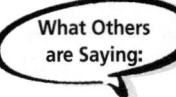
What Others are Saying:

General Wesley Clark: With improved organization and weaponry, 20th century wars killed tens of millions of combatants and civilians. And the march of science and technology continues. . . . World War II forces look pale in comparison to the tanks, armed helicopters, automatic cannon, aircraft and precision-strike capabilities available today, to say nothing of chemical, biological and nuclear weapons. . . . As the destructive potential for conflict has grown, the political efforts to prevent and restrict it have intensified.[3]

TECHNOLOGY: CURSE OR BLESSING?

Many contend that because technology may be used as an instrument of power and oppression that it is inherently evil. Others argue that technology is itself neither inherently good nor inherently evil. Those in this camp maintain that just as a knife can be used for a surgical procedure to save a life, or as an implement of crime to wrongfully take a life, so too with technology. The same technology that makes nuclear weapons possible can also heat the homes of millions without the adverse affects of pollution that come from fossil fuels.

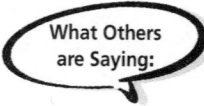

What Others are Saying:

Timothy Demy: Because technology is not developed in a social and ethical vacuum, nor used in one, it is not neutral for either the creator or the consumer. Ethical decisions are always included in the development of new technologies, either directly or indirectly. . . .[4] Because technological activity is a form of cultural activity, it is a way of partially fulfilling the cultural mandate and reflecting the commandment of love.[5]

Technology and Christians

The Christian view is that technology must be used for the honor and glory of God out of recognition of his sovereign lordship over all of creation. If technology assists us to fulfill our obligations to God and to one another, it is being used in the proper way. Not all people, however, recognize the sovereign lordship of God over all things, nor do they believe and honor his Word.

REMEMBER THIS

Christians do not need to fear or be against all technological development. The Bible's account of creation reveals that man, who was created in the image of God, is to "replenish the earth, and subdue it; and have dominion" (Genesis 1:28).

Truth about Tribulation and Technology

A view of prophecy called **preterism** has developed to the detriment of Christianity. This puts forth the erroneous notion that Bible prophecy already has been fulfilled. It says, in effect, that there is no prophecy yet to be fulfilled.

Preterist Gary DeMar denies that the present increase of knowledge and new developments in science and technology has anything to do with prophecy. He labels the notion "nonsense"[6] and claims that there was sufficient know-how in the first century to fulfill the mark of the beast prophecy of Revelation 13. "A simple mark," writes DeMar, "for example a tattoo or a brand, could be easily made on

> KEY TERM
>
> **preterism:** *view of end times that says Bible prophecies have been fulfilled*

the forehead and hand. Branding was a way to identify slaves and idolaters." To make his point, DeMar cites 2 Maccabees 2:29 where we read that Ptolemy Philopater enrolled the Jews of Alexandria and branded them with a red-hot iron. He also mentions Philo, who reported that idolaters were "branded by making indelible, long-lasting marks on their bodies."[7]

DeMar's examples, however, fail to prove what he alleges. Enrolling Jews in Alexandria is far different than enrolling the population of the entire world. Revelation 13:16–17 states: "And he causeth all, both small and great, rich and poor, free and bond, to receive a mark in their right hand . . . And that no man"—not just Jews in Alexandria or the idolaters mentioned by Philo—"might buy or sell, save he that had the mark, or the name of the beast, or the number of his name." All classes are included.

While a simple brand or tattoo might function adequately to keep track of a few hundred people, such a device is totally inadequate for the multitudes described in Revelation 13. Just ask any first grade teacher who has tried to keep track of a group of six-year-olds on a field trip to the zoo.

Mark of the Beast Debate

Preterists also argue that the language of Revelation 13 does not allow for a computer chip or other high-tech device. Futurists believe that the mark of the beast, if it is a microchip, may be placed "in" the hand or "in" the forehead. DeMar, however, observes that the Greek text of Revelation 13:16 uses the Greek preposition *epi,* which means "on," rather than *en* which means "in."[8] This goes along with his belief that the mark is a low-tech brand or mark placed *on* the skin, not some modern electronic device placed *under* the skin.

To be sure, **futurists** do not have to insist that the mark is a microchip. It could be something else. But is it a low-tech brand? Is this a valid conclusion?

Even if DeMar's conclusion that the mark is a kind of brand or tattoo, it does not support his understanding of it being something that is low-tech. Brands on humans and animals that are purely

> ### KEY TERMS
>
> **preterists:** *those who believe Bible prophecies have been fulfilled*
>
> **futurists:** *those who believe Revelation 4–16 portrays future events*

on the surface of the skin have no permanence. Skin cells die and are replaced. Surface injuries may actually hide or disfigure such surface marks. Tattoos can be removed. The use of *epi* ("on") doesn't deny that. It simply indicates that the mark is affixed to the right hand or forehead.

In fact, the word "mark" (*charagma*) comes from the root verb *charasso*, which means "to cut to a point, then to inscribe."[9] It is entirely within the scope of the text to see Scripture as describing some kind of minor surgery— "a cutting to a point"—for the insertion of a chip that will be inscribed with data. If it is a chip, the data must be visible to the scanning device used. In this way the mark is visible as if it were simply *on* the surface of the skin.

Denial of the Prophetic Word

If preterism is correct, then the Bible says virtually nothing about the scientific advances that are taking place in our modern world. Nuclear and biological weapons, state-of-the-art methods of surveillance and tracking, along with many other phenomenal advances in scientific knowledge are not mentioned in the Bible. Those passages in the Bible that speak of a worldwide war that engulfs the entire planet and brings horrible death to great numbers (for example, Zechariah 14:12) must be allegorized and made to apply to a localized event in past history.

REMEMBER THIS

Preterism denies that current events have any prophetic significance whatsoever. Israeli statehood, global education, wars, earthquakes, meteor showers, and so on are not signs of anything and are totally unrelated to the eschatological climax of history. While futurists find catastrophes and disasters to be significant and signs of God's great wrap-up, preterists habitually debunk disasters. They claim that there always have been disasters, tyrants, wars, and epidemics. They regard futurists as fanatics, conspiracy theorists, and assorted half-wits who are trying to frighten people when there is really no cause for alarm.

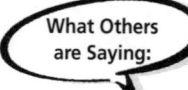

What Others are Saying:

Richard Abanes, *author:* Is war on the increase, as many scholars as well as laymen of our generation have been inclined to believe? The answer would seem to be a very unambiguous negative.

Whether we look at the number of wars, or their severity or magnitude, there is no significant trend upward or down over the past 150 years.[10]

War Reality Check

Abanes's statement is both ludicrous and deceptive. How is it possible to state there is no increase in the "severity" of war? On May 12, 1951, Eniwetok atoll in the South Pacific was vaporized as the Atomic Energy Commission detonated the world's first thermonuclear bomb. The blast was caused by the explosive equivalent of several million tons of TNT. The bomb was so monstrous that it used an atomic bomb of the kind dropped on Hiroshima as a "trigger."

Preterism Stuck in the Past

Preterism insists that the only way to make sense of prophecy is to see a first-century fulfillment. According to Ray Summers, a Southern Baptist, those of us who seek to understand the Book of Revelation from a futurist position have missed the whole point of the book.

What Others are Saying:

Ray Summers: One of the strongest objections to the futurist method is that it leaves Revelation altogether out of relation to the needs of the churches to which it was addressed and which first received it. One of the basic principles of prophecy is that it takes its start with the generation to which it was addressed. Its first purpose is to meet an immediate need—to comfort, to instruct, to warn.[11]

God's Prophecy Comforts

A prediction of an event that is still far in the future can indeed bring great comfort for the present. The apostle Paul wrote about the catching away of the saints and how the dead in Christ will be raised, but then he wrote these words to his immediate audience: "Wherefore comfort one another with these words" (1 Thessalonians 4:18; 2 Peter 3:14, 17). Paul not only knew his words would bring comfort but also encouraged his readers to comfort one another by reminding each other of them.

TOMORROW IS HERE!

For centuries progress stood still. People traveled in essentially the same way in 1000 B.C. as in A.D. 1000. The prophets of the Old Testament had no better remedy for tired feet than did the monks living at the end of the first millennium after Christ. But it is no longer possible for two thousand years to pass without advances in science and technology. Much of the new technology is shrinking the world. Some are even asserting that we are all living in one global neighborhood.

How small has the world become? Small enough so that one body can cover it all. A full-page advertisement for a national insurance company featured the picture of a young woman who is saying: "My body's in New York, but my head's in Bangkok."

Underneath the picture are these words: "From my office in Manhattan, I can manage insurance claims around the world. . . . So whether it's setting up an alternate distribution site after a major Bangkok fire, or finding a good hospital near the Guatemalan jungle, I make sure my customers' businesses stay in business."

High-Tech Snooping

Technology is also making it easier for governments to snoop. D. Ian Hopper, Associated Press writer, reports, "Civil liberties and privacy groups are railing against a new system designed to allow law enforcement agents to intercept and analyze huge amounts of e-mail in connection with an investigation."[12] The system, known as Carnivore, was first revealed on April 6, 2000, in testimony to a House subcommittee and is now in use by the FBI. It can be hooked up at an internet service provider and has the capability of scanning all incoming and outgoing e-mails of a person or persons under investigation by the Bureau.

Even though the FBI has given assurance that it will only tap into the e-mails of a specified target under investigation, various groups remain skeptical. Carnivore does not operate under principles that adequately protect individual rights to privacy, and it breaches fourth amendment search-and-seizure safeguards. Hopper reports, "This 'trust us, we are the government' approach is the antithesis of the procedures required under wire-tapping laws."[13]

The Privacy Invaders

The information superhighway can store all kinds of information about *you*. In fact, so much information of a detailed nature can be captured that it reveals patterns about your life. Machines will soon be able to predict how you will act, what you will choose, and even how you will vote in the next election. All of this can be accomplished through a "cyberstream," defined as an electronic chronicle of one's life, in which records accumulate like baroque pearls on an ever-lengthening string— each arriving phone call and e-mail message, each bill and bank statement, each web bookmark, birthday photo, Rolodex card, and calendar entry.

By feeding all this information into the food processor of statistical analysis, your faithful software servants will be able to make smooth, creamy, startlingly accurate guesses about your plans for the near future. They will find patterns in your life that you didn't know were there. They will respond correctly to terse spoken commands ("Call Juliet," "Buy food," "Print the news") because they will know exactly who Juliet is, what food you need, and what news stories you want to read.[14]

A CLEAR AND PRESENT DANGER

Clearly, the dangers posed by intrusive technology are real. Making the situation even more critical, however, are the repeated attacks against the U.S. Constitution. Constitutional safeguards, written into the Constitution by the founding fathers, protect our national sovereignty and our representative democracy. Knowing that abuses are all too possible at the hands of a government that has no restraints imposed upon it by the general population, the framers of the Constitution built into that document the principle of the separation of powers. This is an ingenious system of checks and balances, which functions among all branches of government and is necessitated by the realization that power has a tendency to bring out what is ugly in human nature.

Important restraints are absolutely necessary to the preservation of human freedom and must be retained in the face of invasive new technologies that threaten every human on the planet. Without them, might makes right. Presidents, government officials, and legislators are fallible and capable of abusing their power. We are all biased to some degree, suffer from incomplete knowledge on any given subject, and are prone to support causes that are personally advantageous. Without checks and balances, private agendas will be advanced even though the majority of the population does not support them.

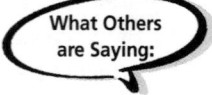

What Others are Saying:

Kenneth Hill and Joan Collins: Congress makes all the laws, but (with minor exceptions) they do not take effect unless signed by the President. The President can veto any act of Congress, but the Congress can pass the law over his veto by a two-thirds majority in both houses. The President is Commander in Chief of the Armed Services, but only Congress may declare war.[15]

REMEMBER THIS

The American system of government is based on a healthy distrust of fallen human nature. In a day of executive orders and presidential decision directives, Christians need to renew their study of the biblical doctrine of fallen human nature.

THINK ABOUT IT

People with a sin nature—and government leaders have one—need to be accountable to others. We are all fallible. Proverbs 11:14 tells us, "In the multitude of counselors there is safety." When one man rules, the rule of law becomes the rule of *his* law.

Easy Mistakes

How serious is the threat posed by technology? To answer that, consider the following two-page ad that appeared in a national magazine. The page on the left showed an out-of-focus photograph with these words in the foreground: "It's never been easier to make a really, really big mistake." The page on the right stated: "These are exciting times. More individuals are taking investing into their own hands with the click of a mouse. And have been empowered to lose more money in less time than they could have possibly imagined . . ."

Yes, technology makes it easier "to make a really, really big mistake"—like an accidental launch of a nuclear missile or misreading data on an object in the sky and taking it to be an enemy **ICBM**. Because of these dangers, governments and nations have never been more willing to surrender their sovereignty and go global as the only solution.

Easy Eavesdropping

Rule by a single individual has always been a bad idea, but modern technology makes it a dangerous idea. Every method by which we communicate with one another is now open to scrutiny. The British and American global spying network that eavesdrops on phone calls, faxes, and e-mails sent via communications satellites is named Echelon. At present, some thirty other nations worldwide have eavesdropping networks, though none as large as Echelon.[16]

> KEY TERM
>
> **ICBM:** *intercontinental ballistic missile*

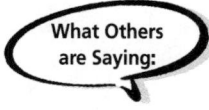

Mike Frost: I think of Echelon as a great vacuum cleaner in the sky which sucks everything up. We just look for the goodies.[17]

Keystroke Cops

While most Americans value their privacy, we may have to get used to the idea that there are others who have no qualms about invading our privacy. A story on the MSNBC internet website for February 7, 2000, and featured in a Southwest Radio Church *Bible in the News* report by Jerry Guiltner relates, "The American workplace has been put on notice that office computers can be monitored. But who would have imagined keystroke cops?"[18]

Some firms are now using a new form of surveillance software that covertly monitors and records each keystroke that employees make. Even materials that are not saved or filed can be monitored. If an employee, for example, writes a grievance about a boss, or even to the boss, but then, after thinking about the possible repercussions and having a change of mind, deletes the letter, every comma, every flick of the fingertip, is still recorded.

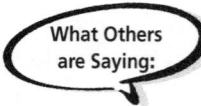

Chris Pauli, *computer-system administrator at an airport in Northern Illinois:* We used to tell our people we could monitor everything—even before we really could—just as a deterrent. Now we really can.

THINK ABOUT IT

Companies using the keystroke cop justify the practice by arguing that some employees may be storing company data that could be used to do irreparable harm to the firm, and that they therefore have a right to keep abreast of what their employees are writing. Furthermore, they want to make sure that the employee is really working, and not just writing personal letters. No doubt, these reasons have a ring of validity to them, but the Bible reminds us that in these last days there will be unscrupulous people lurking and spying. The apostle Paul describes them in 2 Timothy 3:3–4 as false accusers, despisers of those that are good, and traitors.

REMEMBER THIS

One is not paranoid to realize that such technology poses an immense threat to anyone who is regarded as politically incorrect and critical of the globalist elite running the planet in the last days. We are coming into an era in which there is virtually no escape.

Easy Imitations

No doubt, some of today's technology might seem innocuous, such as the ability to digitize scent as the latest in telephone service. The September 8, 1998, edition of *Forbes* featured an article entitled "The Smell Telephone System." It reported that the telephone system of the future won't just extend to eyes and ears around the world but also to noses.

The service has some romantic implications. If you are stuck in Bangkok on Valentine's Day and your sweetheart is thinking about you in Detroit, you will be able to send her an e-mail over a big bandwidth network. As she sits at her computer to connect and opens the e-mail, she'll be greeted by—*ahhh!*—the scent of a hundred roses.

The implications of this new technology reach far beyond romance, something witnessed to by the fact that the military is funding the project. At present there are four types of information that are stored: numbers, words, sounds, and images. But won't it be nice to store smells and the results of other biological processes?

Intimate Brain Scanning

Ray Kurzweil, author of *The Age of Spiritual Machines,* predicts that by the year 2040 computer software will imitate our brains so well that you won't know whether you are talking to a computer or a machine on the telephone. Kurzweil has come up with the idea of "reverse engineering" our brains so that everything we know about ourselves—memories, dreams—that is, the "stuff" that makes you *you* and me *me*—will be downloaded into a computer.[19]

Put plainly, people will be able to scan their brains into a computer and create a self-replica. When this is completed, the computer will actually claim to be that person. It will say something like this: "I grew up in Brooklyn. I graduated from MIT. Then I walked into a scanner and woke up here in this machine."

When Kurzweil was being interviewed about his "spiritual machine," the interviewer was amazed. "Isn't that a frightening scenario?" he asked. "Won't people say, 'Stop the world—I want to get off!'?"

Kurzweil replied: "It's unstoppable. It's part of the fundamental laws of the universe. This is not an alien invasion. It's emerging from within our civilization. We're already pretty intimate with our computers. As we move forward, the **nexus** between machines and humans will become even more intimate."[20]

TECHNOCRAT VERSUS HUMANITY?

It appears that the technocrats who have control of these machines are in a war against humanity. Some of the technologies challenge our basic concepts of human dignity and personhood. Is it possible to discern an affinity between these technologies and what Scripture reveals about Satan's great emissary on earth during the Tribulation, the Antichrist?

KEY TERM

nexus: *connection, link*

"Silent Death"

Some new technologies will be used for the interrogation and torture of prisoners and leaders who might be reluctant to share information—until electroshock and chemical means are used to elicit the desired information.

The military is intensely interested in radio frequency (RF) weapons. Ever since it was first noticed that certain radio frequency energy could have a shattering effect on humans as well as military software, military science has become enamored with RF weapons. Even more sinister is the technology, already on the threshold of deployment, "which can manipulate emotions, control behavior, put you to sleep, create false memories and wipe old memories clean."

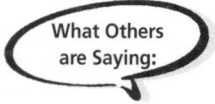

What Others are Saying:

Nick Begich: The use of radio frequency energy as a carrier for silent death has reached varying degrees of completion. It is now possible to disrupt the entire living system with weapons growing out of this research.[21]

CURRENT WORLD EVENTS

Mind Control

The United States Air Force Advisory Board states that it is now possible "to create a high fidelity speech in the human body, raising the possibility of covert suggestion and psychological direction . . . in a fashion that would be most disturbing to them."

Nick Begich comments, "The authors suggest that this would be 'disturbing' to the victim—what an understatement, it would be pure terror. A weapon which could intrude into the brain of an individual represents a gross invasion of one's private life. The idea that these new systems will be perfected in the next several years should be cause for significant discussion and public debate."[22]

Psycho-Terrorism

This kind of technology now makes possible "psycho-terrorism," a term coined by the Russian writer N. Anisimov. He says, "psychotronic weapons can be used to take away part of the information which is stored in a person's brain and send it to a computer which reworks it to the level needed to control the person." The information can be modified and reworked by the terrorist agency and then reinserted into the person's mind. The person thinks these are his own thoughts and operates on the basis of these thoughts, which are not his own but those of another.[23]

Unsuspecting Guinea Pigs

Compounding the problem are the sad stories of medical experimentation performed in the past on human beings without their consent or knowledge. Nick Begich and James Roderick quote reports that appeared in both the *Washington Times* and the *Anchorage Daily News* to demonstrate the readiness of some in the U.S. government to use people as guinea pigs:

- "Government researchers appear to have had a pattern of choosing 'vulnerable people'—minorities, the poor, prisoners and retarded children—for Cold War-era radiation experiments, Energy Secretary Hazel O'Leary said Tuesday . . ."
- "Children in orphanages were used to test experimental vaccines for diphtheria and whooping cough for several decades after WW II . . ."
- "At least 500,000 people were used as subjects in Cold War-era radiation, biological and chemical experiments sponsored by the federal government, a congressional agency said yesterday . . . the tests conducted from 1940 through 1974 ranged from radiation to biological and chemical agents like mustard gas and LSD . . ."[24]

HUMANITY'S BRUTALITY

History, both ancient and modern, confirms the degree of brutality and cruelty that human beings are capable of committing against one another. A society that murders unborn babies has no scruples. If Christians are deemed to be dangerous because they oppose globalism and intolerant because they won't go along with a particular political agenda, their foes will find sufficient reason for their eradication.

Technological Terrorism Justified

Just as the threat of terrorism or the need to crack down on school violence is used to outweigh the objections stemming from appeals to individual rights and prohibitions against the invasion of privacy, the use of technology against Christians will be readily justified. Persecution of a religious group will be seen as a lesser of two evils.

Population Control at All Costs

Stanley Monteith, M.D., in his report entitled "The Population Control Agenda," shows how far unscrupulous people and organizations will go for the sake of some "higher cause" that they believe allows them to transcend God-ordained values. Those who are convinced that the population of planet Earth must be reduced dramatically if society is to survive resort to a shocking solution they find perfectly valid.

What Others are Saying:

Stanley Monteith: One of the most difficult concepts for Americans to accept is that there are human beings dedicated to coercive population control and genocide . . . I shall have to admit that I studied the politics of AIDS . . . for over a decade before I finally came to a horrifying conclusion. The real motivation behind efforts to block utilization of standard health measures to control further spread of the HIV epidemic was "population control."[25]

Citing the comments of Margaret Sanger and her connections with Madame Blavatsky, the founder of a religion that worships Satan, and quoting elitist groups and their official documents, Monteith demonstrates how population control is regarded as "a good and necessary thing." Most will scoff at Monteith's research, and he realizes that. But don't laugh. Remember how Christians failed to speak out during the days of Hitler's reign.

What Others are Saying:

Jacques Cousteau, *French underwater explorer*: [It] is a terrible thing to say . . . In order to stabilize world population, we must eliminate 350,000 people per day. It is a horrible thing to say, but it's just as bad not to say it.[26]

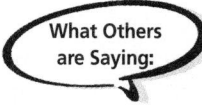

What Others are Saying:

Martin Niemoller: In Germany they came first for the Communists, and I didn't speak up because I wasn't a Communist. Then they came for the Jews, and I didn't speak up because I wasn't a Jew. Then they came for the trade unionists and I didn't speak up because I wasn't a trade unionist. Then they came for the Catholics, and I didn't speak up because I was a Protestant. Then they came for me, and by that time no one was left to speak up.[27]

Console Warfare

Though modern weapons have great destructive potential, modern warfare is even more dangerous because it tends to depersonalize war and therefore desensitize individuals to its horror.

In an age of high-tech weaponry, combatants are now "console warriors." The concept of waging war from computer command centers became a historical reality in both the Gulf and NATO air wars against Yugoslavia. Both of these conflicts involved a heavy dependence on weapons that make it possible for the nation with the most sophisticated weapons to destroy the enemy with a minimum of interaction with hostile air and ground troops.

Though this kept many safe, it also depersonalized war. Begich and Roderick state, "When wars involved direct contact with the enemy the activity of killing was personal and, at the end of the war, all parties understood the impact and could question the morality of their actions."[28] While technology has protected American lives, it has often made the destruction of wars seem less horrible in that war more resembles a video game than combat in which real human beings are maimed and killed.

END-TIME CONCERN

While it is incumbent upon all Americans, and all peoples of the world, to be aware of the ethical and moral issues involved in the implementation of these new technologies, it is difficult to mobilize people to register their protest and to make their voices heard. Evidently, many officials in government resent the concern of certain individuals and groups and would much rather be left alone to pursue their own agenda.

Particular events over the last several years, especially the Oklahoma City bombing and the even more horrific New York City attacks, have made the threat of domestic terrorism an urgent concern for law enforcement officials. Everyone craves security, and large numbers of people are willing to forfeit their liberties in order to feel safe. Consequently, investigating the draconian threat that comes from government surveillance is not always appreciated. Investigations by various groups are often met with scorn and ridicule, and warnings of possible abuses of power often go unheeded.

The line between law-abiding citizens who protest growing government threats to the right of privacy and citizens who are considered to be terrorist threats to U.S. national security is blurring. The patriot movement is one example. Those within the patriot movement define it as organizations with concerned citizens who guard against dictatorship. Those opposed to the movement define it as being comprised of militant, racial supremacists who adhere to an extremely antiauthoritarian ideology.

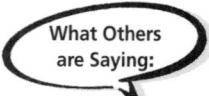

What Others are Saying:

Nick Begich: Overreaction by government is a greater threat to democracy than those posed by real or imagined threats. We have personally met many people associated with the "patriot" movement and the vast majority of these individuals are law abiding citizens with no motives other than to live under the rules of our constitutionally constituted democratic republic and nothing more. The **vilification** of the "patriot" movement proceeds with media assistance under the principles of "guilt by association."[29]

The world stands poised on the brink of disaster. Many of the scenarios created by modern warfare resemble chapters in Revelation. The explosion of knowledge predicted by the prophet Daniel has left a cloud of debris that casts a long shadow over planet Earth. The plethora of technological developments has numerous connections with the prophetic Scriptures. The world is ripe for the **dispensational** change ushered in by the Rapture of the church. There can be little doubt that last-time technology has brought us to the brink of the most tragic seven-year period in the history of humankind.

KEY TERMS

vilification: *defamation, abuse*

dispensational: *the theological view that God deals with humans differently during various times or dispensations*

MSNBC.com

Technology and Science page

**Big Brother Spending Spiked in 2001: GAO Report
Shows $50 Million Spent on Biometrics before 9/11**

By Bob Sullivan

APRIL 15 - Even before Sept. 11, government spending on surveillance technologies had risen sharply in recent years, according to a report released Monday by Congress' General Accounting Office. Over $50 million was spent prior to July 31 of last year researching technologies like biometric identification, including facial recognition software. Twelve different government agencies have researched the technology, with the State Department and Justice Department topping the list. . . .

In a case of unusual political bedfellows, the American Civil Liberties Union and Armey's office made a joint statement last July calling for the data, in the wake of controversial deployments of face recognition cameras at the 2001 Super Bowl and other high-profile events. At the time, Armey's office said in a press release that the technologies have "an alarming potential for misuse."

PROPHETIC IMPACT

Worldwide terrorism is on the rise. Terrorist activity within neighborhoods, in the form of robberies and assaults, are becoming almost a common daily affliction in America today.

Surveillance cameras that smack of Big Brother-type invasion of privacy and liberty would not have been tolerated just a few months ago. Now such intrusive devices are looking more and more like protective big brothers to terrified people wanting security for their lives and possessions.

Bible prophecy in Revelation 13 strongly implies end-time technology, including the mark of the beast that will empower the Antichrist for absolute dictatorship.

Considering computer, satellite, and camera linkages, in conjunction with other technologies developing just as Daniel 12 said they would, the Antichrist's shadow might soon darken an unsuspecting world.

CHAPTER WRAP-UP

- One reason the prophesied time of tribulation will be so horrible is that technology will enable the Antichrist to control and manipulate everyone on earth.

- Revelation 13 foretells the Antichrist's system of control. Everyone will be forced to accept a mark in their foreheads or their right hands, or be killed.

- The twentieth century saw the greatest breakthroughs in technology in history. The tremendous increase of knowledge, which is now said to be doubling every few months, is evidence this generation might be in the time of the end as given in Daniel 12.

- Technological realities today, including an implantable computer chip transceiver and electronic snooping systems, indicate the coming Antichrist control system might be near.

- Technology makes it easier for the government to snoop on its citizens and reduces the checks and balances needed for healthy government.

- New technological advances challenge human dignity and make it easier to torture prisoners, control people's minds, and use people as guinea pigs. War has the feel of a video game.

- Technology is and may be used to control population growth and "errant" religious groups.

The Last Generation

BY J. MICHAEL HILE

Let's Get Started

Jesus gave prophecies about events and world conditions that will be occurring with great frequency and intensity just before he comes back to planet Earth. The prophetic Word indicates that one generation, which is alive just before the end of the age, will not pass away completely; that is, not everyone in that generation will die. Some people will be taken directly from planet Earth to heaven while their minds and bodies are instantaneously and miraculously changed for eternal residence.

Are we living in the time of the last generation?

To answer that question the student of prophecy confronts many other questions:

- What is a generation from God's perspective?
- How long is a generation?
- What is meant by the prophecy Jesus gave about the fig tree in Matthew 24:32–35?
- Is the fig tree in that parable intended to represent modern-day Israel, reborn May 14, 1948?
- Did the generation Jesus talked about begin with Israel's rebirth as a nation?

No one knows the precise answers to these questions since God's Word doesn't tell us, but God does want us to be watching for signs of the last generation. Understanding the meaning of a generation can help us recognize these signs.

There are a number of differing views on what constitutes a generation, as Jesus used the term. The average length of life for human beings has varied greatly over the millenniums according to Bible accounts. Genesis tells us that people lived well over 900 years before the great Flood. Moses lived to be 120 years old. During much of the time between Moses' day and the beginning of the twentieth century, the average life span in many cultures was sometimes less than 50 years. Today, through improved nutrition and modern drugs and medical technologies, people are again living to 80 and well beyond.

Some of the most common theories about what constitutes a generation include the idea that a generation is 70–80 years or that it is 40 years. Examining God's Word and recent events will give us clues about the meaning of the term "generation" and end-time or "fig-tree" generation and help unravel the mystery of the last generation.

Matthew 24:34 Verily I say unto you, This generation shall not pass, till all these things be fulfilled.

THE GENERATION MYSTERY

We know from the Scriptures that the first **generation** began with Adam and Eve. Noah was the tenth generation. Which generation of people was Christ talking about when he said, "This generation shall not pass"? The answer to this two-thousand-year-old question may be closer than we think if the many prophecies we see on the horizon continue toward fulfillment in the twenty-first century.

KEY TERM

generation: normal life span of people born in the same approximate years

Time for Serious Study

The unfolding of the end-time prophetic scenario before our eyes should prompt us to keep our Bible in one hand and the newspaper in the other as we piece the prophetic puzzle together.

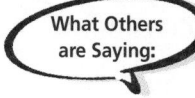

What Others are Saying:

Tim LaHaye: Jesus Christ may not come in this generation, no one really knows! Of that we can be definite! However, our generation has more reason to believe His coming could be during our lifetime than any other generation before us.[1]

Matthew 24:30–33 And then shall appear the sign of the Son of man in heaven: and then shall all the tribes of the earth mourn, and they shall see the Son of man coming in the clouds of heaven with power and great glory. And he shall send his angels with a great sound of a trumpet, and they shall gather together his elect from the four winds, from one end of heaven to the other. Now learn a parable of the fig tree; When his branch is yet tender, and putteth forth leaves, ye know that summer is nigh: so likewise ye, when ye shall see all these things, know that it is near, even at the doors.

The Generation of His Coming

Perhaps the most intriguing and controversial prophetic passage in the Bible is contained in the **Olivet Discourse**, part of which is quoted above. This dynamic end-time message by Jesus in Matthew 24 and 25, Mark 13, and Luke 21, describes major events that will impact the Jewish people just before the Lord returns to set up his kingdom.

After leaving the Temple in Jerusalem, Jesus went to Mount Olivet. Jesus' disciples asked him three burning questions about the future, which are recorded in Matthew 24:3:

> KEY TERM
>
> *Olivet Discourse: prophetic message by Jesus to answer the disciples' questions atop Mount of Olives*

1. When will these things be?
2. What will be the sign of your coming?
3. What will be the sign of the end of the world [age]?

Jesus' answer to those questions alludes to the generation that will be living on the earth when Christ returns. Some believe that the generation Jesus was talking about in the Olivet Discourse was the generation that passed away in A.D. 70. But that does not fit within the context of a literal return of Christ to earth, as described in the verses preceding and following the parable of the fig tree in the passage quoted above.

When the many signals Christ gave for the Tribulation in his Olivet Discourse begin to occur at the same time with greater frequency and intensity, the end-time generation can know Jesus' coming is near.

Signs to Look for Just Before Christ's Return:

- There will be false teachers (Matthew 24:4–5).
- There will be wars and rumors of wars (Matthew 24:6).
- Nation will rise against nation (Matthew 24:7).
- Kingdom will rise against kingdom (Matthew 24:7).
- There will be famines, pestilences, and earthquakes in various places (Matthew 24:7).
- God's people will be greatly persecuted, hated, and killed (Matthew 24:9).
- There will be much betrayal and hatred on the earth (Matthew 24:10).
- False prophets will arise and deceive many (Matthew 24:11).
- Iniquity (lawlessness) will be rampant (Matthew 24:12).
- Real love will not be found (Matthew 24:12).
- The gospel will be preached to the whole world (Matthew 24:14).
- People on earth during the Tribulation will see the Antichrist (Matthew 24:15).

A GENERATION DEFINED

One might raise several questions about the unique generation described by Jesus and about other generations that are described in the Bible.

- What is a generation?
- When does a generation begin?
- When does a generation end?
- How long is a generation?
- Which generation was Christ talking about when he said "this generation"?

What Is a Generation?

According to the *Random House Dictionary of the English Language,* a "generation" can be defined in these ways:

- The entire body of individuals born and living at about the same time
- The average number of years between the birth of parents and the birth of their offspring
- A group of individuals who are roughly the same age and who have similar ideas and attitudes

---

Genesis 17:7 And I will establish my covenant between me and thee and thy seed after thee in their generations for an everlasting covenant, to be a God unto thee, and to thy seed after thee.

When Does a Generation Begin?

The Bible teaches that life begins at **conception**. The word "seed" in the Old Testament was used to describe the **lineage** of offspring at and after conception. God's promises to Abraham and his descendants are given in the Book of Genesis.

Offspring in the Bible were sometimes referred to as "seed" and other times associated with "generations," as shown in the Book of Psalms: "A seed shall serve him; it shall be accounted to the Lord for a generation" (Psalm 22:30).

Jeremiah's life began at conception as shown by God's plans for him. God told Jeremiah that he planned Jeremiah's ministry before he formed him in the womb: "Before I formed thee in the belly I knew thee; and before thou camest forth out of the womb I **sanctified** thee, and I **ordained** thee a prophet unto the nations" (Jeremiah 1:4–5).

KEY TERMS

conception: *moment when life is formed*

lineage: *historical line of blood relatives*

Jeremiah: *prophet in Judah who predicted Jerusalem's fall to the Babylonians and the Jews' return from exile 70 years later*

sanctified: *made holy*

ordained: *officially commissioned for a special task*

FURTHER STUDY

Luke 1:31 (conception)
Jeremiah 1:1–2 (Jeremiah)

Promises God Made to Abraham and His Descendants

Reference	God's Promise...	The Promise Kept...
Genesis 12:2	I will make you into a great nation.	From Abraham sprang both the Jewish and Arab peoples.
Genesis 12:2	I will bless you.	God protected and enriched Abraham during his lifetime.
Genesis 12:2	I will make your name great and you will be a blessing.	Jews, Muslims, and Christians honor Abraham as founder of their faith.
Genesis 12:3	I will bless those who bless you, and whoever curses you I will curse.	Throughout history peoples who have persecuted the Jews have experienced national disaster.
Genesis 12:3	All peoples on earth will be blessed through you.	Abraham's descendents gave the world the Bible and Jesus.
Genesis 12:7	To your offspring I will give this land.	Israel remains the promised land of the Jewish people, to be occupied at history's end.

Judges 2:10 And also all that generation were gathered unto their fathers: and there arose another generation after them, which knew not the Lord, nor yet the works which he had done for Israel.

When Does a Generation End?

A generation ends at the death of a notable individual or at the death of those individuals who are living at about the same time. For example, the death of **King David** is described in Acts 13:36 and that event implies the end of that era: "For David, after he had served his own generation by the will of God, fell on sleep, and was laid unto his fathers. . . ."

The men who led Israel after the death of **Joshua** represented a new generation that was displeasing to God. Joshua's generation ended when he and those who were about his age died (Judges 2:8–10). An abundance of evidence in the Scriptures points to physical life beginning at conception and ending at death.

KEY TERMS

King David: *Israel's second and most famous king, from whose line came Mary, Jesus' mother*

Joshua: *leader of Israel after Moses' death*

FURTHER STUDY

2 Samuel 5:3 (King David)

LENGTH OF A GENERATION

KEY POINT

A generation ends when a key person dies or when most people of one age group die.

One of the most perplexing issues among students of Bible prophecy is the length of a generation. There is much disagreement among secular and religious writers concerning the length of a generation. One common theory says a generation is 40 years. The idea behind this theory is that since the Israelites were punished by having to <u>wander</u> in the wilderness for 40 years until that disobedient <u>generation died</u>, God sees a generation as 40 years.

FURTHER STUDY
Numbers 14:30–33 (wander)
Hebrews 3:8–11
(generation died)

Mark 13:28–33 Now learn a parable of the fig tree; When her branch is yet tender, and putteth forth leaves, ye know that summer is near: So ye in like manner, when ye shall see these things come to pass, know that it is nigh, even at the doors. Verily I say unto you, that this generation shall not pass, till all these things be done. Heaven and earth shall pass away; but my words shall not pass away. But of that day and that hour knoweth no man, no, not the angels which are in heaven, neither the Son, but the Father. Take ye heed, watch and pray: for ye know not when the time is.

Israel as a Fig Tree

KEY POINT

Many people believe that the birth of Israel in 1948 marks the beginning of the generation that will be alive at Christ's return.

When Israel became a nation in 1948, some believed that Israel's birth date marked the beginning of the generation that would see all the events leading up to the Second Coming of Christ. This theory was based upon the generation alluded to in the parable of the fig tree. The fig tree is symbolic of the nation Israel.

If that theory is true and if a generation is 40 years, then Christ should have raptured the believers on or before 1988.

To study more about the parable of the fig tree, check out these references.

Judges 9:8–15
Isaiah 66:8
Jeremiah 24:1–10
Matthew 21:17–21
Matthew 24:32–51
Mark 11:11–14, 20–21
Mark 13:28–37
Luke 13:6–9
Luke 19:41–44
Luke 21:29–36
Romans 11:1–2, 25–27
Revelation 6:13

End-Time Generation Puzzle

After 1988 passed uneventfully, the 40-year theory fell into disrepute. Either 1948 had not been the starting date for the generation described in the fig tree parable or a generation must be longer than 40 years.

Some argued that 1967, the year Jerusalem was captured by Israel, or some other future date could be the birth of the generation that would see the return of Christ. Some proponents of the **end-time generation** theory questioned whether 40 years was actually the length of a generation today. A few sources hold that a generation is now 20 to 30 years in length. Other people's opinions range from 30 to 100 years.

> **KEY TERM**
>
> **end-time generation:**
> people alive during the time
> of Christ's return

The Longevity of Humankind

> *KEY POINT*
>
> *After 1988 the 40-year theory was no longer commonly accepted.*

Numerous theories have been put forth concerning the length of a generation without defining clearly what a generation is, when it begins, or when it ends. Remember, a generation, as described in the Bible, begins at conception and ends at death. The length of a generation is not an arbitrary period of time that occurs within the life span of an individual or group of people.

Joshua's age at the time of death, 110 years (including nine months **gestation**), was the length of the generation he represented. Some of his generation died before him and some after him. Consequently, the average life span of a person or group of people living at about the same time constitutes the length of that generation.

REMEMBER THIS

The length of a generation has not always been constant since the days of Adam and Eve. Before the Flood, the average life span of people was over 900 years. Today, if a person lives to be 100 years old, it is a special occasion in which the person is afforded celebrity status.

The Flood's Effects

To understand how long a generation is today, it will be helpful to know what the length of a generation was before the Flood and what happened to the life span of humans immediately following the Flood. Before the Flood the life span of the **patriarchs** averaged around 930 years (see illustration, page 184). One exception should be noted. <u>Enoch</u> did not live a full life because God took him; Enoch did not die.

The life span of the patriarchs decreased from generation to generation as a result of the earth's <u>changed</u> environment brought about by the breakup of the "**fountains of the deep**" located within the earth and the "**windows of heaven**" spoken of in Genesis 7:11.

These catastrophic occurrences, according to some scientific authorities, disrupted a protective environmental shield that had prevented the earth from receiving damaging ultraviolet rays from the sun. With the deterioration of that shield, things on earth, including human life, began to degenerate and deteriorate at a much faster rate. The average life span decreased as a result.

KEY TERMS

gestation: *when a baby is in a mother's womb from conception to birth*

patriarchs: *founding fathers of Israel*

fountains of the deep: *vast underground sources of water*

windows of heaven: *supernatural openings in the skies through which tremendous amounts of rain fell*

FURTHER STUDY

Deuteronomy 3:26–28;
31:23; 34:9 (Joshua)

Genesis 5:23–24 (Enoch)

Genesis 2:6 (changed)

Noah and his family lived on both sides of the Flood. Noah was 600 years old when the floodwaters <u>covered</u> the earth. He lived 350 years after the Flood and was 950 years of age at his <u>death</u>. Shem, Noah's son, lived to be 600 years old. Shem was nearly 100 years old when the Flood occurred. He lived an <u>additional 500</u> years after the Flood. The age of each successive generation continued to decrease to the point that Abraham lived to be only 175 years old. The regression of age continued with Abraham's descendants (see illustration, page 185). Abraham's son Isaac lived to be 180; Jacob, 147; Joseph, 110; Levi, 137; Kohath, 133; and Amram, who was Moses' father, 137.

Numbers 32:11, 13 Surely none of the men that came up out of Egypt, from twenty years old and upward, shall see the land which I sware unto Abraham, unto Isaac, unto Jacob; because they have not wholly followed me: Save Caleb the son of Jephunneh the Kenezite, and Joshua the son of Nun: for they have wholly followed the Lord. And the Lord's anger was kindled against Israel, until all the generation, that had done evil in the sight of the Lord, was consumed.

KEY TERMS

Noah: *righteous man who built the ark and was saved from the Flood*

Joshua and Caleb: *God-fearing men who spied out the Promised Land and who encouraged the Israelites to obey God and occupy it*

FURTHER STUDY

Genesis 7:11 (covered)

Genesis 9:29 (death)

Genesis 11:10–11
(additional 500)

Numbers 14:6
(Joshua and Caleb)

The Wilderness Generation

Those who hold to the 40-year generation concept do not take into account the total age of those who had sinned against the Lord. The curse was against the men who had reached 20 years of age and older.

After the 40-year judgment period was completed, there were no men left older than 60 years of age except **Joshua and Caleb**. Although Joshua was not a descendant of Moses or Aaron, he represented the succeeding generation that was to enter the Promised Land. Joshua and Caleb were the

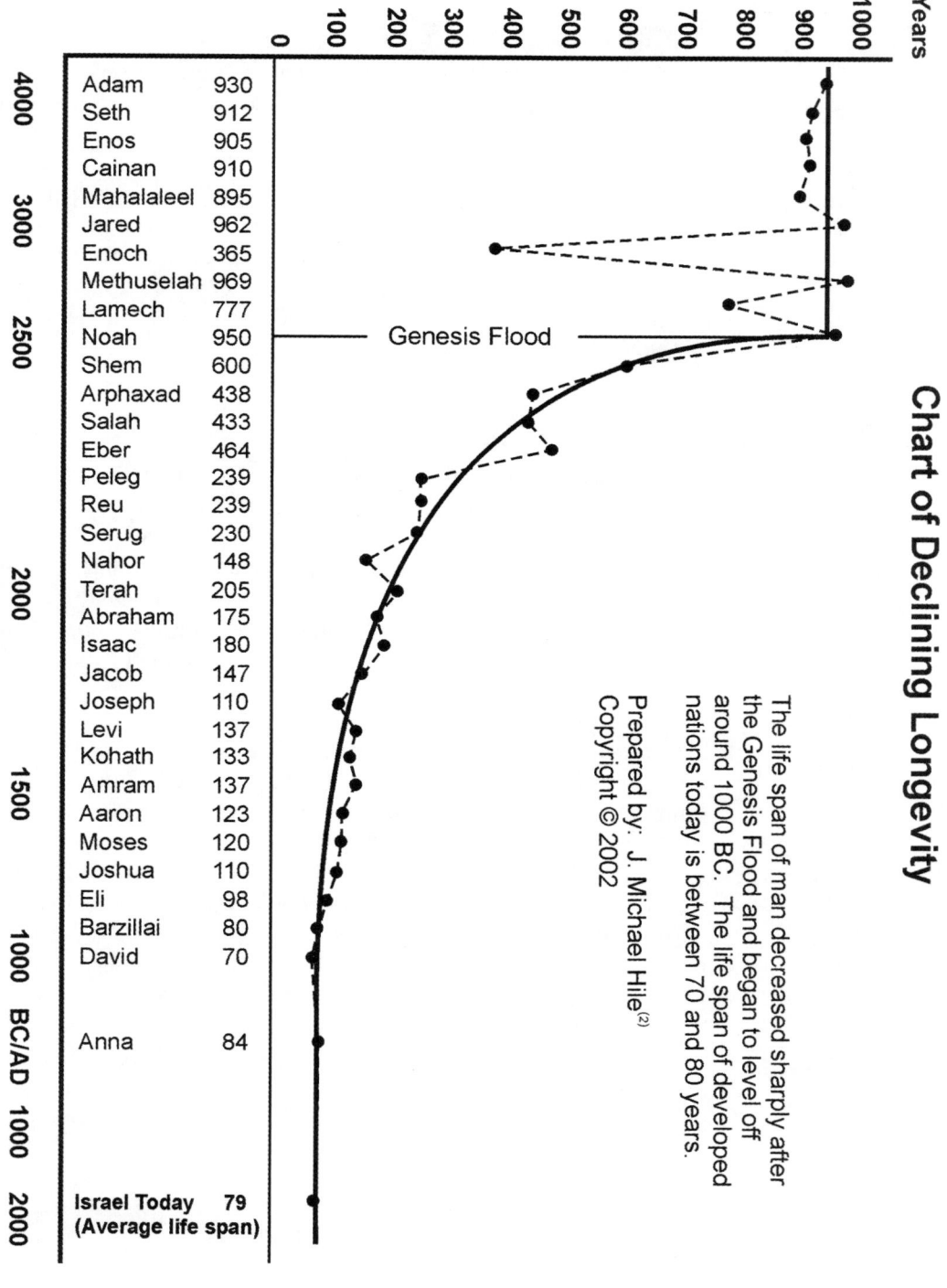

Chart of Declining Longevity

Years	
Adam	930
Seth	912
Enos	905
Cainan	910
Mahalaleel	895
Jared	962
Enoch	365
Methuselah	969
Lamech	777
Noah	950
Shem	600
Arphaxad	438
Salah	433
Eber	464
Peleg	239
Reu	239
Serug	230
Nahor	148
Terah	205
Abraham	175
Isaac	180
Jacob	147
Joseph	110
Levi	137
Kohath	133
Amram	137
Aaron	123
Moses	120
Joshua	110
Eli	98
Barzillai	80
David	70
Anna	84
Israel Today **(Average life span)**	**79**

Genesis Flood

The life span of man decreased sharply after the Genesis Flood and began to level off around 1000 BC. The life span of developed nations today is between 70 and 80 years.

Prepared by: J. Michael Hile[2]
Copyright © 2002

only two males permitted to live after the Lord cursed the rebellious generation that would not return and retake their land in Canaan.

REMEMBER THIS

Forty years could not have been the length of that generation, but it was the time God allotted for that generation to die off. Most of the recorded life spans during this time were well over 40 years. Aaron was 123; Moses, 120; Joshua, 110; and Caleb was over 85 when their generations died off.

The Life Span of Humans Stabilizes

FURTHER STUDY
Samuel 4:15 (98 years)

The average length of a generation was about 930 years for those living before the Flood but decreased to around 120 years by the time Moses crossed the Red Sea and began his 40-year sojourn in the wilderness of Sinai. Since there are not very many 120-year-old men walking around today, it is apparent that the average life span is no longer 120 years (see illustration, page 185).

Eli, a high priest and judge of Israel whose life bridged the thirteenth and twelfth centuries B.C., died at the age of 98 years. According to 1 Samuel 2:22, he was considered to be a "very old" person at the time of his death.

REMEMBER THIS

The oldest, fully authenticated age in recent times (122 years) was Jeanne Louise Calment, who was born in France on February 21, 1875, and died on August 4, 1997. Maud Farris-Luse, recognized in 2001 as the world's oldest person (115 years) by the *Guiness Book of World Records*, was born on January 21, 1887, in the state of Michigan and died March 18, 2002. Obviously, these cases are exceptions and do not represent the average life span of humankind today.

Additional views for the life span of humans (that is, the length of a generation) include 100, 80, 70, 60, 50, and 20 years. A more recent theory divides the 2,166 years from Abraham's birth to the birth of Christ by the fifty-two generations listed in Matthew chapter 1 to give a generation the length of 51.57 years.

> **Psalm 90:10** The days of our years are threescore years and ten; and if by reason of strength they be fourscore years, yet is their strength labour and sorrow; for it is soon cut off and we fly away.

KEY POINT

The 70–80 year generation theory holds the most promise.

KEY TERM

exodus: *when the Israelites escaped Egyptian bondage*

A View from the Psalmist

Disregarding untimely or unnatural deaths due to epidemics, famine, and war, there is evidence in the Scriptures and in recent history to support a 70–80 year life span for the past 3,000 years. The evidence for a 70–80 year lifespan was present during the tenth century B.C. during the reign of King David (about 1010–970).

About 400 to 500 years after the **exodus** (about 1450 B.C.), the life span of humans seemed to level off at around 70–80 years. This was around 1000 B.C. during the days of kings Saul, David, and Solomon.

Perhaps the most significant declaration in the Bible for the life span of humans is given in Psalm 90. The psalmist states that the life span of people is 70 years with 80 years being the upper range of normal life expectancy.

Ironically, Moses, who lived to be 120 years old, is credited with writing Psalm 90 during the fifteenth century B.C. Moses may have been suggesting a new life span for people, since the 70–80 year statement does not coincide with his age or the age of his contemporaries, Aaron and Joshua.

> **2 Samuel 5:4** David was thirty years old when he began to reign, and he reigned forty years.

The Generation of David

About 400 years after Moses' death, David began his reign of 40 years that would end around 970 B.C. As David approached the end of his life, he was considered to be an old man by those living at that time. First Chronicles 23:1 says, "So when David was old and full of days, he made Solomon his son king over Israel."

Acts 13:36 concludes, "For David, after he had served his own generation by the will of God, fell on sleep, and was laid unto his fathers and saw corruption." The Scriptures reveal that David served his generation and was 70 years old when he died.

A contemporary of David, Barzillai the Gileadite, was considered to be an old man during the days of King David's reign. Second Samuel 19:32a says, "Now Barzillai was a very aged man, even fourscore years old. . . ."

> **Jeremiah 7:29–30a** Cut off thine hair, O Jerusalem, and cast it away, and take up a lamentation on high places; for the Lord hath rejected and forsaken the generation of his wrath. For the children of Judah have done evil in my sight saith the Lord:

The Babylonian Captivity

Around 200 years after David's death, Isaiah prophesied: "**Tyre** shall be forgotten seventy years, according to the days of one king" (Isaiah 23:15).

The concept of 70 years as the life span for kings may have been established after David's death at 70 years. When **Judah** was taken into Babylonian captivity in 606, 597, and 586 B.C. by **King Nebuchadnezzar**, it was to be for 70 years. The verses in Jeremiah 7 above explain God's judgment on that generation.

KEY TERM

Daniel: *captive prophet of Judah who became great in the Babylonian court of Nebuchadnezzar*

FURTHER STUDY

Daniel 1:6 (Daniel)

Matthew 23:33–38; Luke 11:29 (generation)

Luke 17:25 (rejected)

When King Nebuchadnezzar captured the southern kingdom of Judah, Ezekiel and **Daniel** were carried off to the land of Babylon. After Babylon's capture by the Medes in 539 B.C., Daniel began reading from the Book of Jeremiah about the captivity that had been prophesied by Jeremiah: "In the first year of his reign, I Daniel understood by books the number of the years, whereof, the word of the Lord came to Jeremiah the prophet, that he would accomplish seventy years in the desolations of Jerusalem" (Daniel 9:2).

The length of time appointed for the rejection of this "evil" generation was 70 years. If the age of the Jewish generation rejected by God was 20 years and up, as with Moses' generation in the wilderness, then those still living in Babylon would have been over 90 years old when the 70-year period ended. Most of the generation taken into captivity had already died or were too old to make the journey back to the Promised Land. Daniel was a youth when taken captive and was probably in his 80s or 90s.

> **Luke 2:36–37a** And there was one Anna, a prophetess, the daughter of Phanuel, of the tribe of Aser: she was of a great age, and had lived with an husband seven years from her virginity; and she was a widow of about fourscore and four years,

The Generation of Christ

Shortly after Christ's birth, Jesus was brought to Jerusalem to be dedicated to the Lord. Anna, who was considered to be very old at the time Christ was born, was present at the Temple. She was 84.

Christ described the generation of his day as evil and accused them of killing, crucifying, and persecuting the prophets, wise men, and scribes that he had sent to them. He also prophesied that he would be rejected by his generation. Because of their stubbornness and failure to recognize "the time of their <u>visitation</u>," Christ pronounced judgment upon the city of Jerusalem and declared: "All these things shall come upon this generation" (Matthew 23:26). Jesus was talking about the generation of people that were alive during his lifetime.

We know that Christ did not live the full length of his generation, which raises the question: "Who shall declare his generation? For his life is taken from the earth" (Acts 8:33; Isaiah 53:8). Christ said in Luke 11:30, "For as **Jonas** [Jonah] was a sign unto the Ninevites, so shall also the Son of man be to this generation."

Has God appointed a "man of God" to be a sign to each generation of people? Jesus Christ, who was "cut off" or killed as prophesied in Daniel 9:26, was to represent the evil generation of his day. How long would Christ's generation have been if he had not died an early death?

Most Bible scholars believe Christ was crucified about A.D. 30–33. If that was the case, the wicked generation that the time of Christ represented was judged 40 years later when Jerusalem was destroyed by the Romans in A.D. 70. When the last **vestige** of Jewish resistance was wiped out at Masada in A.D. 73–75 (see illustration, page 191), the destruction of Jesus' generation was complete.

Historians tell us that Jesus Christ was born sometime before the turn of the century (2–8 B.C.) with 4 B.C. being the most popular view. Assuming that the generation that Christ described had expired by A.D. 75, the length of that generation would have been between 70 and 80 years.

The extra-biblical book of Jubilees, which was found among the Dead Sea Scrolls during the middle of the twentieth century (1947–1956), has an interesting account of the regression of man's age that coincides with the description given in Psalm 90:9–10. This ancient document, believed to have been written sometime between 150 and 105 B.C.,

Masada

This drawing depicts the remains of the high plateau fortress built by King Herod on the western shore of the Dead Sea where the Jews last defied Rome. Masada was excavated in the 1960s and 1970s.

describes the regression of man's age from the generation of Adam down to a generation that will receive a great punishment from the Lord (see illustration, page 185).

Life Span of Humans Today

The life span of humans leveled off at around 70 to 80 years during the reigns of kings Saul, David, and Solomon and has remained about the same for the past 3,000 years (1000 B.C. to A.D. 2000). Fluctuations in life span have occurred due to war, famine, disease, and other factors. People are most likely to grow old in rich countries where there are sufficient medical and sanitary facilities, clean drinking water, and adequate food.

According to the U.S. Census Bureau's International Data Base, life expectancy today is only 37.13 years in Zimbabwe, 47.49 years in Kenya, and 48.09 years in South Africa, but it is 63.24 years in Brazil, 63.69 years in Egypt, 67.34 years in Russia, 71.62 years in China, 79.87 years in Australia, and 80.80 years in Japan. Most of the countries in Europe and North America have life spans between 70 and 80 years. The life expectancy of those living in the United States in 1850 was less than 40 years but increased to 47.3 years by 1900 and then mushroomed to 76.7 years (1999) by the end of the twentieth century.[3]

If 70 to 80 years still represents the length of a generation, as described in Psalm 90:9–10, one would expect the life span of those living today to be close to that figure. According to the *2002 World Almanac and Book of Facts*, the average life expectancy in the United States is 77.26 years (74.37 years for males and 80.05 years for females). For Israel it is 78.71 years (76.69 years for males and 80.84 years for females). The average life expectancy at birth for Israel is projected to be 81.6 years in the year 2025.[4]

THE FIG TREE GENERATION

In the parable of the fig tree, Jesus talked about a generation of people (perhaps Jews and Gentiles) that would be living at the time he returned to earth to establish his kingdom. With Israel back in their land after almost 2,000 years of dispersion and with other end-time prophecies coming into focus, the Jewish people now living in Israel could very well be the generation Christ was talking about.

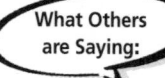

What Others are Saying:

Hal Lindsey: It is my unwavering conviction that this is the terminal generation. By this I mean that this generation is witnessing the coming together of all the prophetic signs into the exact pattern that Jesus and the other prophets predicted would immediately precede His return.[5]

Luke 21:29–33 And he spake to them a parable; Behold the fig tree, and all the trees; When they now shoot forth, ye see and know of your own selves that summer is now nigh at hand. So likewise ye, when ye see these things come to pass, know ye that the kingdom of God is nigh at hand. Verily I say unto you, This generation shall not pass away, till all be fulfilled. Heaven and earth shall pass away: but my words shall not pass away.

Perhaps This Generation?

In Luke's version of the fig tree parable, he mentions the fig tree (Israel) and all the <u>trees</u> (nations of the world).

If the length of David's generation, Christ's generation, and today's generation is 70–80 years (a 3,000 year span), it would be reasonable to conclude that the generation Christ was talking about in the parable of the fig tree will also be 70–80 years in length. If the fig tree in this parable represents the nation of Israel, as many prophetic scholars believe, and the generation that is described has a life span of 70–80 years, then we see several strong indicators that the generation Christ was talking about has already been born. That would mean that the return of Jesus Christ to establish his reign for 1,000 years is close at hand.

> FURTHER STUDY
> Judges 9:8–20 (trees)

The indicators we have seen include the following:

- The rebirth of Israel as a nation in 1948 (Isaiah 66:8)
- The controversy over Jerusalem in the end times (Zechariah 12:1–3)
- Preparations for rebuilding the Jewish Temple (Revelation 11:1–2)
- Ongoing negotiations for a peace treaty between Israel and the Palestinians (Daniel 9:27)

> What Others are Saying:

Dr. James Dobson: Jesus himself said that we could take a lesson from the fig tree. In other words, you can look at the signs and get a notion of where we are in the history of mankind. . . . It would appear that we are moving towards some kind of endpoint. . . . It all seems to lead in the direction that the scripture has told us . . . that there is an age that will end . . . and we may not be far away from it. . . . I believe he's coming and I believe his return is imminent. I'm not going to select a date . . . because people have gotten in trouble with that. But we can see the fig tree. We are the generation of the fig tree, I believe. And we can see that the time is right.[6]

The Most Significant End-Time Prophecy

Israel's return to the land of Abraham, Isaac, and Jacob in the twentieth century after dispersion by the Roman armies in A.D. 70 is the most important event that signals the soon return of Jesus Christ. The end-time events described in the Olivet Discourse and the Book of Revelation could not take place without Israel being back in their land.

Israel's rebirth as a nation has also served as a catalyst for other end-time prophecies that are beginning to converge. The pieces necessary for development of the end-time prophetic puzzle began to fall in place between the middle of the nineteenth and first half of the twentieth centuries when the Jewish people began coming back to their homeland in record numbers.

REMEMBER THIS

KEY TERM

Zionism: *Jewish political movement to establish a Jewish state*

A movement called **Zionism** encouraged the Jewish people to return to the Promised Land and brought about the Balfour Declaration in 1917, a statement by Great Britain that supported a home for the Jewish people. After much negotiation and endorsement of a partition resolution by the United Nations in 1947, the rebirth of Israel (Isaiah 66:7–9) took place on May 15, 1948. Following a period of wars between the Jewish and Arab nations in 1948, 1956, 1967, and 1973, peace negotiations have been ongoing and will continue until a covenant (Daniel 9:27) is confirmed between the Antichrist and the nation of Israel.

God's Blueprint for the Future

Christians who take the Bible seriously should be actively watching the prophetic shadows that are appearing in today's headlines. The primary purpose of God's prophetic Word is to point people to Jesus Christ, "the author and finisher of our faith" (Hebrews 12:2).

As we entertain the possibility that we may be the generation Jesus was talking about nearly 2,000 years ago in the fig tree parable, we are admonished by the Scriptures to watch

KEY TERMS

Issachar: *one of twelve sons of Jacob, founder of a tribe or clan*

dispensation: *specific era in which God deals with people a certain way*

FURTHER STUDY

Matthew 24:37–51
   (be prepared)

Matthew 16:3 (signs)

Luke 19:44 (time)

1 Thessalonians 4:13–5:11
   (into heaven)

Revelation 13:11–18
   (global dictatorship)

and <u>be prepared</u>. No one knows the day or the hour of his coming but the Father. The same Jesus, however, was angry with the Pharisees and scribes for not discerning "the <u>signs</u> of the times" and not knowing the "<u>time</u> of their visitation." In these thought-provoking and challenging days in which we are living, we need to be informed and discerning like "the children of **Issachar**, which were men that had understanding of the times, to know what Israel ought to do" (1 Chronicles 12:32).

One day there will be a generation of Christians that will escape the grip of death and be ushered <u>into heaven</u>, the final frontier for believers. The generation of unbelievers that is left behind will face the ruthless tyranny of a <u>global dictatorship</u>. The world stage is now being set for the closing act of this **dispensation**, and the climax of world history, Christ's return, is drawing near. As God's children, we may very well be the generation that is chosen to "escape all these things that shall come to pass, and to stand before the Son of man" (Luke 21:34–36). That possibility is certainly worth pondering!

THINK ABOUT IT

What Others are Saying:

Billy Graham: There is only one authoritative book in the world that accurately predicts what is going to happen in the future—and that is the Bible. . . . The question arises: Who will restore order? Who can counter the danger of the nuclear holocaust? Who alone can govern the world? The answer is Jesus Christ! . . . Yes, God has promised this planet to His Son, Jesus Christ, and someday it will be His. He will bring an end to all the injustice, the oppression, the wars, the crime, the terrorism that dominate our newspapers and television screens today. . . . The promised coming of the Lord has been the great hope of true believers down through the centuries. . . . Virtually everything has been fulfilled that was prophesied in the Scriptures leading up to the coming of Christ. We know His coming is near!"[7]

**HEADLINE
HIGHLIGHT**

Israel Defends Destruction in Jenin

By Joshua Brilliant
United Press International
April 18, 2002

NAHAL GINAT, West Bank, April 18 (UPI) - Two bulletproof buses brought the reporters and TV crew to the tree-covered hilltop of what used to be called Nahal Ginat, a military settlement west of Jenin. It was a military attempt to pre-empt world criticism of the deaths and destruction in Jenin. . . .

Thursday morning Palestinian human rights groups convened a news conference in Jerusalem alleging hundreds had died, that an Israeli truck dumped bodies into a pit and then retrieved them. They alleged people were executed and soldiers allowed women into a house to evacuate a crippled man only to begin demolishing the building when they went inside. . . .

The Israelis denied there had been a massacre. . . .

The army operated "with tweezers," the division's commander, Brig. Gen. Eyal Shlein said. The Israelis paid for it, he said, with 23 soldiers killed and 75 wounded in Jenin . . .

[Shlein] said one of his officers saw Palestinians force two women to stand in front of a gunman who stuck his gun between them and fired. . . .

Shlein said soldiers called out to people to leave their homes and gave them time to do so. When they heard civilians in distress who wanted to leave, "we stopped the fire and stopped the tractors," he added.

PROPHETIC IMPACT

Jesus foretold through prophecy that all eyes will be upon Jerusalem and God's chosen people of Israel just before he returns. The world's attention is turned to Israel every day. World leaders instinctively know that tiny bit of land is the most important place on planet Earth.

Israel is the nation symbolized as a fig tree throughout the Bible. Just prior to his words in Matthew 24:32–35, Jesus laid out a number of signals involving Israel that will mark the last generation of earth dwellers immediately before his Second Coming. He said that those who are watchful will know just how close his coming is when all of these signals for Israel are coming together at the same time.

Then Jesus gave the fig tree (meaning Israel) as the key signal to anticipate. When it is a tender or very young nation in the land and when it is critically prominent in the world scene, the observant student of prophecy will know that Jesus' coming is very near.

Can there be any serious argument against the truth that Israel is the most troublesome spot in the world at this moment? Daily, the world community condemns Israel for aggressing against her neighbors even though Israel is only doing what it must to defend itself. If these signals are end-time signs, Jesus Christ's Second Coming must be very near. The Rapture, which will occur at least seven years before the Second Coming, can take place at any moment. It is likely that ours is the last generation of this age.

CHAPTER WRAP-UP

- The prophetic Word indicates that one generation will be alive at Christ's return to planet Earth and gives signs to help in discovering if we are living in this last generation.

- Jesus' parable of the fig tree, found in Matthew 24:32–35, holds the key to understanding what generation will be alive at the time of Christ's Second Coming. The fig tree is used often in the Bible to symbolize the nation Israel.

- There are various definitions of what constitutes a generation of people. These differences present a puzzle when trying to pin down exactly what Jesus meant by "this generation."

- The theory that a generation is 40 years long collapsed after the prophecies Jesus mentioned were not in view by the time of Israel's fortieth anniversary.

- Defining the length of a generation is difficult because life expectancy has increased thanks to modern medicine.

- Most likely a generation today is between 70 and 80 years long. Not everyone in a generation will die within that time span. Some will live to be 100 years or older. Therefore, the exact number of years the last generation, spoken of by Christ, will live is impossible to determine.

- Every major prophetic signal Jesus gave in his Olivet Discourse is already in view, although he gave these as signs for the Tribulation. This means the Rapture of the church, which will take place at least seven years before Christ returns, must be very near. It could happen at any moment!

SECOND-COMING COUNTDOWN

12

Suddenly
Gone!

BY WILLIAM T. JAMES

Let's Get Started

Planet Earth reels with foreboding that something unknown and uncontrollable is about to thrust terrifying events upon our generation. Anxiety swells while the new millennium rumbles like a storm across the twenty-first-century landscape. While optimism abounds that this new century will produce a brighter, better world, apprehension eerily warns that the years ahead harbor perils of apocalyptic dimension.

> **KEY TERM**
>
> **Rapture:** *Christ snatching the church from earth*

The Bible foretells of a phenomenal event that will have a far greater impact on Christians and non-Christians alike than any happening that has occurred since Jesus' crucifixion, burial, and resurrection. The **Rapture** will happen suddenly. Its impact will be tremendous. God's Word has forewarned every generation since the earliest days of the church to watch expectantly for this event.

What is the Rapture? When will it occur? What will it mean to the world? And, most importantly, how will it affect you?

EVENT WILL SHOCK EARTH

> **1 Corinthians 15:51–52** Behold, I show you a mystery: We shall not all sleep, but we shall all be changed, In a moment, in the twinkling of an eye, at the last trump; for the trumpet shall sound, and the dead shall be raised incorruptible, and we shall be changed.

Likely Scenarios

A young mother will be walking the aisles of a Wal-Mart store with her two-year-old daughter riding securely and happily in the shopping cart while they both look over all the brightly packaged goods on the shelves. A businessman will be entering an on-ramp to a freeway near Los Angeles, giving a nervous glance to his left to make sure he will have room to merge smoothly into the flow of traffic.

Half a world away, the captain of a 747, having just received permission to take off, will push the throttles fully forward and the gigantic bird will begin its roll between the runway lights that appear to come together in a sharp point in the distant darkness. A mother-to-be will reach for a ringing telephone, a broad smile on her face anticipating talking with her husband who had promised to call once he was settled in his hotel where his company is holding its quarterly sales meeting. Then, in a split-second, it will happen!

A surgeon in a Boston hospital who has just started moving his scalpel along the man's chest suddenly finds the blade cutting only air. The patient is gone!

A mortician in Dallas recoils in astonishment when the suit he is smoothing on the corpse collapses. The body is no longer there!

The mother pushing the cart in the store turns back toward the basket with the items she has gotten from the shelf. Her little girl is missing! Only her toddler's colorful little dress and shoes remain in the cart in a crumpled heap. The woman's scream pierces the air, joining other screams of similar panic reverberating throughout the store.

At the same moment, the commuting businessman in Los Angeles sees the big semi rig directly in front of him swerve sharply right and begin tumbling down the steep embankment while the roadways ahead and on either side of him explode with violent wrecks.

Precisely at that instant, the copilot in the 747's right seat panics when he realizes that the huge jet, now screaming down the runway at more than 100 miles per hour, is totally out of control, its pilot having disappeared!

The young father-to-be is shouting into the telephone, wanting to know what is wrong with his wife, whom he hears crying hysterically. She has fallen to the floor and is desperately groping her abdomen, nearly insane because she cannot feel the baby who is no longer in her womb.

When all Christians vanish in the rapture, billions of people around the world will suffer shocks similar to those depicted above. Or they will awaken to find they live in a world phenomenally different from the one they knew when they went to bed the night before.

Although today's world has its share of confusion and chaos, when this astonishing event takes place, near-insanity will for a time rule this panicked planet. It will be far different from the attitude of apathy that rules at present.

What Others are Saying:

KEY TERM

ambassadors: Christ's representatives

Hal Lindsey: If God is going to remove His **ambassadors**, you can expect there will be some repercussions that will shake people up and I really believe that when every living believer is snatched out, there's going to be planes crashing, cars crashing; there's going to be all kinds of weird things happening because God wants to shake up the world and let them know that something supernatural has intervened.[1]

WHAT IS THE RAPTURE?

1 Thessalonians 4:16–18 For the Lord himself shall descend from heaven with a shout, with the voice of the archangel, and with the trump of God; and the dead in Christ shall rise first; Then we who are alive and remain shall be caught up together with them in the clouds, to meet the Lord in the air; and so shall we ever be with the Lord. Wherefore, comfort one another with these words.

Disappearing Act

What is this electrifying instant that will rock the world? As Paul describes in 1 Thessalonians, it is the moment when Jesus, with a voice that sounds like a trumpet, will summon all those who have believed in him since the day of **Pentecost**—living and dead—to heaven to be with him forever.

Each believer will then be changed. Earthly bodies that age and decay will be transformed into bodies that are eternal and beautiful beyond imagination. This will happen so quickly that God's Word calls it "in the twinkling of an eye" (1 Corinthians 15:52).

Christians will be instantly changed from mortal beings to supernatural beings. As exhilarating as that transformation will be, it will pale beside their joy of seeing Jesus Christ face-to-face. As Christians we will understand—through our transformed and perfected senses—the width and height and depth of God's holiness and love. We will suddenly know Christ as he truly is. Each believer will be like Christ in that moment and will be eternally in his majestic presence. Scripture says, "But we know that, when he shall appear, we shall be like him; for we shall see him as he is" (1 John 3:2).

KEY TERM

Pentecost: *place and moment Holy Spirit came to dwell in believers*

FURTHER STUDY

Acts 2 (Pentecost)

---

2 Peter 1:19–21 We have also a more sure word of prophecy; whereunto ye do well that ye take heed, as unto a light that shineth in a dark place, until the day dawn, and the day star arise in your hearts: Knowing this first, that no prophecy of the scripture is of any private interpretation.

For the prophecy came not in old time by the will of man: but holy men of God spake as they were moved by the Holy Ghost.

Literal Interpretation

To interpret Scripture **literally**—in this instance, Scriptures about prophecy—is to take God's Word as meaning, in real terms, exactly what it says. The Holy Spirit has given us the prophecy about the Rapture and the resurrection of all believers just as he gave the <u>prophecy of</u> Jesus' first coming during Old Testament times.

Paul says all Christians will in one moment be changed into bodies that cannot grow old or decay. To believe this will happen precisely the way Paul says it will happen is to interpret his words literally.

Some who study these matters don't believe the Bible is meant to be interpreted literally. They view many passages in the Bible as symbolic or as spiritual ideas. Some who spiritualize the Rapture passages, for example, believe 1 Corinthians 15:52–55 and 1 Thessalonians 4:13–18 mean that Christ comes into the believer and changes him instantly. Thus, the believer will never die but live in eternity with Christ.

I believe that when Christ comes to live in the believer at the time of salvation, the believer is instantly changed into an eternal saint of God who will forever be with Christ. But this is not the Rapture. The Rapture is a literal moment in time when *all* Christians since the day of Pentecost (both living and dead) will be snatched into the air above planet Earth to go to heaven and the <u>Father's house</u> with Jesus Christ.

> **KEY TERM**
>
> ***literally:*** *not symbolically*
>
> **FURTHER STUDY**
> Micah 5:2 (prophecy of)
> John 14:1–4
> (Father's house)
> Genesis 12:1–3; 26:2–6;
> 28:1–3, 15
> (God's promises)

What Others are Saying:

Tertullian: Words ought to be taken and understood in the sense in which they are written, especially when they are not expressed in allegories and parables, but in determinate and simple declarations.[2]

THINK ABOUT IT

Theologians who spiritualize prophetic truth believe that the church has replaced Israel in God's plans. They believe Israel is no longer heir to <u>God's promises</u>.

This is called "replacement theology." These theologians say that the church (all those saved since Pentecost) are the heirs to all of God's promises to his chosen people, the Jews. The Jews (Israel) threw away the right to their inheritance when they rejected the Messiah, Jesus, when he came to earth the first time.

According to this theological line, all Christians are now, spiritually speaking, Jews. Replacement theologians teach and preach this despite the tremendous, unconditional promises God gave his wayward but beloved chosen people he chose for himself long before the church was born.

WHEN WILL THE RAPTURE TAKE PLACE?

> FURTHER STUDY
> Matthew 24:36
> (God knows)

In his Olivet Discourse, Jesus gave great details of what would come to pass just before he returned. God has not seen fit to give the precise time of the Rapture. Jesus indicated that only his Father, <u>God, knows</u> the timing of that spectacular event. All of the signs Jesus gave in the Olivet Discourse were for his Second Coming when he will reign on earth, not for the Rapture.

Although there are no signs given for the Rapture, we in this pre-Tribulation era have graciously been allowed to see the foreshadowing of the dramatic signs of the Tribulation and Second Coming.

God's Gracious Signposts

Signs Pointing to the Tribulation	Reference
1. Israel back in their land	Ezekiel 36:8–11
2. Prophetic nations in alignment	Ezekiel 38:1–6,18; 39:1; Daniel 9:26
3. Revived Rome in form of European Union	Daniel 9:26
4. Developing one-world government; one-world economy; one-world religion	Revelation 13; 17:12–13
5. Great increase in knowledge, communication, and travel	Daniel 12:4
6. Apostasy	2 Thessalonians 2:3
7. Perilous times	2 Timothy 3:1

REMEMBER THIS

Jesus and the prophets gave many signs for the Tribulation, the last seven years of unprecedented trouble. The Rapture will take place before the Tribulation. Therefore, because these signs are already occurring in this pre-Tribulation era, we know the Rapture must be very near.

THINK ABOUT IT

Today many Christians ignore the prophetic Word. Why did the Lord give such in-depth signs for the end of the age if he didn't intend for his followers to recognize and understand prophetic matters?

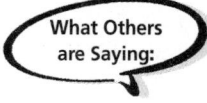

What Others are Saying:

Peter LaLonde: We are to be expectant at all times. . . . What we see now in the world today are signs of the second coming of Christ. . . . [I]f we as Christians could come to grips with this—in a moment we will be in the presence of our Lord forever . . . [h]ow it would transform our lives![3]

KEY POINT

Christians today can understand the truth about coming events by watching and being alert to the signs of Jesus' coming.

John Walvoord: I've been teaching prophecy for more than 50 years on the seminary level. It's a very precious truth and a very practical one, but it's more than just a doctrine to me. The idea of being able to see Christ—perhaps any day—face to face, is an amazing, electrifying anticipation. And that's what the Bible teaches, and I believe that's what God wants us to realize and hope for. And so as I am dealing with this subject, perhaps from a theological, biblical standpoint, it is also from the standpoint that if you really love Christ, you are going to love His appearing. And this is going to be a precious truth to you.[4]

Differing Views of Rapture's Timing

Here are the main views about the timing of the Rapture. While they differ considerably, each viewpoint revolves around that period known as Jacob's trouble or Daniel's seventieth week.

FURTHER STUDY
Jeremiah 30:7
(Jacob's trouble)

- *Post-Tribulation Rapture:* the Rapture will take place at the end of the seven-year Tribulation.
- *Mid-Tribulation Rapture:* the Rapture will take place somewhere near the three and one-half year point of the seven-year Tribulation.

- *Pre-Tribulation Rapture:* the Rapture will occur before the seven-year Tribulation.

There are a number of stark variations within these Rapture views. To review an in-depth look at the Rapture, please see chapter 1 where that stunning future event is dealt with at length.

This book presents Bible prophecy from the pre-Tribulation viewpoint. It is the only viewpoint that sensibly fits together with all aspects of the prophetic Word man has been given.

To the detriment of proclaiming the prophetic Word, there has developed of late a viewpoint called preterism. This view puts forth the unscriptural proposal that all prophecy was completed in A.D. 70 with the <u>destruction</u> of Jerusalem prophesied by Daniel the prophet and by Jesus in the Olivet Discourse. Any reasonable examination of prophetic passages throughout the Bible tells the reader that there are tremendous prophecies yet to be fulfilled.

> **Revelation 22:20** He which testifieth these things saith, Surely I come quickly. Amen. Even so, come, Lord Jesus.

Christ's Imminent Return

God's prophetic Word points absolutely to the coming of Jesus Christ at any moment. In fact, the word "quickly" in Revelation 22:20 means suddenly or abruptly. This truth is termed the **doctrine** of **imminence**. The early church fathers eagerly longed for, even expected, Jesus Christ to return during their lifetimes. They were most assuredly believers in the pre-Tribulation Rapture!

If they had believed that the Great Tribulation had to occur before Christ returned, they would have certainly and ceaselessly warned others. They would have urged those around them to watch for the catastrophic occurrences and for the Antichrist,

KEY TERMS

doctrine: *central precept of Bible truth*

imminence: *any moment*

FURTHER STUDY

Daniel 9:26; Matthew 24:2 (destruction)

both of which Scripture tells us will have to come onto the scene before Jesus physically returns to earth to judge the nations and set up his millennial kingdom. Instead, the early church fathers urged us to look for Christ's return.

THINK ABOUT IT

The doctrine of imminence is a wonderful truth at the very heart of the pre-Tribulation view of the Rapture. Imminence was a part of Paul's thinking, and of his hope. He thought it possible for Christ to come at any moment during his lifetime.

This is evident from many things he wrote under the Holy Spirit's direction:

- *1 Corinthians 15:51–52:* "Behold, I shew you a mystery; We shall not all sleep, but we shall all be changed, In a moment, in the twinkling of an eye, at the last trump: for the trumpet shall sound, and the dead shall be raised incorruptible, and we shall be changed."
- *Titus 2:13–14:* "Looking for that blessed hope, and the glorious appearing of the great God and our Saviour Jesus Christ; Who gave himself for us, that he might redeem us from all iniquity, and purify unto himself a peculiar people, zealous of good works."

KEY POINT _____

Christ's coming for Christians is imminent, and it will happen before the Tribulation begins!

Notice the apostle Paul's use of the pronouns "we," "our," and "us." He included himself among those who could be raptured during his lifetime. Notice also that in the Titus account above, he was not looking for the Antichrist nor for Tribulation, but for his Lord and Savior, Jesus Christ, the blessed hope.

What Others are Saying:

Charles Stanley: Jesus said, "I don't know when I'm coming back . . . not even the angels in heaven know; only my Father knows." Matthew 24:27 and Matthew 24:36–41 . . . remind us of His warnings. He's coming without a warning; He's coming instantly without a warning. The skies are going to break open. The shout, the sound of a trumpet. And I believe that only believers are going to hear and only believers are going to know what is taking place. . . . I wonder how many of us really do watch, wait, look forward to, think that at any moment Jesus Christ could come. There's not a single thing that has to be done before Jesus comes. . . . I don't have to worry about when it's going to happen. All I have to do is be ready.[5]

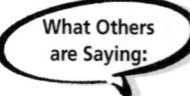

J. Dwight Pentecost: The church was told to live in the light of the imminent coming of the Lord to translate them in his presence. . . . Such passages as 1 Thessalonians 5:6; Titus 2:13; Revelation 3:3 all warn the believer to be watching for the Lord himself, not for signs that would precede his coming.[6]

Renauld Showers: The Bible makes it clear that nobody living on Planet Earth knows exactly when the Lord Jesus will come for His bride, the Church. It's an imminent event. It could happen at any moment. In fact, it could even happen today! . . . [A]fter Jesus has caught up His bride the Church from the earth to meet Him in the air, we are convinced in light of [John 14] that He will return with His bride from the air above the earth back to His Father's house in heaven to begin living in the living accommodations He has prepared there.[7]

REMEMBER THIS

The apostle Paul gives Christians wonderful assurance regarding the imminent coming of Christ in 1 Thessalonians 4:18: "Wherefore comfort one another with these words." Today's increasing problems on every hand make this a comforting promise.

Daniel 9:24 Seventy weeks are determined upon thy people and upon thy holy city, to finish the transgression, and to make an end of sins, and to make reconciliation for iniquity, and to bring in everlasting righteousness, and to seal up the vision and prophecy, and to anoint the most Holy.

Daniel's Seventy Weeks

To understand the Rapture and its timing, it is crucial to comprehend the prophecy of Daniel's seventy weeks (see illustration, page 211). Much of the disagreement involving the subject of the Rapture revolves around misunderstandings regarding God's dealings with the nation Israel on the one hand and his program for the church on the other. The distinctions between these two separate programs are not easily or clearly discerned without a careful and prayerful study of the seventy weeks mentioned in Daniel 9.

In Daniel 9, God outlines his program for "thy people"—meaning Daniel's people, Israel—and tells Daniel that there is a specific period of time set for human history to conclude. Daniel is told that seventy weeks are set to bring things to a close. The seventy weeks are "prophetic" weeks; that is, each week represents seven literal years, based upon the 360-day Jewish calendar year. Therefore, 490 years are set to bring things to a close before the Messiah will come.

Daniel 9:25–27 Know therefore and understand, that from the going forth of the commandment to restore and to build Jerusalem unto the Messiah the Prince shall be seven weeks, and threescore and two weeks: the street shall be built again, and the wall, even in troublous times. And after threescore and two weeks shall Messiah be cut off, but not for himself: and the people of the prince that shall come shall destroy the city and the sanctuary; and the end thereof shall be with a flood, and unto the end of the war desolations are determined.

Timeline of Daniel's Seventy Weeks

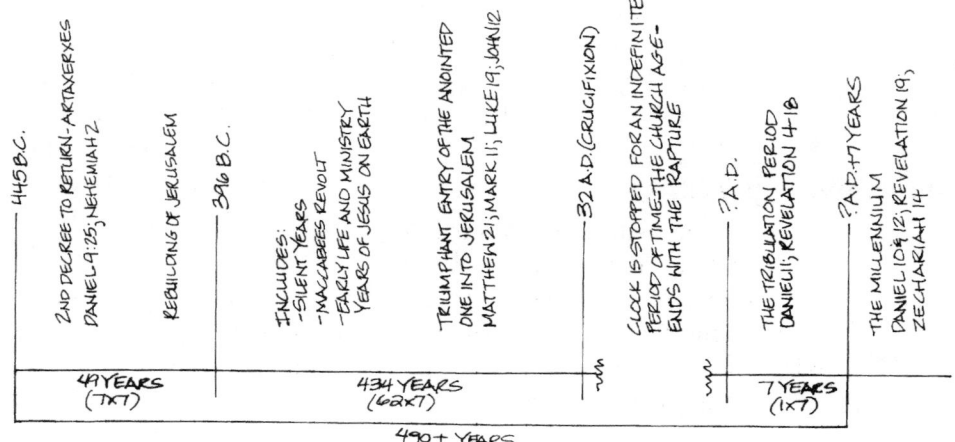

The Disruption

Daniel 9:25–26 mentions a disruption of unspecified time between the sixty-ninth and seventieth weeks. The prophecy says Messiah, Jesus, will be put to death but not for any offense he commits. In other words, he will die for our sins on the cross. This disruption or "cutting off" ends the sixty-ninth week of Daniel's prophecy in 9:24.

The sixty-ninth week Daniel describes is history. Jesus lived, died, and rose again. The seventieth week Daniel describes is the seven-year tribulation period spoken of <u>by Jeremiah</u> the prophet and <u>by Jesus</u>. It is yet to be fulfilled; it is in the future. This age of disruption for God's nation Israel, this period in which you and I are privileged to live, is the church age.

Increase in Knowledge

The prophet Daniel foretold that as the time for the end of God's plan for the present earth nears, "knowledge shall be increased" (Daniel 12:4). That knowledge, many biblical scholars believe, refers to revealed biblical truths. Since the angel of God told Daniel, "Seal the book, even to the time of the end" (Daniel 12:4), it is obvious that God planned to make at least some portion of his **mysteries** understandable to the generation alive at the end of this present earth system.

The discipline of **eschatology**—the study of end-time matters—is a recent development in the mining of the deep truths of God's prophetic Word. It is just one example of today's increase in knowledge.

There are many who still do not have an accurate understanding of Daniel's seventy weeks, especially about the all-important prophetic **interlude**. This has caused much controversy and debate among Christians. Some, because of this lack of understanding, are so against the pre-Tribulation Rapture position that they angrily mock those who hold that view.

KEY TERMS

mysteries: *unknown things*
eschatology: *study of the end times*
interlude: *pause*

FURTHER STUDY

Jeremiah 30:7 (by Jeremiah)
Matthew 24:21 (by Jesus)

> **2 Peter 3:3–4** Knowing this first, that there shall come in the last days scoffers, walking after their own lusts, And saying, Where is the promise of his coming? for since the fathers fell asleep, all things continue as they were from the beginning of the creation.

Peter's Scoffers?

Peter warned about scoffers in the last days who would **malign** the truth and encourage others to follow their false ways. The pre-Tribulation view of the Rapture of the church has come under attack from many sides. Christian theologians as well as non-Christians have increasingly scoffed at the belief that there will be a Rapture or a partial Rapture at any intervening moment in history.

Christians who believe Christ will keep them from the **hour of temptation** by calling them to himself in the air are accused of having a Star Trek mentality. The pre-Tribulation Rapture view in particular is disparaged as a Beam-me-up-Scotty fantasy. Those who mock this view fail to understand the distinctions within God's family. God has a plan for Israel, and he has a plan for the church. When one comprehends these two separate programs, the Rapture and its timing become clear.

> KEY TERMS
>
> **malign:** *speak evil of*
> **hour of temptation:** *time of trial or Tribulation*
>
> FURTHER STUDY
> Revelation 3:10
> (hour of temptation)

> **Daniel 12:1** And at that time shall Michael stand up, the great prince which standeth for the children of thy people: and there shall be a time of trouble, such as never was since there was a nation even to that same time: and at that time thy people shall be delivered, every one that shall be found written in the book.

Daniel's Reference to the Israelites

Many critics of the pre-Tribulation Rapture view proclaim that Daniel 12:1 proves that the church will be on earth during the Tribulation. The critics say the phrase "children of thy people" is talking about Christians.

But Daniel's prophecies here involve the only people who were considered God's children in the Jewish sense of the term; that is, he was talking about the children of Israel—the Israelites. Daniel was saying that Michael the archangel was the "prince" among God's heavenly hosts assigned to protect the Jewish nation during this coming time of trouble—the Tribulation. The church is nowhere in view.

All Christians who lived and died during the church age will, by this time, have been raptured and resurrected and taken to the Father's house by Jesus, their Savior and Lord. At the time Daniel was given this prophecy, of course, the church was centuries away from being born.

What Others are Saying:

Dr. J. Vernon McGee: Scripture clearly states that at the rapture those "which sleep in Jesus will God bring with Him" (1 Thessalonians 4:14). Only, "the dead in Christ shall rise first" (1 Thessalonians 4:16). We are in Christ by the **baptism of the Holy Spirit**, which began on the day of Pentecost and will end at the Rapture. This particular body of believers is called the Church.[8]

Good Company

So are we who believe in a pre-Tribulation Rapture and take a **premillennial** view of Christ's return in good company?

Again, many mock the view that Jesus is coming back to reign on earth for one thousand years. And many who share a premillennial view deride the idea of a pre-Tribulation Rapture of the church. They believe the church will go through the horrific seven years of Tribulation that immediately precede the Millennium.

Some critics of pre-Tribulation Rapture say the idea came from a young woman in England in the 1800s who had a demonic vision. They say a theo-

> **KEY TERMS**
>
> **baptism of the Holy Spirit:** God, the Holy Spirit, dwelling in Christians
>
> **premillennial:** belief Christ will return before the Millennium

logian named John Darby took the girl's vision and came up with the pre-Tribulation Rapture "theory."

While specific documentation of early church leaders giving their views on the Rapture of the church is rare, research has brought to light an early church leader's pre-Tribulation Rapture writing. Ephraem of Nisibis (A.D. 306–373), considered to be the greatest figure in the history of the Syrian church, said this: "All the saints and elect of God are gathered together before the tribulation, which is to come, and are taken to the Lord, in order that they may not see at any time the confusion which overwhelms the world because of our sins."[9]

Clearly, the fact that some early church leaders who lived well before the 1800s held a view that the Rapture could occur at any moment, and that it would be pretribulational, means the John Darby could not have invented the theory. In addition, there are many documented writings about a general belief in Christ's coming again for Christians before the time of God's wrath.

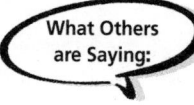

What Others are Saying:

Dr. J. Vernon McGee: I am going to give you the viewpoints of many men in the past to demonstrate that they were looking for Christ to return. They were not looking for the Great Tribulation, they were not even looking for the Millennium, but they were looking for him to come. This expectation is the very heart of the premillennial viewpoint as we hold it today.

- Barnabas, who was a coworker with the apostle Paul, has been quoted as saying, "The true Sabbath is the one thousand years . . . when Christ comes back to reign."
- Clement (A.D. 96), bishop of Rome, said, "Let us every hour expect the kingdom of God . . . we know not the day."
- Polycarp (A.D. 108), bishop of Smyrna and finally burned at the stake there, said, "He will raise us from the dead . . . we shall . . . reign with Him."
- Ignatius, bishop of Antioch, who the historian Eusebius says was the apostle Peter's successor, commented, "Consider the times and expect Him."
- Martin Luther said, "Let us not think that the coming of Christ is far off."

• John Calvin, in his third book of Institutes, wrote: "Scripture uniformly enjoins us to look with expectation for the advent of Christ."

My friend, I have quoted these . . . men of the past as proof of the fact that from the days of the apostles and through the church of the first centuries the interpretation of the Scriptures was premillennial. When someone makes the statement that premillennialism is something that originated one hundred years ago with an old witch in England, he doesn't know what he is talking about. It is interesting to note that premillennialism was the belief of these very outstanding men of the early church.[10]

WHAT WILL THE RAPTURE MEAN TO THE WORLD?

Those who remain on earth after the Rapture will be left gasping in fear and wonderment. Although termed a <u>mystery</u> by the apostle Paul, the taking away of <u>Christ's bride</u>, the church, will no longer be a mysterious prophetic doctrine. It will be a reality.

Revelation 4:1 After this I looked, and, behold, a door was opened in heaven: and the first voice which I heard was as it were of a trumpet talking with me; which said, Come up hither, and I will shew thee things which must be hereafter.

When the Church Age Ends

FURTHER STUDY
1 Corinthians 15:51–58
(mystery)
Ephesians 5:23–32
(Christ's bride)

The church is spoken of nineteen times in the first three chapters of the Book of Revelation. Then John, the prophet who was given the revelation, hears these words from heaven: "Come up hither" (Revelation 4:1). The church isn't mentioned in Revelation again until chapter 19 when Christ returns with the armies of heaven to put an end to man's rebellion at Armageddon.

This shows that the church is nowhere in view during chapters 4 through 18. These chapters of Revelation cover the time during which God's wrath falls upon earth.

When the church is raptured and <u>returns</u> to the Father's house with Christ, great changes will occur on earth. God will then begin dealing with Israel as he dealt with that people during the Old Testament period. That is, he will bring great pressures to bear upon his chosen people, the Jews, through judgment.

During the age of grace, the period or dispensation in which we currently live, God is not judging sin. He is correcting his children, the Christians. He is still ultimately in control of this fallen planet, but he is not judging at present in the Old Testament sense.

The Tribulation will bring God's judgments. They will increase while humankind grows more and more evil in its sinful activities. The last three and one-half years of that seven-year period will bring God's most concentrated wrath. He will send twenty-one judgments in three series, consisting of seven judgments each (see illustration, page 111).

Here are the three series:

1. The Scroll (or Seal) Judgments (Revelation 6:1–8:1)
2. The Trumpet Judgments (Revelation 8:2–15:6)
3. The Vial (or Bowl) Judgments (Revelation 15:7–18:24)

KEY TERMS

purge: to bring forth
purify: cleanse
remnant: remaining number
redemptive plan: God's way of salvation

FURTHER STUDY
John 14:1–4 (returns)

REMEMBER THIS

God's judgments have four purposes:

1. To judge earth's rebellious inhabitants
2. To **purge** or **purify** a **remnant** of Jews (Israel) who believe in his **redemptive plan** and his Messiah, Jesus Christ
3. To purge or purify a remnant of Gentiles who believe in his redemptive plan for mankind
4. To bring Messiah to his millennial reign upon the throne of David

> **John 14:1–3** Let not your heart be troubled: ye believe in God, believe also in me. In my Father's house are many mansions: if it were not so, I would have told you. I go to prepare a place for you. And if I go and prepare a place for you, I will come again, and receive you unto myself; that where I am, there ye may be also.

What the Rapture Means to Christians

Christians who hold the pre-Tribulation view of the Rapture are often accused of looking for an escape from terrible times and of being foolish or cowardly. Critics sometimes add that anyone with such an escapist viewpoint will sit back and wait for Christ to rescue them rather than be about God's business of fighting the good fight in this life.

Living with the constant, expectant hope of Christ's return at any moment, however, is an incentive for Christians. Rather than encouraging them to relax, Christians who expect the Rapture desire to work even harder to obey God's Word and to share the gospel with their unbelieving friends. We do so because we love him and because we want to hear his words, "Well done, [thou] good and faithful servant: thou hast been faithful over a few things, I will make thee ruler over many things: enter thou into the joy of thy lord" (Matthew 25:21). Belief in the Rapture is a comforting promise of God's goodness to his children as they look forward to a future life with him.

What Others are Saying:

Dave Breese: The Scripture says to Christians, "Because you have kept the word of my patience, I will keep you from that hour of trial, temptation, tribulation, that will come upon the whole world to try them that dwell on the earth." Therefore, we see in Scripture that the Bible says that Christ will come for His saints before the beginning of the Tribulation and take all believing Christians up to be with him in heaven.[11]

> **2 Thessalonians 2:7–8** Only he who now
> hindereth will continue to hinder until he be taken
> out of the way. And then shall that wicked one be
> revealed.

What the Rapture Means for Those Who Remain

The apostle Paul tells us that there will come a startling change in the moral order for the end-time generation of humankind. The one referred to in this Scripture, "he who now hindereth," is God the Holy Spirit. The Holy Spirit is presently restraining Satan's evil influence upon the world.

Media news analysts, people on the street, and even many theologians wonder about the bad things happening in the world today. What causes these bad things? Why can't people and nations just get along with each other? Why the cruelty and hatred against other races, religions, and types of people?

Of course, the fallen nature of humankind—sin—and Satan are the causes of such things. If people think things are bad now, they will, if they are on earth at that future time, look back on our present era as a pleasant time to be alive.

Conditions during the tribulation period will be unprecedented. Even Adolf Hitler and Josef Stalin's regimes of horror will pale by comparison. The Antichrist world leader and his False Prophet will ultimately make that era hell on earth. But God's judgments on rebellious human beings will be even more horrific!

REMEMBER THIS

There is a reason why that last seven years known as the Tribulation will be so bad. When God the Holy Spirit stops restraining evil as he does today, a world of almost total lawlessness will be the result. Paul prophesies in 2 Thessalonians 2:7–8 that the most wicked man ever to live will then gain control of almost the whole world system. This won't happen until the church is removed.

What Others are Saying:

Hal Lindsey: There could have been no Church before the Holy Spirit came and started His ministry of taking each believer at the moment of salvation and baptizing into living union with Christ himself, joining us in a living, organic union with Christ, so that we are in Christ from that moment on. He takes up permanent residence in every believer. . . . So these are the days of the Holy Spirit. This is the age of the Holy Spirit. What does 2 Corinthians say is going to happen before the Antichrist is revealed? The restrainer is going to be removed. You see, the Holy Spirit resident within the Church is the restrainer. So when you remove the restrainer, you also have to remove the containers in which He dwells, i.e., you and me. So, you see, it was a miracle the way the Church began; it's going to be another miracle the way it departs. And that is when the Holy Spirit resident in the Church is taken out, and we with Him.[12]

LIVE IN EXPECTATION

It is unfortunate that most Christians have their noses so down on the earthly grindstone that they never look up toward their hope from heaven. The way many Christians live today shows that a significant portion of Christ's bride, the church, disregards the commandment of Jesus, their bridegroom. He said: "Watch ye, therefore; for ye know not when the master of the house cometh, at evening, or at cockcrow, or in the morning; Lest, coming suddenly, he find you sleeping. And what I say unto you I say unto all, Watch" (Mark 13:35–37).

This generation is experiencing, to one degree or another, every signal the Lord Jesus gave. Today should be a time of great expectation!

Antithesis.com

Monday, April 29, 2002
http://www.antithesis.com/features/lastdays_03.html
The End Is Near—Again

HEADLINE HIGHLIGHT

The small and the great, the sane and the insane, the sacred and the profane have been quick to predict when the end might come. For example, Billy Graham and Barbra Streisand—two people on different ends of the spiritual spectrum—have at least one thing in common:

They both believe that we cannot hold out much longer.

Barbra Streisand believes "the world is coming to an end." She just feels "that science, technology, and the mind have surpassed the soul—the heart. There is no balance in terms of feeling and love for fellow man."

Billy Graham, equally pessimistic, writes: "If you look in any direction, whether it is technological or physiological, the world as we know it is coming to an end. Scientists predict it, sociologists talk about it. Whether you go to the Soviet Union or anywhere in the world they are talking about it. The World is living in a state of shock."

Billy Graham does not "want to linger here on the who, what, why, how, or when of Armageddon." He simply states that "it is near." What does Graham mean by "near"? The Book of Revelation states that the time was "near" for those who first read the prophecy (Rev. 1:1, 3). Since Revelation was written during Nero's reign, prior to the destruction of Jerusalem in A.D. 70, the prophetic events of Revelation were fulfilled during the lifetime of those who first read the prophecy.

PROPHETIC IMPACT

This short article from the internet, written by an unnamed author, makes it chillingly clear just how near we might be to Armageddon. Thrillingly, however, the author's scoffing is evidence that the time of Rapture cannot be far off.

The writer is presumably a confessing Christian because other information on the website seems to indicate the site owners champion Christianity.

God's Word speaks of those who will claim to be a part of the church in the last days, but who will scoff at the idea of Christ's imminent return. No one—especially not the Holy Spirit with his perfect knowledge—would think it unusual for an unbeliever to scoff. Peter must have been prophesying, at least in part, about those claiming to be believers when he said, "Knowing this first, that there shall come in the last days scoffers, walking after their own lusts, And saying, Where is the promise of his coming? for since the fathers fell asleep, all things continue as they were from the beginning of the creation . . . " (2 Peter 3:3–4).

CHAPTER WRAP-UP

- People will be shocked and stunned when the Rapture occurs. For a time, the world will be turned upside down.

- At the present, although worries about the future of our world grow daily, the overwhelming majority of earth's inhabitants go along with life as usual. Most people are not concerned about doomsday.

- At some shocking instant, before the Tribulation is initiated by the Antichrist guaranteeing the seven-year peace covenant (Daniel 9:26–27), the Rapture will happen. All Christians who are living and all who have died since Pentecost will disappear from earth. Christ will take them home to heaven.

- Although many scoff at the Rapture theory and even some Christian theologians hold a spiritual or symbolic interpretation of end-time events, early church leaders believed and taught that Jesus would return at any moment for believers.

- The Rapture will take Christians out of the world before the reign of the Antichrist.

Antichrist: The Last Cult Leader

BY AGUSTA HARTING

Let's Get Started

What do we know about the Antichrist, this dreaded creature whom we hope *never* to see in person? What will he be like, and what will be his attributes?

Speculations about the Antichrist abound, and much has been written as well as fabricated about him. Even though we have a rather sketchy revelation concerning him in the Bible, it has become somewhat of a national pastime in recent decades to portray him in all sorts of ridiculous situations.

It is sometimes interesting and informative to read about the Antichrist's future activities when it is merely a speculative scenario written by biblically informed Christians. But Christians are not the only people who like to imagine things about the Antichrist.

Secular movies starring the Antichrist have amused and titillated vast audiences, beginning with films like *The Omen*, where he was supposedly the child of Satan and a jackal. Although audiences worldwide were on the verge of hysteria with terror as they gawked at the film (yet later begged for *Omen II*), they did not think that there *really* was such a person as the Antichrist. Today, the Antichrist is still as unreal to most people as Satan himself, whom the intelligentsia of the world views as the bogeyman of Christianity.

THE ANTICHRIST'S IDENTITY

The body of Christ and those who count themselves among the ranks of Christianity differ greatly on the details concerning the Antichrist. Some say that he will be a Jew, while others insist that he must be Roman. Some are positive that he will be a Russian. Still others say he will be an American.

Some even claim that he isn't really a person at all but merely a world system or an evil empire. Others say he has already been here in the person of Emperor Nero, who made a game of brutally torturing and killing hundreds of the early followers of Christ. Some propose that the Antichrist's False Prophet, of Revelation 13, might be a future Roman pope.

Hitler: Type of Antichrist

Another would-be Antichrist on the world's screen of horrors was the German fuhrer Adolf Hitler. Those of us who are over sixty remember the terror Hitler evoked in us. His brutality is widely known. Hitler slaughtered over 6 million Jews. What is less known, however, is that Hitler was an avid occultist.

Seldom did Hitler plan any move without consulting spirit mediums, psychics, and astrologers. From his deep involvement in the occult, Hitler was introduced to the lie that a superior race existed on the earth. This was supposedly the Arian race of fair-skinned, blue-eyed people scattered all over Scandinavia and northern Europe. So obsessed was Hitler with this demonic doctrine that he set out to destroy anyone whom he deemed unworthy of this "superior" racial membership.

THINK ABOUT IT

Hitler certainly gave a formidable performance as the supposed Antichrist. He was so demon-possessed that his followers boasted that there was an invisible, otherworldly power that overtook him and energized him in his evil works. Hitler also claimed that he was doing the crimes he committed on the Jews "for Christ."

Unimaginable Evil

Although there is disagreement among Christians about the identity, chronology, and timing of the Antichrist's appearance, all agree he will be the epitome of *evil*. You and I cannot imagine how evil he will be. He will make Adolf Hitler and his cohorts, with all their unspeakable treacheries against the Jewish people, seem weak by comparison.

The closest we can come to imagining the horror of the Antichrist is to picture Satan in all his unbridled fury. Look at his person and his diabolical works! Picture, if you can, all his perverted malice gone amok!

The Antichrist will be exactly like his father the devil. All his powers and characteristics will be exactly like those of the ancient enemy, himself, because he will be completely possessed by Satan.

Even if we never see the Antichrist in person, we see a little bit of him every day. We catch glimpses of him in the evil, distress, lies, murder, and mayhem in our world as well as the increasing interest in and activities of the cults and the occult.

Antichrist, Cults, and the Occult

Even though the Bible offers rather sketchy details about the Antichrist, it still reveals many truths we should study and examine, especially as they relate to the cults, the occult, and counterfeit religions. This is where the Antichrist will truly be in his element. How do we know that? We know it because those are Satan's favorite territories and Satan is his father. Satan has been inventing and reinventing false religions, embellishing them for thousands of years, ever since he lied to Eve in the Garden of Eden in Genesis 3.

In the Garden of Eden, Satan convinced the first woman that she and Adam could become autonomous from God. Then Satan proceeded to make up the first <u>false religion</u> after which *all* the rest have been patterned for over six thousand years.

FURTHER STUDY
Genesis 3:4–5; 4:3–8
(false religion)

By studying cult leaders and their occult teachings and techniques, we begin to glimpse a small portion of the deception and machinations of the Antichrist when he comes into power. By studying the tactics of the enemy, we become more discerning and better equipped to rescue others out of the devil's pernicious net of deception.

REMEMBER THIS

We should be ever mindful, of course, to put on the whole armor of God, as described in Ephesians 6 and also to heed the exhortation from 2 Timothy 2:24–26: "And the servant of the Lord must not strive; but be gentle unto all men, apt to teach, patient, In meekness instructing those that oppose themselves; if God peradventure will give them repentance to the acknowledging of the truth; And that they may recover themselves out of the snare of the devil, who are taken captive by him at his will." We are not better or smarter than cultists. We have just become the recipients of God's infinite mercy and grace.

THE PROBLEM OF CULTS

It is almost impossible to fathom the rapid multiplication and growth of cults in the world during the last century. Studies conservatively estimate the number of cults in America as anywhere from three thousand to five thousand. Some of these cults are now so large that they are almost household names. Some have grown so wealthy and powerful that they rank right up there with the Fortune 500. Others are so obscure that few of us ever hear of them until some earthshaking disaster happens.

Cults and Their Leaders

When we study the bloody trails of cult leaders, gurus, occultists, and false prophets through the centuries, we could say that they are and have been a kind of dress rehearsal for the future workings of the Antichrist. Since the late 1950s we have seen this clearly in this country. Here are some of America's recent cults:

- People's Temple (1978). This cult began in Indiana, but ended in Jonestown, Guyana, where almost one thousand people committed suicide at the bidding of their crazed master, Jim Jones.
- Branch Davidians (1993). Eighty-one members of this cult died in a blazing fire in Waco, Texas. Even though the Waco tragedy is still under suspicion for the government's blunder in the matter, the fact remains that most chose to die as they followed their self-proclaimed messiah, David Koresh, by remaining with him in the blazing inferno.
- Heaven's Gate (1997). In San Diego, California, America watched in horror as the body bags of members of this cult were carried out of a peaceful looking villa that had been rented by their guru, Marshall Applewhite. Applewhite had promised his followers a trip to a "level above human" via the trail of the Hale-Bopp Comet.

KEY POINT _____

Many in the media see little or no difference between the cults and evangelical Christianity.

Cults in the Closet

Unfortunately, it takes grotesque tragedies like the ones listed above to wake up the world to the problem of cults. But publicized deaths are not the only ones that occur. We rarely hear about cult members who die one by one from suicide, murder, and other circumstances.

CURRENT WORLD EVENTS

The media lump cultists and evangelical Christians into one group with white supremacy groups like the Christian Identity Movement and fanatical neo-Nazi hate mongers like the Skinheads. The press corps see little difference between Christian philosopher Dr. Francis Schaeffer and the Grand Dragon of the Ku Klux Klan. Today's news media describe both Muslim terrorists and right-wing evangelical Christians as "fundamentalists."

PROPHECY TO WATCH FOR

We can expect to see Christianity mocked publicly and the persecution of Christians accelerate as time draws nearer to the end or to the introduction of the greatest cult leader of them all— the Antichrist. The Bible says, "Therefore the world knoweth us not, because it knew him not" (1 John 3:1).

> **2 Thessalonians 2:9–11** Even him, whose coming is after the working of Satan with all power and signs and lying wonders, And with all deceivableness of unrighteousness; because they received not the love of the truth, that they might be saved. And for this cause shall God send them a strong delusion, that they should believe a lie:

THE DANGER OF CULTS

We know from Scripture that the world will enthusiastically welcome the Antichrist, thinking that he is a great worker of miracles and a great man of peace.

> **Matthew 7:14** Beware of false prophets which come to you in sheep's clothing, but inwardly they are ravening wolves.

False Pretenses

Jesus foretold a danger far more serious than the end-of-the-age disdain for Christians that will be held by the majority of the media. He warned about false teachers who are not what they appear.

We are dealing with things of a spiritual nature, things that are dangerous for our souls: the false prophets of the cults and the occult of today.

KEY POINT

Many people have ignored the danger of cults.

Why are they so dangerous to us? Because these particular wolves *look, talk,* and even *act* like the sheep! The problem, of course, is that while they may use the *vocabulary* of the sheep, they do not *believe* like sheep. Neither do they teach the *doctrine* of the sheep.

This is definitely one of the signs that Jesus said would precede the Antichrist. And this is a sign that the church has basically ignored. The body of Christ has been far too lax for far too long in dealing with the cults and the occult. We have ignored their danger, allowing them to grow like an out-of-control cancer for centuries. The result is the wolves have devoured millions of lambs!

> **Acts 20:28** Take heed therefore unto yourselves, and unto all the flock, over which the Holy Spirit hath made you overseers, to feed the church of God, which he hath purchased with his own blood. For I know this that after my departing shall grievous wolves enter in among you, not sparing the flock. Also of your own selves shall men arise, speaking perverse things, to draw away disciples after them. Therefore watch, and remember that by the space of three years I ceased not to warn every one night and day with tears.

Damage Prophesied

The apostle Paul prophesied about the tremendous suffering that would befall the church in connection with false prophets. In Acts he warned the church of wolves or false teachers that would come among them. Paul understood that damage would come both from without and within the church.

THE MARKS OF A CULT

A Christian can recognize a cult by two key signs: a false gospel and false writings.

Cults proclaim a false gospel. One short definition of a cult from a Christian viewpoint is this: A cult is a group of people centered around a leader (or leaders) who teaches a false gospel. Most Christians I talk with are not sure just what to look for when discerning cults. They are afraid that they will insult someone or that they will be name-calling if they use the word "cult." They are timid and afraid God will judge them for being negative about another's religion.

But Paul showed no such timidity. He warned the church in Galatians 1:6–9: "I marvel that ye are so soon removed from him that called you into the grace of Christ unto another gospel: Which is not another; but there be some that trouble you, and would pervert the gospel of Christ. But though we, or an angel from heaven, preach any other gospel unto you than that which we have preached unto you, let him be accursed. As we said before, so say I now again, If any man preach any other gospel unto you than that ye have received, let him be accursed."

A second way to recognize cults is by their false writings. Satan has always hated God's Word, the Bible. He has endeavored to cast a dark shadow on it, to undermine and pervert it, ever since the Garden of Eden. Satan loves to cast doubt. He asked Eve, "Hath God really said . . . ?" (Genesis 3:1). Cult leaders are usually prolific writers who constantly supplement the Bible with their own false writings. They not only add to the Bible but also they delete from it or claim it is "mistranslated."

Prominent Cults and Their False Writings

- *Mormons:* The Book of Mormon, The Doctrine and Covenants, and The Pearl of Great Price
- *Jehovah's Witnesses:* A "retranslation" of the Bible called The New World Translation of the Holy Scriptures
- *New Age:* A Course in Miracle, The Urantia Book, and The Celestine Prophecy

THE SEDUCTION OF THE OCCULT

Cults are seductive. Many people—this writer included—have been involved in the occult simply because they did not *know* that it was the occult. One in four Americans is, or has been, in some way involved in the occult.

REMEMBER THIS

Discerning the Difference

Understanding the difference between a cult and the occult can be difficult because cults often practice the occult and the occult often results in the formation of a cult. Confused?

Here's the difference:

- Cults need at least two people: a leader who teaches falsehoods out of harmony with the Bible and a follower who believes that leader. Unfortunately, cults are usually larger than two people.
- The occult is something that can be believed and practiced alone. It involves a ritual, formula, or technique of some sort used to make something "supernatural" happen.

Deuteronomy 18:9–14 When thou art come into the land which the Lord thy God giveth thee, thou shalt not learn to do after the abominations of those nations. There shall not be found among you anyone that maketh his son or his daughter to pass through the fire, or that useth divination, or an observer of times, or an enchanter, or a witch. Or a charmer, or a consulter with familiar spirits, or a wizard, or a necromancer. For all that do these things are an abomination unto the Lord: and because of these abominations the Lord thy God doth drive them out from before thee. . . . For these nations, which thou shalt possess, hearkened unto observers of times; and unto diviners: but as for thee, the Lord thy God hath not suffered thee so to do.

Divination: One of Satan's Trap Doors

Satan has many traps in his occult kingdom. The passage above, in which God is speaking to the Israelites as they are headed to the Promised Land, offers a good list. The words "useth divination" in particular have a great deal of meaning in the Deuteronomy passage because divination is the basis for *all* occultism.

Funk and Wagnall's Standard Desk Dictionary defines the word "divination" thus: "The act or art of knowing the future or that which is hidden or unknown." The word "divine" is defined as "of or pertaining to God or a god."

Can we see the connection here? Of course! When one practices divination, one is in reality playing God because things pertaining to the future <u>belong</u> to him alone, not to us—unless he has revealed them to us in the Bible. If we need wisdom or knowledge in order to know how to act, he has promised to <u>guide</u> us through the Holy Spirit. We do not go to psychics or others who use divination of any sort to arrive at the answer!

Satan has never been satisfied with this arrangement and therefore fallen humans aren't either. "Your eyes shall be opened," Satan promised Eve

> FURTHER STUDY
> Isaiah 46:10 (belong)
> Proverbs 3:5–6 (guide)

in the Garden of Eden (Genesis 3:5). Those who seek special knowledge of the future may *think* they will be well informed. The information will be false just as Eve's <u>eye-opening</u> experience was not what Satan had promised.

Some Christians believe they can read their horoscopes or astrological charts just for fun. But astrologers are <u>scorned</u> in God's Word, because they are practitioners of divination, pretending to forecast the future through information from the cosmos. They are consulting the *creature* rather than their Creator. It is crucial that Christians keep astrologers entirely out of their lives. Astrology has been the gate through which Satan has for centuries lured gullible people deeper into the occult.

2 Thessalonians 2:9 Even him, whose coming is after the workings of Satan with all power and signs and lying wonders,

Signs and Wonders

If we had only to worry about psychics on late-night TV shows we would be pretty well off. Unfortunately, the counterfeiters and **shamans** are becoming so pedestrian and mainstream that children these days are thoroughly familiar with most terminology for the occult. When you tell some children about the miracles of Jesus Christ, they respond with an I-can-top-that attitude and tell about something they read or saw on TV.

The Antichrist will display many supposed miracles, astounding his audiences everywhere on the earth. This will be no small feat since today's generation already thinks "miracles" are everywhere.

We probably cannot imagine the power that the Antichrist will display with his signs and false wonders. Like the Antichrist, both the cults and the occult can boast of various and sundry

> KEY TERM
>
> **shamans:** *people who use magic to cure the sick, divine the future, or control nature*
>
> FURTHER STUDY
>
> Genesis 3:7 (eye-opening)
> Deuteronomy 18:10–12;
>   Isaiah 47:13–14; Daniel
>   2:27–28 (scorned)

"miracles." Claims have been made concerning them, which have resulted in the conversion, or as I like to call it *perversion,* of millions of people. Many of these so-called miracles have been and are being done in the name of Jesus Christ.

REMEMBER THIS

Cultists think that the end justifies the means when it comes to cover-ups and blatant lying to promote the cult. The Jehovah's Witnesses call these deliberate deceptions, which they feel they must occasionally employ, "theocratic warfare." The followers of Rev. Moon call theirs "Heavenly Deception." God calls them *sin!*

2 Corinthians 11:3–4 But I fear, lest by any means, as the serpent beguiled Eve through his subtlety, so your minds should be corrupted from the simplicity that is in Christ. For if he that cometh preacheth another Jesus, whom we have not preached, Ye might well bear with him.

DEMOTING JESUS

Being filled with the spirit of the Antichrist, cult leaders as well as all occultists will usually change the person and nature of Jesus Christ to seduce their followers and cause them to worship "another Jesus." Satan, the subtle liar, wants them to use the name "Jesus" but to pervert their understanding about who he *really* is, thus demoting him to a mere creature.

Second Corinthians 11:3 is the only place in Scripture where we read about the apostle Paul being afraid. Paul had <u>been through</u> shipwrecks, imprisonments, starvations, and stonings. He had explicitly said that he preferred death rather than life so that he could be with the Lord. Yet he spoke here of being afraid. And just *what* frightened this great hero of our faith?

FURTHER STUDY

2 Corinthians 11:24–28
(been through)

Paul feared exactly that which we should all fear today—that the church has been too negligent in warning the sheep about the cult wolves and their false Christs. How clever Satan is not to *deny* the existence of Jesus, but to make a game of lowering Christ to a level equal to himself. And Satan uses cult leaders to do it!

Many cult leaders deify themselves and humanize God; they raise themselves as gods and bring Christ down to mere human status. The false Christs of the cults are idols, and the Bible warns explicitly that when we bow down to *any* idol, we are worshiping devils. "But I say that the things the Gentiles sacrifice, they sacrifice to devils and not to God: and I would not that ye should have fellowship with devils" (1 Corinthians 10:20).

True Belief Must Be Belief in Truth

KEY POINT

Perverting the interpretation of Christ is an effective, devilish ploy to prepare people for embracing the Antichrist.

Many people believe that it does not matter which "Jesus" we worship or believe in as long as we are sincere. They believe that all roads lead to the same God. Nothing could be further from the truth. In the Gospel of John, Jesus taught the opposite: "I said therefore unto you, that ye shall die in your sins: for if ye believe not that I am he, ye shall die in your sins" (John 8:24).

The question is to whom does "he" refer? The translators of the King James Bible added "he." If we read the verse without the "he," the Greek reads *ego eimi,* or "I AM," which is the name God revealed to <u>Moses</u> at the burning bush when God sent him before Pharaoh to free the people of Israel from slavery in Egypt. Jesus says that if you do not believe that he is *God,* you will die in your sins! It is tragic and serious to alter the person of Christ, and the devil knows it. He knows that a false Christ cannot save us.

> FURTHER STUDY
> Exodus 3:3 (Moses)

REMEMBER THIS

The word "antichrist" also means "instead of Christ"! When people do not know the true Messiah, Jesus Christ (God the Son), they stand defenseless against the false Christs of today *and* tomorrow.

> **Matthew 24:24** For there shall arise false Christs, and false prophets. . . .

Joseph Smith Is a False Prophet

Are false Christs being preached today? Oh yes, in many places. For example, there are now 11 million Mormons who, like most other pseudo-Christian cults, believe in "another Christ." The false prophet Joseph Smith Jr. invented the blasphemous doctrine that Jesus is not God, but *a god* who is the "spirit brother" of Lucifer, the devil. This Jesus of Mormonism *had* to come here to the earth to gain a physical body for himself in order to progress to godhood, just like his Father supposedly had to do on another planet. Jesus would then become a *God among many other Gods*.

This is pure blasphemy and out of harmony with all valid Scripture. The Bible states that there is only *one* God. "Before me there was no God formed, neither shall there be after me" (Isaiah 43:10), and that God is <u>eternal</u>.

In teaching his doctrine, Joseph Smith used almost the exact wording the prophet Isaiah used to describe Lucifer the devil.

FURTHER STUDY
Psalm 90:2 (eternal)

Isaiah said, "How art thou fallen from heaven, O Lucifer, son of the morning? How art thou cut down to the ground, which didst weaken the nations! For thou hast said in thine heart, I will ascend into heaven, I will exalt my throne above the stars [angels] of God: I will sit also upon the mount of the congregation . . . I will ascend above the heights of the clouds; I will be like the most High. Yet thou shalt be brought down to hell, to the sides of the pit" (Isaiah 14:12–15).

What Others are Saying:

Joseph Smith: God himself was once as we are now, and is an exalted man, and sits enthroned in yonder heavens. I am going to tell you *how God came to be God*. We have imagined and supposed that God was God from all eternity. I will refute that idea, and take away the veil, so that you may see. . . . Here, then is eternal life—to know the only wise and true God; *and you have got to learn how to be gods yourselves* . . . the same as all gods have done before you . . . until you arrive at the station of a god, and ascend the throne of eternal power, the same as those who have gone before."[1]

Jehovah's Witnesses Demote Jesus

The false prophets of the Watchtower Organization (Jehovah's Witnesses) likewise teach that Jesus is not God, but merely a "Spirit Creature" created by Jehovah-God as the angel Michael. They deny that Jesus is Almighty God and demote him to *a god* with a little *g*. Since the Witnesses believe *correctly* that Lucifer is an angel, we see here another "Jesus" who is the devil's brother!

New Age Messiah Promised

False Christs abound in our nation today. The New Agers teach that a "Christ" is coming who will solve all problems on earth and lead us into another age of unity, peace, and enlightenment, or the New Age. They have been touting for years that this Christ, "Matreya," is now here and in hiding until the fullness of time when people become spiritually adept enough to welcome him. Jesus Christ is supposedly *one* of his disciples! Of course, nobody can see Matreya except the very elite of the occult, who mainly communicate with him "**telepathically**."

Many **necromancers** (or "channels" as they prefer to call themselves today) are being taught about Jesus by their "spirit-guides." Some of them have the audacity to claim that they are channeling Jesus of Nazareth! And who is this "Jesus" of the New Age? Let the "enlightened ones" speak: "There is nothing about me [Jesus] that you cannot attain . . . Christ waits for your acceptance of Him as yourself . . . Is [Jesus] the Christ? O yes, along with you."[2]

This blasphemy of our supposed *equality* with Jesus Christ is unfortunately being taught by a hoard of spiritual leaders in just about every country on the globe. Unified in its promotion, the gurus and false prophets do not know that they are fulfilling Bible prophecy by deceiving humankind into believing it is no different from Jesus, who is God! While enthusiastically proclaiming that they believe in Christ, they deny that he is uniquely *the* Christ! The Bible says those who do this are <u>liars</u>.

KEY POINT

False Christs and false prophets will increase before the end of the age and will pave the way for the Antichrist.

KEY TERMS

telepathically: *through means beyond the ordinary senses*

necromancers: *those who summon spirits of the dead so they can see the future or influence events*

FURTHER STUDY

1 John 2:22 (liars)

REMEMBER THIS

It is vital that Christians be alert to the dangers of the false Christs of the cults, as well as to the false prophets who proclaim them. Since so many of them will not submit to the authority of the Word of God, one can see how easily they will follow the Antichrist—the world's last cult leader. He will set himself up in the Temple of God, claiming to be God: "Who opposeth and exalteth himself above all that is called God, or that is worshipped; so that he as God sitteth in the temple of God, showing himself that he is God" (2 Thessalonians 2:4).

---

2 Timothy 4:4 And they shall turn away their ears from the truth, and shall be turned unto fables.

FROM FABLES TO FAITH

Star-studded Hollywood California is not only the headquarters for most of our film industry but also a hotbed for the cults and the occult. Movies and television programs today are, literally, evangelists for the occult. Many entertainers and film producers are zealous and dedicated missionaries for occultism of all kinds, including the fable of reincarnation.

The false doctrine of reincarnation has taken such a grip on the world that it seems unlikely it will ever be released. Even some Christians now claim that reincarnation in no way contradicts the resurrection! "Ye surely shall not die," said the serpent to Eve in the Garden. But God says: "And so it is appointed unto men once to die, but after this the judgment" (Hebrews 9:27). No happy returns here!

It is incredible that the world cannot look to the fruit of the *real* reincarnation doctrine, India. Bound by their hopeless superstitions, people in India are starving to death while worshiping rats and cows. The caste system of India is so evil that it is a sheer wonder that all of India has not perished long ago from hunger and pestilence.

The westerner who travels there is often shocked at the misery and filth of cities like Bombay and Calcutta. Hindus themselves do not like reincarnation, but erroneously believe that they are trapped in the wheel of **Karma**. They go on and on in their misery, sadly believing that they are doomed to be born again and again in order to achieve perfection, or nirvana. They multiply for themselves any combination of gods (idols) in order to change their bad fortune while living on earth. Hindus who can afford to hire **gurus** use them in hopes of shortening their paths through the pitiless system of Karma and thus insuring that they do not have to pass again through this vale of tears.

KEY TERMS

Karma: *the supposed force from a person's actions that determines his or her next life*

gurus: *personal spiritual guide*

Hollywood stars and New Agers in the Western world have such high self-esteem that they almost invariably think they were someone quite fabulously important in their former lives. Many claim to have been "Atlantians," citizens of the fictional continent Atlantis. If they are right, Atlantis would have had more inhabitants than Los Angeles!

What Others are Saying:

Hank Hanegraaff: *Time Magazine* documented the pervasive impact of reincarnation on Tinsel Town: Glenn Ford was a Christian martyr, eaten by a lion. Loretta Lynn was a Cherokee princess and a mistress of one of the King Georges, she is not sure which. Shirley MacLaine and Sylvester Stallone were both beheaded, she by Louis XV, he during the French Revolution. Stallone thinks he may have been a monkey in Guatemala, and MacLaine is sure she was a prostitute in a previous life. Many Hollywood stars and other celebrities are firm believers in reincarnation.[3]

THINK ABOUT IT

It will be sad when all the people who have died while involved with cults and the occult stand before the throne of God and realize that their prophets were just con men.

THE GREATEST CON MAN IN HISTORY

The greatest con man of them all is yet to come. We neither know his name nor the exact time of his coming. In the Bible he is called, among other things, the Antichrist. He will give the world what it thinks it must have—peace and prosperity. But it will be false peace and false prosperity.

He will do the following:

- Work many supposed miracles the Bible calls "signs and lying wonders" by using the occult techniques of the devil
- Be welcomed and adored by his followers
- Persecute and kill all those who will not be marked by the number 666
- Order anyone who becomes a believer in Jesus Christ to be beheaded
- Sit in the Temple of God and declare that he is God

We have seen a smattering of the Antichrist's tactics reflected in the cult leaders we've mentioned in this chapter, but we've seen nothing as enormously evil as the Antichrist will be. The false prophets of today can deceive only millions, perhaps a billion. The Antichrist will deceive most of the world.

Christians are fond of saying that they have "read the end of the Book!" And so they should because the Bible tells us the ultimate destiny of the Antichrist and his cohorts is destruction: "And fire came down from God out of heaven, and devoured them.

> **FURTHER STUDY**
> John 8:31 (free)

And the devil that deceived them was cast into the lake of fire and brimstone, where the beast and the false prophet are, and shall be tormented day and night forever and ever" (Revelation 20:9b–10).

The world we live in is thoroughly polluted with sorceries of every kind. Many nations have regressed to the paganism they practiced before the gospel came to them. Only we, the body of Christ, can set them <u>free</u> by bringing them to Christ.

REMEMBER THIS

While we wait for Christ's appearance, let us be about our Father's business, bringing many cultists and occultists to Christ. Ask God to kindle in your heart a holy passion for truth. Let us then embrace the truth, live the truth, and teach the truth. And most important of all, let us know him who said, "I am the way, the truth and the life: no man cometh unto the Father but by me" (John 14:6).

Nando.net

On the Furthest Fringes of Millennialism

Copyright © 1997 The New York Times and Nando.net

The mass suicide in a wealthy Southern California enclave casts a brutal light on a millennialist sect that earned notoriety in California 22 years ago, before disappearing into isolation to teach its members that the Earth was corrupt, that civilization was doomed and that only the disciplined few could be saved, rescued by a UFO.

San Diego police linked the 39 people to a group called Heaven's Gate that maintained an elaborate Internet site under that name. . . . In its documents, the group described a world view on the furthest fringes of millennialism, with disconnected elements of Christianity interpreted through a thick lens of science fiction.

In essence, its teachings boiled down to a belief in exalted purpose for a few, combined with an exceptionally grim view of life on an Earth where evil was in control—a heady mixture of profound hope amidst utter isolation.

. . . The urgent belief in a coming end to a hopelessly corrupt world is a long and recurrent tradition in American religious culture. In one of its best-known episodes, followers of the Bible student William Miller, anticipating Christ's return in 1843, gathered on hillsides, anticipating transport to Heaven. . . .

[The biblical book of Revelation's] dense allegory has long attracted all manner of religious believers seeking prophetic knowledge of the future. (It was Revelation that David Koresh insisted he was in the process of de-coding as federal agents besieged the Davidians' compound.)

PROPHETIC IMPACT

Satan's ultimate humanist cult leader, the Antichrist, will ensnare most of the world's population by "speaking great words" (Daniel 7:8; Revelation 13:5).

The minds of fallen humankind are readily susceptible to deceit. The devil is working his cunning and deceitful mind games today. The media, although perhaps without fully realizing it, lump evangelical Christians who believe in the Rapture with the foolish but deadly cults of our time.

<table>
<tr><td>

FURTHER STUDY
2 Thessalonians 2
(man of sin)

</td></tr>
</table>

The attempt by the author of the preceding Headline Highlight to draw similarities between true Christian beliefs and the spaced-out beliefs of cults cannot be missed. Antichrist's spin machine against God's truth is moving full throttle.

When the prophesied <u>man of sin</u> steps upon earth's stage, he will find a world of willing followers.

CHAPTER WRAP-UP

- The Antichrist is a frightening although fascinating character. The Bible has much to say about this coming world dictator, yet he remains a mysterious figure.

- Some clergy and others within Christianity have claimed the Antichrist is a representative system of satanic influence rather than a real person. Some believe the Antichrist is a spirit of evil. Others believe the Antichrist is a person who has already lived and died.

- The Antichrist will be the manifestation of his father, the devil. The cults and the occult are the devil's favorite territories today.

- Cult leaders, gurus, occultists, and false prophets through the centuries have been forerunners of the future workings of the Antichrist.

- True Christianity is being linked to or lumped with dangerous, fanatical cults. The average media person sees little or no difference between the cults and fundamental, evangelical Christianity.

- Jesus prophesied about false teachers who would pass themselves off as believers but who would lie and twist God's Word.

- A cult is marked by a leader who teaches a false gospel and followers who believe false writings.

- The occult can be practiced alone and involves a ritual to make something supernatural happen. Divination, signs, and deceptive miracles are marks of the occult.

- Cults and the occult demote Jesus. For example, Mormonism claims Jesus is a "spirit brother" of the devil, not *the* one and only Son of God. The cults' false teachings will pave the way for the Antichrist.

- The world is immersed in cultic and occult paganism. God expects Christians to carry the message of hope to the lost, the victims of the Antichrist spirit.

- The Antichrist is a man who one day will rule the world. He will do supposed miracles, be welcomed, kill those who don't believe him, and declare he is God.

The Armageddon Campaign and the Second Coming

BY ARNOLD G. FRUCHTENBAUM

Let's Get Started

The two climactic events of the Great Tribulation are the Campaign of Armageddon[1] and the Second Coming of Jesus the Messiah. A considerable amount of data is given about this time period in the Scriptures. One of the greatest difficulties in the study of **eschatology** is placing these events in chronological sequence to discover exactly what will happen in the Campaign of Armageddon.

While the term "Battle of Armageddon" has been commonly used, it is really a misnomer. For this reason many prophetic teachers have stopped employing that term and are now using "Campaign of Armageddon," because there is not one battle but several as part of an overall campaign.

The Bible indicates there will be stages in the Campaign of Armageddon. The Antichrist will

> **KEY TERM**
>
> **eschatology:** branch of theology concerned with the end times

gather his army. The enemy will destroy Babylon, capital city of the one-world government. Jerusalem will fall to the Antichrist, and then he will chase the Jews, as they escape into Petra. The Jews will confess their sin, plead for Christ to return, and be regenerated. Then Jesus will return and fight the forces of the Antichrist. Christ will victoriously ascend the Mount of Olives.

BACKGROUND AND PRELUDE

Before the Second Coming of Messiah, the nation of Israel must experience **regeneration**. Until Israel as a nation is saved, until Israel as a nation looks to the one "whom they have pierced," until Israel as a nation cries out for him to return with the words: "Blessed is he that comes in the name of the Lord" (Matthew 21:9 ASV); there will be no Second Coming.

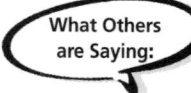

What Others are Saying:

Arthur Kac: Israel's spiritual rebirth will not be the work of man; it will not be brought about by human means or effort. It will be the work of God. God will pour out upon them His spirit of grace and supplication. The Jew of today cannot pray. Even if he does pray he merely recites words. It is only when God shall grant them the spirit of grace and supplication will the Jews be able to pray. This new spirit in them will remove their spiritual blindness.[2]

Satan's Hatred of the Jewish Race

KEY TERM

regeneration: *spiritual revival*

FURTHER STUDY

Leviticus 26:40–42;
Jeremiah 3:12–18;
Hosea 5:15–6:3;
Zechariah 12:10;
Matthew 23:37–39
(regeneration)

While the Rapture of the church has no preconditions and can happen at any moment, the Second Coming does have one precondition: Israel's spiritual revival. If we understand the basis of the Second Coming of Messiah, we can understand the theological foundations of anti-Semitism. Satan knows that once Jesus returns his career is over. Satan also knows there will be no Second Coming until the Jewish people ask Messiah to return. Therefore, if Satan could ever succeed in destroying the Jews once and for all *before* they have a chance to plead for Jesus to return, there would be no Second Coming and his career would then be eternally safe.

REMEMBER THIS

Satan is behind all the wars and persecutions against the Jews. He seeks to destroy them at every opportunity. That explains the Holocaust under Nazi Germany, and that explains the unique activities of Satan during the Tribulation.

Satan's Confinement

During the second half of the Tribulation, Satan will be <u>confined</u> to the earth. Once Satan is confined, he knows his time is <u>short</u>. Knowing his time is short, he <u>persecutes</u> the Jews. He must try to destroy the Jews before they have a chance to plead for the Messiah to return.

Tribulation Era Persecution

The persecution of the Jews will begin in the middle of the Tribulation and will continue until the beginning of the Campaign of Armageddon.

During this period approximately two-thirds of the Jewish population of that day will be killed, but <u>one-third</u> will be left in the closing days, weeks, or months of the Tribulation. Satan specifically organizes the Campaign of Armageddon to annihilate once and for all the remnant of Jewish people still living.

Two Tribulation Political Systems

During the seven years of the Tribulation, there will be two distinct political systems, one for each half of the Tribulation. The political system during the first half of the Tribulation will consist of the entire world being subdivided into ten distinct nations ruled by ten kings. If Daniel 7 is taken literally, one cannot limit these ten nations merely to western Europe; they will have to cover the entire world. Perhaps the European Union may someday become one of these ten, but it could never, biblically speaking, become all ten.

During the first half of the Tribulation, ten men will rule the political affairs of the world coequally.

> FURTHER STUDY
> Revelation 12:7–12
>   (confined)
> Revelation 12:12 (short)
> Revelation 12:17
>   (persecutes)
> Zechariah 13:9 (one-third)

In the middle of the Tribulation, the Antichrist will declare war against these ten kings. In the course of this war, he will succeed in killing three of them and then the other seven will submit to his authority. At that point the Antichrist will institute the second political system of the second half of the Tribulation: He will proclaim himself the one-world political ruler.

Two Tribulation Religious Systems

KEY POINT

During the last half of the Tribulation, the Antichrist will establish a one-world political system.

There will also be two distinct religious systems: one for each half of the Tribulation. The religious system of the first half of the Tribulation is described in Revelation 17 in terms of "ecclesiastical" Babylon.

All false denominations and all false religions will unify into a one-world religious system. This system will control the religious affairs of the world during the first half of the Tribulation. Those who do not submit to its religious authority will suffer persecution.

KEY TERMS

Holy of Holies: *inner room of the Temple, containing the ark of the covenant*

sixth bowl judgment: *Euphrates River dried up*

FURTHER STUDY

Revelation 16:12–16 (sixth bowl judgment)

In the middle of the Tribulation and after the Antichrist takes political control, he will destroy this one-world religious system. He will then take over the Jewish Temple, seat himself in the **Holy of Holies** of the Jewish Temple, and declare himself to be the one true god.

Thus, the religious system of the second half of the Tribulation will be the worship of the Antichrist. Those who accept him as god must signify it by taking his mark of 666. During this period of tremendous Jewish persecution, one man will serve as both the one-world political ruler and the one-world religious ruler.

STAGE 1: ARMIES ASSEMBLE

The Campaign of Armageddon will begin with the **sixth bowl judgment** (see illustration, page 111) recorded in Revelation 16:12–16. With the outpouring of the sixth bowl judgment, the Euphrates River will be dried up, making it easier for the Antichrist to assemble his forces for the Campaign of Armageddon. A decree will be issued from the capital city of Babylon,

KEY TERMS

counterfeit trinity: *imitation of the godhead of Father, Son, and Holy Spirit*

Har-magedon: *combination of two Hebrew words that mean "the mountain of Megiddo"*

FURTHER STUDY

Revelation 16:16
(Har-magedon)

which is located on both banks of the Euphrates River, ordering the allies of the Antichrist to gather their armies.

The gathering for this final campaign against the Jews is clearly the work of the **counterfeit trinity**. All three members of the counterfeit trinity are involved: the dragon, or Satan, who is the counterfeit Father; the Beast, or the Antichrist, who is the counterfeit Son; and the False Prophet who is the counterfeit Holy Spirit. The summons will be reinforced by demonic activity to make sure the nations will cooperate in assembling their armies. They will gather in **_Har-magedon_**, or "the mountain of Megiddo."

REMEMBER THIS

One can see the entire Valley of Jezreel from the mount upon which the city of Megiddo (see illustration, page 248) stood. What is known as the Valley of Armageddon in Christian circles is actually the biblical Valley of Jezreel. The term "Armageddon" is never applied to the valley itself, but only to the mount at the western end.

THINK ABOUT IT

The phrase "Campaign of Armageddon," while more accurate than the term "Battle of Armageddon," is a misnomer to some extent. There will be no fighting in Armageddon itself; all of the fighting will take place elsewhere. The Valley of Jezreel, which is guarded by the mountain of Megiddo, will merely serve as the gathering ground for the armies of the Antichrist. A more biblical name for this final conflict is found in the closing words of Revelation 16:14 ASV: "the war of the great day of God, the Almighty."

Isaiah 13:1 The burden of Babylon, which Isaiah the son of Amoz did see.

Map of Megiddo

This map of Israel during the time of Christ shows the location of the city of Megiddo.

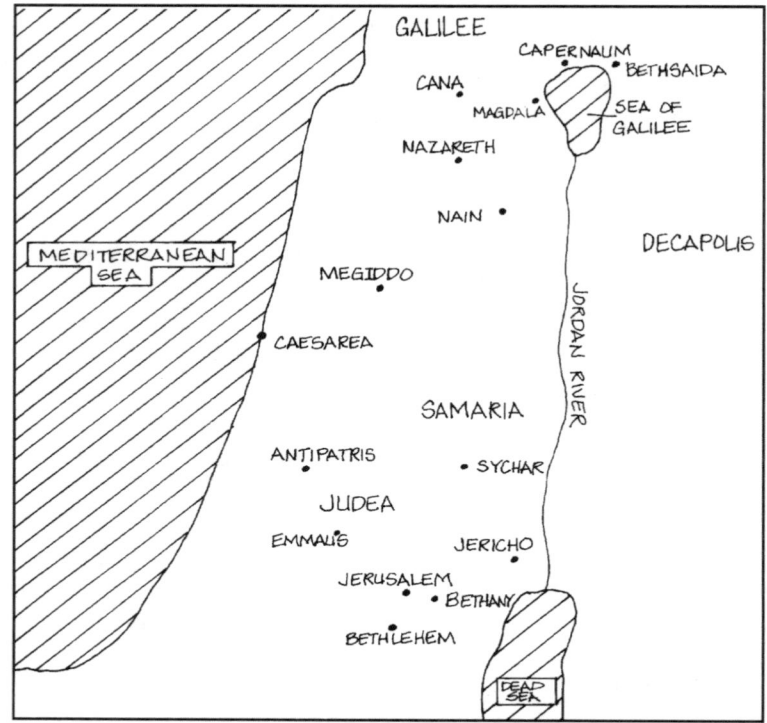

STAGE 2: THE DESTRUCTION OF BABYLON

KEY POINT

The "war of the great day of God, the Almighty" is an accurate description of the Battle of Armageddon.

The burden of Babylon that Isaiah saw in Isaiah 13:1–5 was another gathering of many peoples. Whereas the gathering in the first stage will be of *pro*-Babylon and *pro*-Antichrist forces, the gathering at this stage will be of *anti*-Babylon and *anti*-Antichrist forces. Their purpose will be to destroy Babylon.

According to Isaiah 13:3, the ones who are destroying Babylon are God's consecrated ones or God's "sainted ones," meaning believers. Gentile believers in the Tribulation comprise these armies that destroy the city of Babylon.

Isaiah 13:6–14:23 offers a detailed description of the means by which Babylon will be destroyed. Isaiah 13:6–9 places these events within "the Day of Jehovah," the most common biblical term for the Tribulation. In other words, this was not a prophecy fulfilled in ancient history, but one to be fulfilled during the Tribulation.

In Jeremiah 50:9–10, 41–42, Jeremiah had a vision of the same thing Isaiah had seen over a century earlier: groups of armies gathering to destroy the city of Babylon, the capital of the world under the Antichrist.

Revelation 18 also deals with this topic and emphasizes that when Babylon is destroyed it is destroyed suddenly, quickly, and massively. Before anyone really knows what is happening, Babylon, the capital of the world, is burning.

Jeremiah clearly indicates that the <u>king</u> of Babylon is not in the city when Babylon is destroyed. So where is he? By comparing the Scriptures of the first stage with those of the second stage, it appears that while the Antichrist is meeting his forces in the Valley of Jezreel, his enemies take this opportunity to gather and destroy his capital city quickly, suddenly, and massively.

> **FURTHER STUDY**
> Jeremiah 50:43; 51:32–33 (king)

One messenger must run to meet another in a relay situation until they have reached the king of Babylon, the Antichrist, to inform him that his capital city has now been destroyed.

STAGE 3: THE FALL OF JERUSALEM

Zechariah describes the third stage in the Campaign of Armageddon in Zechariah 12:2–3 and 14:1–2. Although the Antichrist will have all his allied forces with him when he receives the news that his capital city has been destroyed, he will not move eastward to destroy his enemies. Satan is in control, and his program—to destroy the Jews—will be uppermost in his mind. Instead of moving east, the Antichrist will move south against Jerusalem.

From the Valley of Jezreel, the armies of the Antichrist will move south, and all the armies of all the nations will gather against Jerusalem. Some very heavy fighting will occur in the attack on Jerusalem described in Zechariah 10:4–9 and Micah 4:9–5:1, which deal with this stage of the Campaign of Armageddon. Although the forces of the Antichrist will suffer heavy losses, eventually Jerusalem will fall.

STAGE 4: THE ARMIES AT BOZRAH

While Jerusalem falls in the third stage of the Campaign of Armageddon, the majority of Jews no longer will be in Jerusalem. In fact, they no longer will be in the land of Israel. According to Matthew 24:15–22 and Revelation 12:6–17, the state of Israel as it now exists will collapse in the middle of the Tribulation and there will be another dispersion out of the Promised Land. The majority of the one-third remnant that survives will make its way into a special place.

According to Matthew 24:16, the special place is in "the mountains"; in Revelation 12:6, 13–14, it is in "the wilderness"; and in Isaiah 33:12–16, it is in a very rocky place that is easily defended. These are all clues, but no specific place is named. However, Micah 2:12 ASV does name a specific place: "I will surely assemble, O Jacob, all of you; I will surely gather the remnant of Israel; I will put them together as the sheep of Bozrah, as a flock in the midst of their pasture; they shall make great noise by reason of the multitude of men."

The specific place where the remnant of Israel is said to be hiding is a city known in Hebrew as *Bozrah*. That same city is better known today by its Greek name of Petra (see illustration, page 251). Petra means "cliff-rock," which is a good name for this city of buildings carved out of the rocks of the cliff.

In Hebrew, *Bozrah* means "sheepfold" because that is how the city is shaped. An ancient sheepfold had a narrow entrance so that the shepherd could count his sheep as they entered the sheepfold to make sure none were lost. The narrow passageway opened into a larger, circular area where the sheep had more freedom of movement. The only way into Petra is through a narrow passageway, which extends about one and one-quarter miles in length. Once through this narrow passageway, which can be defended by only two men against a whole army, you are inside a huge, circular area.

REMEMBER THIS

Petra is a place that is easily defended. It is within *the wilderness* of the area of Jordan. It is also in *the mountain* ranges of Mount Seir. It is part of the ancient territory known as Edom or modern-day southern Jordan.

Petra

The city of Petra, or Bozrah, is hidden at the end of a long, deep gorge. You can enter it only from a narrow passageway.

Daniel 11:41 ASV He shall enter also into the glorious land, and many countries shall be overthrown; but these shall be delivered out of his hand: Edom, and Moab, and the chief of the children of Ammon.

Three Nations Escape

Daniel describes the conquest of the Antichrist in the middle of the Tribulation as the Antichrist begins his world political takeover. While the Antichrist gains political control, Daniel says three nations will escape his domination. These three nations are the ancient nations of Edom, Moab, and Ammon. Today, all three of these ancient nations comprise only one nation: Jordan. The city of Petra, or Bozrah, is within the territory of ancient Edom—today's southern Jordan.

God's Principle of Refuge

As always in Jewish history, whenever there has been persecution of the Jews in one part of the world, God has opened up a place—a <u>city of refuge</u>—in another part of the world. For example, in 1492 when the nations of Europe began expelling their Jews, God allowed Columbus to discover the New World, which has become one of the greatest havens for Jewish refugees fleeing persecution elsewhere.

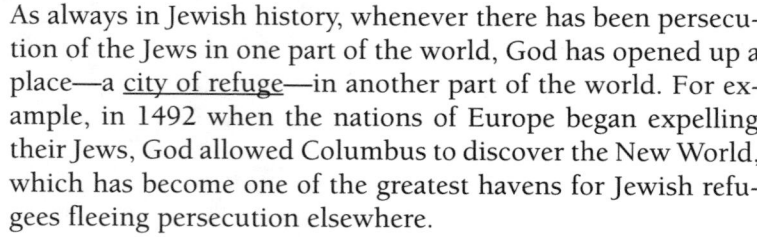

In the Tribulation when the whole world turns against the Jews, God will make certain there is one place in the world outside the political domination of the Antichrist: the land of Edom or modern, southern Jordan. That is the only place to which the Jews will be able to flee, and that is where they will go. The bulk of the remnant of Israel will be hiding there, in Petra, during that time.

Armies Move toward Bozrah

Since the purpose of the Antichrist's campaign is the total annihilation of the Jews, after Jerusalem falls in the third stage, the armies of the world will move south from Jerusalem to Bozrah

as Jeremiah 49:13–14 ASV makes clear: "For I have sworn by myself, says Jehovah, that Bozrah shall become an astonishment, a reproach, a waste, and a curse; and all the cities thereof shall be perpetual wastes. I have heard tidings from Jehovah, and an ambassador is sent among the nations, saying, Gather yourselves together, and come against her, and rise up to the battle."

In stage four the nations of the earth will gather at Bozrah to destroy the remnant of Israel that will be gathered there. The armies will begin applying pressure upon the bulk of the remnant now hiding in the city of Bozrah, or Petra.

STAGE 5: THE REGENERATION OF ISRAEL

Two preconditions must be met for the Second Coming of Messiah:

1 *National Confession of Israel.* According to Leviticus 26:39–42, before Israel can enjoy the full benefits of the **Abrahamic covenant** as it pertains to the borders of the Promised Land, they must first confess the **iniquity** of their fathers. Jeremiah 3:12–18 teaches that before Israel can enjoy the full benefits of the millennial or **messianic kingdom** they must also confess their iniquity.

Again, iniquity was both singular and specific: one specific sin has to be confessed before they can enjoy the full benefits of the millennial or messianic kingdom: "I will go and return to my place, till they acknowledge their offence, and seek my face: in their affliction they will seek me earnestly" (Hosea 5:15 ASV).

THINK ABOUT IT

Before anyone can go back to a place, he must first leave it. Only after he has left it can he return to it. God says that he will *return* to his place. God's place is heaven, so before God can return to heaven, he must first leave it. When did God leave heaven? He left heaven at the incarnation when he became man in the person of Jesus of Nazareth. But because of one specific offense committed against him, he went back to heaven at the ascension from the Mount of Olives. He will not return to this earth until that offense is confessed.

REMEMBER THIS

The Jewish national offense committed against the person of Jesus is not in killing him, because it was Gentiles who killed Jesus. It was Gentiles who put Jesus to death. The Jewish national offense lies in the rejection of his messiahship. Until that rejection is confessed, there will be no Second Coming.

2 *A Pleading for Christ to Return.* Zechariah 12:10 states that before there can be a national cleansing of Israel's sins and before there can be a Second Coming and kingdom, Israel must first look unto the one "whom they have pierced," and they must "mourn for him as one mourns for an only son." According to Matthew 23:37–39, before Jesus will come back, Israel must plead for him to come back with the words: "Blessed is he that comes in the name of the Lord."

Hosea 6:1–3 Come, and let us return unto the Lord: for he hath torn, and he will heal us; he hath smitten, and he will bind us up. After two days will he revive us: in the third day he will raise us up, and we shall live in his sight. Then shall we know, if we follow on to know the Lord: his going forth is prepared as the morning; and he shall come unto us as the rain, as the latter and former rain unto the earth.

Jews' Blindness Taken Away

At this stage of the Campaign of Armageddon, one way or another the Jewish leaders will finally discover why all this has fallen upon them. They will realize that the root problem has been the rejection of the messiahship of Jesus. When the Jewish leaders learn this, they will then issue the decree of Hosea 6:1–3. When this decree is issued, the last three days before the Second Coming will begin.

During the first two of these last three days, Israel will confess her national sin: the rejection of the messiahship of Jesus. The words of that confession are contained in Isaiah 53:1–9. While this passage is often looked upon as a prophecy of the **crucifixion**—and it certainly is that—it is also more than that.

It contains the actual words of Israel's confession during these first two of the last three days of the Great Tribulation. This will fulfill the first part of the basis of the Second Coming.

On the third day of the last three days Israel, as a nation, will be saved. As Isaiah 66 puts it, Israel will "be born in one day"; or as Paul puts it in Romans 11:26, "all Israel shall be saved." At that point—on the third day of these last three days—they will plead for the

Messiah to return. This will fulfill the second part of the basis of the Second Coming. The words of that pleading are contained in Isaiah 64, Psalm 79, and Psalm 80. The specific person they are pleading for is the one on God's right hand. This is none other than Jesus the Messiah who has been sitting at the <u>right hand</u> of God the Father ever since his ascension from the Mount of Olives. He is *the son of man.*

STAGE 6: THE SECOND COMING

KEY POINT

Jews will ask Jesus to come down from his throne to deliver Israel, and he will do so.

Jesus will return at the Jewish request for him to do so. The initial *place* of his return will not be the Mount of Olives, as is commonly taught, but the place known as Bozrah. <u>Four passages</u> place the Second Coming at the city of Bozrah or Petra, where the remnant of Israel will be gathered and be besieged by the forces of the Antichrist.

They are finally able to break the siege, because Jehovah the King is leading them. At the Second Coming, the Messiah will enter into battle with the forces of the Antichrist, which have gathered at Bozrah. With his return to the remnant of Israel in Bozrah, Jesus will "save the tents of Judah first," before saving the Jews of Jerusalem, as Zechariah 12:7 ASV predicted: "Jehovah also shall save the tents of Judah first, that the glory of the house of David and the glory of the inhabitants of Jerusalem be not magnified above Judah." The term "tents" points to temporary abodes rather than permanent dwellings. The fact that Judah is living in tents shows that Judah is not home *in* Judah, but is temporarily living elsewhere. That elsewhere is Bozrah.

FURTHER STUDY

1 Peter 3:21–22 (right hand)

Isaiah 34:1–7; 63:1–6; Habakkuk 3:3; Micah 2:12, 13 (four passages)

STAGE 7: FROM BOZRAH TO JEHOSHAPHAT

Joel 3:12–13 ASV Let the nations bestir themselves, and come up to the valley of Jehoshaphat; for there will I sit to judge all the nations round about. Put ye in the sickle; for the harvest is ripe: come, tread ye; for the winepress is full, the vats overflow; for their wickedness is great.

KEY TERM

Akaba: *alternative spelling: Aqaba*

FURTHER STUDY

Isaiah 63:3 (tramples)

While the battle between the Messiah and the Antichrist will begin at Bozrah, it will apparently continue all the way back to the eastern wall of Jerusalem where the battle will end. This wall overlooks a section of the Kidron Valley, which is also known as the Valley of Jehoshaphat. The fighting that begins in Bozrah continues as the Messiah "<u>tramples</u> the armies of the nations." It finally terminates in the Valley of Jehoshaphat where the "winepress" is pictured as being situated.

This is the same winepress found in Revelation 14:19–20 where John sees a winepress spewing forth blood for the range of about two hundred miles. The two-hundred-mile distance extends from the city of Jerusalem all the way down to the Gulf of **Akaba** (see illustration, page 68).

STAGE 8: CHRIST'S VICTORY ASCENT

> **Zechariah 14:3–4a** ASV Then shall Jehovah go forth, and fight against those nations, as when he fought in the day of battle. And his feet shall stand in that day upon the mount of Olives, which is before Jerusalem on the east.

After the bloody fighting in the Valley of Jehoshaphat is completed, Christ will go up the Mount of Olives in victory. Even in this passage the fighting against the nations precedes the time when Christ's feet stand upon the Mount of Olives. The same order of events is evident in Zechariah 12:7. Zechariah clearly says that God intends to "save the tents of Judah first"—meaning the tents of the people living outside Judah—before he rescues the inhabitants of Jerusalem.

Along with this victory ascent upon the Mount of Olives, a number of cataclysmic events will occur as the Great Tribulation comes to an end. These cataclysmic events will be a result of the seventh bowl judgment described in Revelation 16:17–21.

With the seventh bowl, a voice cries out, "It is finished," because the seventh bowl brings the Tribulation to an end. After this declaration, the following things will occur:

- There will be convulsions of nature, including the greatest <u>earthquake</u> ever to occur in the history of the earth (Revelation 16:18).
- The city of Jerusalem will split into three divisions (v. 19).
- The Mount of Olives will split in two, creating a valley running east and west.
- The city of Babylon will suffer the full wrath of God (v. 19).
- Earth will undergo many geographical changes (vv. 19, 20).
- Hail weighing 120 pounds will fall (v. 21).
- There will be a <u>worldwide blackout</u> (v. 15).

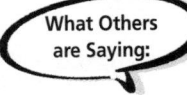

What Others are Saying:

Randall Price: This splitting of Jerusalem into three divisions (apparently through the great earthquake described in Zechariah 14:5) will be in preparation for the building of Messiah's Temple and His Millennial reign (Zechariah 14:4–8; Ezekiel 47:1–12; Revelation 20:4). . . . Earthquakes happen frequently in the Jerusalem area, and evidence indicates that the Mount of Olives is set to split should an earthquake of sufficient size strike the region.[3]

REMEMBER THIS

God will not forget his people, the Jews. He will provide a refuge for them from these cataclysmic events by means of the valley cutting through the Mount of Olives spoken of by Zechariah. This newly formed valley will provide a way of escape for the Jewish inhabitants of Jerusalem from the earthquake that will destroy the city. In this way they will be rescued following the deliverance of the other Jews in Bozrah.

FURTHER STUDY
Joel 3:14–17; Zechariah
    14:4b–5; (earthquake)
Joel 3:14–17; Matthew
    24:29 (worldwide
    blackout)

Jewish World Review
Friday, April 12, 2002
http://www.NewsAndOpinion.com
Lebanon: The Fuse for Armageddon
By Charles Krauthammer
Copyright © 2002 Washington Post Co.

Watch Lebanon. If you want to know where the Israeli-Palestinian war is going, watch Lebanon. If the war goes—literally—ballistic, the fuse will have been lit by the Iran-backed Hezbollah guerrillas now firing rockets into Israel from Lebanon. . . .

[Hezbollah leaders threaten to unleash] Katyusha rockets against Israel if Israel dared to respond to Hezbollah attacks. Were that to happen, the northern front would explode. Israel has been sending urgent messages through the United Nations and the United States that it would not tolerate such aggression. It would be forced to counterattack—on Lebanon, on Syrian army positions in Lebanon and possibly on Syria itself, Syria being Hezbollah's boss and patron.

Syria could not withstand such an Israeli attack conventionally. It might then launch its missiles equipped with chemical weapons into Israeli cities. And that could trigger Armageddon. Israel was established so that never again would the gassing of Jews be permitted. . . .

Just end the occupation of the West Bank, say the Arabs, and we will guarantee Israel peace. Do you want to see Israel's future if it caves in to that demand?

Look at Lebanon, where Israel gave up a defensive occupation and is now looking squarely in the face of Armageddon.

PROPHETIC IMPACT

The highly studied opinion in the column above accurately reflects just how near the region might be to an Armageddon-like nuclear conflict. The columnist puts his finger on the specific spot that God's Word seems to indicate will suffer complete nuclear devastation. Zechariah 17:1 ASV foretells: "The burden of Damascus. Behold, Damascus is taken away from being a city, and it shall be a ruinous heap."

The prophecy also declares that Israel will not escape the devastating consequences of a future conflict involving the ancient city of Damascus. Zechariah prophesies further: "The fortress also shall cease from Ephraim, and the kingdom from Damascus, and the remnant of Syria: they shall be as the glory of the children of Israel, saith the Lord of hosts. And in that day it shall come to pass, that the glory of Jacob shall be made thin, and the fatness of his flesh shall wax lean" (Zechariah 17:3–4 ASV).

Bible prophecy foretells Damascus and Syria will suffer almost total loss, and Israel will lose two-thirds of its people, by the time the Armageddon campaign plays out.

CHAPTER WRAP-UP

- The Battle of Armageddon should be called the Campaign of Armageddon because it will be a series of events rather than one battle.

- Since Satan knows there can be no Second Coming of Messiah until the Jews plead for Messiah to return, Satan will try to destroy all Jews.

- The persecutions of the Jews will begin in the middle of the Tribulation and will continue until the beginning of the Campaign of Armageddon. About two-thirds of the Jewish population of that day will be killed.

- The Campaign of Armageddon is specifically organized by Satan to annihilate the remaining one-third of the Jewish people.

- The Campaign of Armageddon will have eight stages beginning with the sixth bowl judgment and the assembling of the Antichrist's armies.

- In stage two Babylon will be destroyed.

- In stages three and four Jerusalem will fall and the Jews will escape to Bozrah where the Antichrist's forces will regroup.

- In stage five Israel will confess its sin and plead for Christ to return.

- In stage six Christ will return.

- In stage seven Christ will lead the battle against the Antichrist.

- In stage eight Christ will stand victoriously on the Mount of Olives.

CHAPTER **15**

Day of the Lord

BY JOHN F. WALVOORD

CHAPTER HIGHLIGHTS

- Time of Judgment
- Day of the Lord Yet Future
- Prophetic Ages Contrasted
- Rapture Precedes Wrath
- Literal Judgment!

Let's Get Started

The day of the Lord is pictured as coming on the world unexpectedly like "a thief in the night" (1 Thessalonians 5:2) and is predicted as happening immediately after the Rapture of the church. Though the expression "day of the Lord" does not occur frequently in the New Testament, it occurs many times in the Old Testament, which gives a clear description of its character. A student of this doctrine finds an abundance of scriptures that describe it, including these:

- Isaiah 2:12–21; 13:9–17; 34:1–8
- Joel 1:15–2:11, 28–32; 3:9–16
- Amos 5:18–20
- Obadiah 15–17
- Zephaniah 1:7–18; 3:14–17

The day of the Lord is a period much longer than twenty-four hours in which God directly judges the world, especially the nation of Israel for its wandering from God.

By examining various passages we can better understand the day of the Lord is a time of literal judgment that will occur in the future after the Rapture.

261

TIME OF JUDGMENT

> **Isaiah 2:17–18** The loftiness of man shall be bowed down, and the haughtiness of men shall be brought low; the Lord alone will be exalted in that day. And the idols he shall utterly abolish.

Frightening Picture of God's Wrath

The prophets Isaiah and Joel both speak about the day of the Lord. Isaiah describes the day of the Lord as the day of judgment coming "upon every one that is proud and lofty" (Isaiah 2:12). Isaiah describes those being punished as fleeing to clefts in the rocks in an effort to escape "for fear of the Lord, and for the glory of his majesty, when he ariseth to shake terribly the earth" (Isaiah 2:21).

Isaiah further depicts the day of the Lord as "the day of the Lord's vengeance, and the year of **recompenses** for the **controversy** of Zion" (Isaiah 34:8). In preceding verses Isaiah indicates great destruction of human property, the stench of their corpses and the mountains covered with blood (Isaiah 34:3). "And all the host of heaven shall be dissolved, and the heavens shall be rolled together as a scroll: and all their host shall fall down, as the leaf falleth off from the vine, and as a falling fig from the fig tree" (Isaiah 34:4).

> KEY TERMS
>
> **recompenses:** compensations, payment
> **controversy:** cause

KEY POINT

Various passages picture the day of the Lord as a horrible time of God's judgment.

The Book of Joel focuses on the day of the Lord as its major theme and most of the contents of the book describe this time of judgment. Joel pictures the day of the Lord as a time of gestation of locusts that eat all of Israel's crops. It will be a time of destruction. Joy will be lacking. Crops will die. Even the animals will suffer: "How do the beasts groan! the herds of cattle are perplexed, because they have no pasture; yea, the flocks of sheep are made desolate" (Joel 1:18). Joel 2:3 sounds the alarm that the day of the Lord is coming, illustrating it as a flame that devours everything.

Joel 2:28–29 And it shall come to pass afterward, that I will pour out my spirit upon all flesh; and your sons and your daughters shall prophesy, your old men shall dream dreams, your young men shall see visions: And also upon the servants and upon the handmaids in those days will I pour out my spirit.

A Bright Spot

On a brighter note, Joel 2:28–32 mentions promises that even in this time of judgment, God's spirit will be poured upon those who will prophesy. Joel 2:30–31 speaks of the signs that will precede this time of mercy:

- God will show wonders in heaven and earth.
- God will send blood, fire, and smoke.
- The sun will be turned to darkness.
- The moon will be turned into blood.

KEY POINT

Despite his judgment God will provide mercy and blessings for those who trust him.

Joel's predictions are similar to the predictions of Revelation 6 and Matthew 24:29. The day of judgment, however, will be followed by a day of the Lord's deliverance. Joel states: "And it shall come to pass, that whosoever shall call on the name of the Lord shall be delivered: for in mount Zion and in Jerusalem shall be deliverance, as the Lord hath said, and in the remnant whom the Lord shall call" (Joel 2:32).

Similar prophecies are found in other references to the day of the Lord, including the account of Israel's restoration in Zephaniah 3:14–20. Zephaniah mentions the rejoicing of Israel along with the pouring out of the Lord's mercies upon them in their regathering in the land of their fathers.

DAY OF THE LORD YET FUTURE

While some of the passages in the Old Testament about the day of the Lord have been partially fulfilled, the future day of the Lord will eclipse all of this.

First Thessalonians 5:2 pictures the day of the Lord as a future time that will come as a thief in the night. Further, 1 Thessalonians 5:3 indicates that it will begin with a time of peace and then end suddenly: "For when they shall say, Peace and safety; then sudden destruction cometh upon them, as travail upon a woman with child; and they shall not escape."

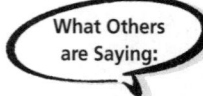

Tim LaHaye: [The day of the Lord] is not a single day but a period of time filled with many prophetic events. The context must be considered to determine what time or event is considered. Here [1 Thessalonians 5:3] the context is that of the Tribulation, confirmed by it overtaking some who are unprepared as a "thief." Events classified as "the day of the Lord" appear over thirty times in the Old Testament and refer to any time God intervenes in judgment in the affairs of men. This verse is the first place it is used in the New Testament and refers to the Tribulation and end-time events that lead up to the physical coming of Christ.[1]

Sequence of Events

KEY POINT

The day of the Lord will come suddenly.

If the various scriptures on the day of the Lord are put together, they bear out that the time between the Rapture and the Second Coming is a period of somewhat more than seven years. That time will begin with the Rapture. At approximately that time, according to Daniel 7, the Roman Empire will be revived with a ten-nation group.

The Roman Empire will be formed on a friendly basis, with the major nations of Europe and perhaps North Africa and western Asia involved, though the Bible does not name countries. After the revived Roman Empire forms, the Antichrist will appear.

Daniel 7:8 I considered the horns, and, behold, there came up among them another little horn, before whom there were three of the first horns plucked up by the roots: and, behold, in this horn were eyes like the eyes of man, and a mouth speaking great things.

Man of Sin Imposes Peace

The Antichrist will appear as the little horn Daniel mentions as coming up from among them. Daniel 7:7 speaks of ten horns, and in Daniel 7:24 the horns are declared to be ten kingdoms or kings. The Antichrist will conquer the first three kings or kingdoms and after that will be regarded as ruler of all ten countries involved in the revived Roman Empire. When he achieves this place of prominence after he has consolidated his power, the Antichrist will impose a seven-year covenant upon Israel, which will begin the last seven years leading up to the Second Coming of Christ.

Ezekiel 39:4 Thou shalt fall upon the mountains of Israel, thou, and all thy bands, and the people that is with thee: I will give thee unto the ravenous birds of every sort, and to the beasts of the field to be devoured.

KEY POINT

After three and a half years the peace will be broken.

Peace Shattered

For three and a half years, the false peace covenant will be observed until it is interrupted by a sneak invasion from the north. The invading entity will be composed of six countries: five of which are named and the sixth is described as coming from the far north. Apparently this refers to one of the states of the former Russian union. As Ezekiel 38 and 39 indicate, the invasion will be met by a series of catastrophes from God, which will wipe out the army.

Great Tribulation Begins

After the period of peace is broken, the Great Tribulation will begin. Because the Great Tribulation will begin without warning as indicated in Matthew 24:15, it will fulfill the prediction that it will bring sudden destruction upon the world. The Great Tribulation is described as a period during which the Antichrist proclaims himself as god over the whole world as well as world ruler and attempts to kill all who will not honor him both as god and ruler.

FURTHER STUDY

Daniel 9:27
(covenant upon)

Ezekiel 38:2, 5–6
(six countries)

Matthew 24:15–28
(Great Tribulation)

1 Thessalonians 5:3
(sudden destruction)

Daniel 11:36–37; Revelation 13:7 (world ruler)

Revelation 13:15
(attempts to kill)

PROPHETIC AGES CONTRASTED

The day of the Lord contrasts our present day of grace when God is not attempting to judge sin or bring it into final judgment. Since the church will be raptured before this day, people who are Christians today do not have to fear this period.

> **1 Thessalonians 5:4–5** But ye, brethren, are not in darkness, that that day should overtake you as a thief. Ye are all the children of light, and the children of the day: we are not of the night, nor of darkness.

Day and Night Contrasted

The day of grace contrasts the night of the <u>Great Tribulation</u>. We have further confirmation that those who are raptured who belong to the preceding period will not experience the wrath of God in 1 Thessalonians 5:9: "For God hath not appointed us to wrath, but to obtain salvation by our Lord Jesus Christ." This provides further evidence that the church will not go through the Tribulation and will be raptured before the day of the Lord begins.

REMEMBER THIS

We who have the hope of salvation are urged in 1 Thessalonians 5 to watch and be sober, or vigilant. Our lives are to be characterized by faith and love. We are to comfort each other with the hope of seeing Christ face-to-face and spending eternity in heaven. Such knowledge helps us persevere through all life's sufferings and trials now. We are also to encourage each other to good Christian life and conduct.

FURTHER STUDY
1 Thessalonians 5:11–24;
Revelation 6–18
(Great Tribulation)
Revelation 7:1–8 (144,000)

Saints in Heaven and on Earth Contrasted

Revelation 7 pictures <u>144,000</u> Israelites who are sealed, or saved, and protected through the Great Tribulation. By contrast, Revelation 7:9 pictures the saints in heaven as a multitude of kingdoms, tongues, and peoples. The question is asked, "Who are these people?" The answer: "These are they which came out of great tribulation, and have washed their robes, and made them white in the blood of the Lamb" (Revelation 7:14).

Millions will be saved and become Christians during the Tribulation. Those who do so are not promised to be kept physically safe from God's wrath as it falls on unbelievers on the earth. The believers will be sealed, however, or kept spiritually safe. Although most people who become believers during the Tribulation will be <u>martyred</u> for their faith, their souls will enter God's eternal presence.

> FURTHER STUDY
> Revelation 7:9–17; 17:6;
> 19:2; 20:4 (martyred)

Horrific judgments on earth will cause such carnage that billions will die, including some of those who have become Christians during the Tribulation. Tremendous death and suffering are particularly prophesied for Israel in that period. Zechariah 13:8 declares: "And it shall come to pass, that in all the land, saith the Lord, two parts therein shall be cut off and die; but the third shall be left therein."

What Others are Saying:

Dr. Spiros Zodhiates: During the time period of the Day of the Lord, there will be those who truly repent and are saved, but those who remain enemies of the Lord, whether Jews or Gentiles, will be punished.[2]

RAPTURE PRECEDES WRATH

2 Thessalonians 2:1–2 Now we beseech you, brethren, by the coming of our Lord Jesus Christ, and by our gathering together unto him, That ye be not soon shaken in mind, or be troubled, neither by spirit, nor by word, nor by letter as from us, as that the day of Christ [the Lord] is at hand.

Fighting Satan's Deception

Properly interpreted, Scripture confirms that the day of the Lord will not begin before the Rapture takes place. The Rapture is not a part of the day of the Lord. Second Thessalonians 2 gives background that indicates false teachers came into the church at Thessalonica after Paul left. These false teachers proclaimed that because sufferings and persecutions were prophesied to be a part of the day of the Lord—and since Christians of Paul's day were undergoing suffering and persecution—believers were already in the day of the Lord. Further, the false teachers taught that this view had been Paul's view.

The Thessalonians were deceived since they had not understood they were to be raptured before the day of the Lord began. Accordingly, Paul was indignant at this misrepresentation from the mind of Satan and wrote to correct their thinking.

Paul says that the day of the Lord will not come until after the "falling away." The day of the Lord will not come until after the man of sin assumes his position. This man of sin will exalt "himself above all that is called God, or that is worshipped; so that he as God sitteth in the temple of God, showing himself that he is God" (2 Thessalonians 2:4).

Exact Definitions Important

Second Thessalonians brings up a point that is often overlooked by teachers of prophecy: Exact wording should be observed. There is a difference between the day of the Lord "beginning" and the day of the Lord "coming." The expression "the day of the Lord comes" refers to the event that marks it. The phrase "the day of the Lord begins" refers to a time period. This is natural in our way of thinking. For instance, we might say, "When the Fourth of July comes we will have a parade." Obviously we won't have a parade when the Fourth of July begins because that would be at midnight; this statement refers to the event.

In 2 Thessalonians, Paul is saying that the full revelation of the Antichrist will come when he becomes world dictator and claims to be God. This will occur at the beginning of the Great Tribulation. He will be identified, however, long before this—more than three and a half years before the Second Coming of Christ when he conquers three of the ten nations and then all ten (Daniel 7). Paul is telling the Thessalonians that they are not in the day of the Lord because these major events have not occurred.

FURTHER STUDY
2 Thessalonians 2:6–12
(one who restrains)

Confirmation of this is mentioned concerning <u>one who restrains</u>. In the present age of grace after Pentecost, the Holy Spirit indwells the church and is a major force in restraining evil in the world. Christians form only a small percentage of the world's population, yet they strongly influence morality and rules of law in all nations. While interpreters have argued about this, the only true force in the world that holds back evil is God in the person of the Holy Spirit who indwells the church.

REMEMBER THIS

One of God's major means of holding back the flood tides of evil is to use the power of the Holy Spirit working in and through believers. If the Holy Spirit is not in the world then he cannot be in his church. Conversely, if the Holy Spirit is in his church then he is in the world. When the Holy Spirit is removed from earth it means the removal of the church has occurred. This will not happen until the Rapture.

Holy Spirit Taken Out

Clarification is also necessary on what it means to have the Holy Spirit taken out. He will be removed from the world scene at the Rapture in the same sense that he came on the day of Pentecost. The Holy Spirit cannot be restrained from being in the entire world. A similar situation is found in the case of Christ. Although Christ came to earth, lived among people, and then left and went to heaven, he said, "I am with you always." In other words, he is still everywhere, present in his deity, and indwelling the church along with the Holy Spirit.

LITERAL JUDGMENT!

Speaking as a whole, the revelation of the day of the Lord clearly indicates that following the Rapture of the church there will be a terrible time of literal divine judgment on the world that far exceeds anything God has ever done in the past. The description of Revelation 6–18 is graphic. It is not symbolic, as some have said. It is realistic as it affects all humankind.

When the Second Coming of Christ occurs, a great majority of the world's population will have already been killed and the cities will have been reduced to rubble by the earthquake of Revelation 16:18–20.

REMEMBER THIS

The Rapture is a blessed hope (Titus 2:13) and means of deliverance from this present evil world for those who put their trust in Christ in this day of grace. Our hope is not deliverance *through* the Great Tribulation but deliverance *from* it. The church will be caught up to meet the Lord in the air and will be in heaven while the great events of the day of the Lord are fulfilled on earth.

THINK ABOUT IT

The exhortation to live a life that is in keeping with God's high calling is the main teaching of the Bible. Believing that we will escape God's wrath during the Tribulation does not give Christians an excuse to sin or to give up and wait on a hilltop for the Rapture. If Christ appears today, will he find us busy about his Father's business?

HEADLINE HIGHLIGHT

CNN.com

U.S. page
Doomsday Clock Advances 5 Minutes: Asian nuclear tests bring 'midnight' closer
Posted June 11, 1998

CHICAGO (CNN) - Doomsday drew closer on Thursday and is now just nine minutes away, according to the keepers of the symbolic Doomsday Clock. Worried by recent nuclear test explosions in India and Pakistan, the minute hand of the clock—a measure of how close humankind is to destroying itself—was moved to nine minutes before midnight, with midnight representing a worldwide nuclear holocaust . . .

The decision on what the Doomsday Clock should read is made by officials from the Bulletin of the Atomic Scientists, a publication that has been tracking the world's slide toward nuclear confrontation since 1947 . . .

History of the Doomsday Clock

The Doomsday Clock was created in 1947—two years after the United States used nuclear weapons against Japan in World War II—and set at seven minutes to midnight.

Since then, the clock has been moved both forward and backward, 15 times in all, reflecting international tensions and the developments of the nuclear age. The closest it ever came to "doomsday" was in 1953, not long after the United States and the Soviet Union both tested hydrogen bombs. In that year, the clock read two minutes until midnight . . .

The Doomsday Clock first began ticking beneath a monument at the University of Chicago where nuclear energy was born in 1941 during the Manhattan Project.

The atomic scientists who founded the Bulletin—and created the clock—did so in hopes of ensuring that nuclear weapons were never again used in war.

PROPHETIC IMPACT

Atomic scientists, who are among the most intelligent people on earth, believe this planet is ticking down toward nuclear Armageddon. They are right about humankind's rush to that biblically prophesied event. How much of the destruction will be nuclear is fodder for speculation.

The scientists miss the mark, however, when they believe Armageddon could take place at any given moment in time, based upon who is willing to pull the thermonuclear trigger or who first accidentally starts man's final war.

God is in total control. He will determine the timing of these catastrophic events. God terms the time of apocalypse "the day of the Lord." That day will begin with a specific event, according to 2 Peter 3:10: "But the day of the Lord will come as a thief in the night; in the which the heavens shall pass away with a great noise, and the elements shall melt with fervent heat, the earth also and the works that are therein shall be burned up."

Peter prophesies the whole period known as the "day of the Lord." The beginning of the day of the Lord will be as much a surprise as a burglar breaking into a home. This is the Rapture of the church!

After the Rapture will come the era of the Tribulation, the Second Coming of Christ, the Millennium, the white throne judgment, and the remaking of the heavens and the earth.

FURTHER STUDY
Revelation 20:11–15
(white throne)
Revelation 21:1 (remaking)

The atomic scientists are right about one thing: The catastrophic intervention that could lead to Armageddon could begin at any moment. But it will not be thermonuclear bombs raining down. It will be when millions of Christians suddenly disappear from the earth.

CHAPTER WRAP-UP

- Old Testament prophets, especially Isaiah and Joel, speak of the day of the Lord in terms of terrible judgments from God that will disastrously affect the heavens and the earth.

- God shows his mercy by promising in Joel 2:28–32 that he will pour out his spirit on his people (those who are believers at that time).

- First Thessalonians 5 pictures the day of the Lord as a future time that will come as a thief in the night.

- Scripture shows that the time between the Rapture and the Second Coming is more than seven years. The sequence of events will begin with the Rapture and the revival of the Roman Empire.

- The Antichrist, the man of sin, will come onto the end-time scene during the first part of the Tribulation. He will appear to be a peacemaker, but he will actually cause great death and destruction.

- Contrasts can be drawn between this present age (the age of grace) and the tribulation era. God is not presently judging the world for sin in the sense that he will during the Tribulation. Now is the time of God's gospel light; the Tribulation is a time of sin-filled darkness and wrath.

- The day of the Lord will not begin until the Rapture takes place and the Holy Spirit is taken out of this world. During the Tribulation, Christians of the church age will be enjoying comfort, peace, and joy in heaven.

- The day of the Lord will be a literal time of judgment from which the Christians in the age of grace will be delivered.

Millennium

BY DAVID ALLEN LEWIS

Let's Get Started

Revelation chapter 20 expresses the concept of an observable and fully operational Millennium, or thousand-year kingdom of God on earth. The earthly manifestation of this kingdom endures for a short time. It is only a small, though extremely important, part of the kingdom of God.

THE MILLENNIUM PROPHECY

Isaiah 9:6–7 For unto us a child is born, unto us a son is given: and the government shall be upon his shoulder: and his name shall be called Wonderful, Counsellor, The mighty God, The everlasting Father, the Prince of Peace. Of the increase of his government and peace there shall be no end, upon the throne of David, and upon his kingdom, to order it, and to establish it with judgment and with justice from henceforth even for ever. The zeal of the Lord of hosts will perform this.

A Kingdom Promised

Even before Christ was born, Isaiah prophesied about a coming kingdom ruled by God. The millennial kingdom is but one segment of God's prophetic plan. It will follow a time of great tragedy and horror—the Great Tribulation—and it will be the transition era between this present world and the eternal state.

Jesus will set up his millennial kingdom, claiming the throne of David atop Mount Moriah in the millennial temple. Christ will restore the earth to a beautiful status from the decimation of the seven-year period of the apocalypse that immediately precedes his Second Coming.

> **Revelation 20:6** Blessed and holy is he that hath part in the **first resurrection**: on such the **second death** hath no power, but they shall be priests of God and of Christ, and shall reign with him a thousand years.

Ruling Promised

Humankind has for centuries talked and written about a glorious somewhere, someday, some way, but it all has been fiction. Utopia, Shangri-la, nirvana, or whatever the fallen minds of humans have conjured—all of their desires to bring heaven to earth have been empty, hopeless gestures.

God's Word, the Bible, promises an earthly kingdom where peace prevails, health abounds, and prosperity overflows beyond measure. The millennial reign of the Lord Jesus Christ will one day fulfill that prophetic promise. It is not pie-in-the-sky fantasy. It is truth from the very heart and mind of the living God!

That glorious future kingdom of Jesus Christ, the King of kings and Lord of lords, will be home to all who love, obey, and worship him.

> **KEY TERMS**
>
> **first resurrection:** *Christ's arising from death*
> **second death:** *eternal separation from God in hell*

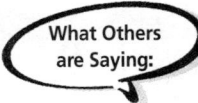

What Others are Saying:

Daymond R. Duck: During the Millennium, there will be no need for the United Nations and the World Court because nations and leaders will place themselves under the rule of Christ. There will be no poverty, no theft, no war, only one God, and pure worship. With Jesus on the throne, this world will be the wonderful place God always intended.[1]

KEY POINT

The Millennium is not the end; it is the beginning, the precursor to eternity.

Luke 1:31–33 And, behold, thou shalt conceive in thy womb, and bring forth a son, and shalt call his name Jesus. He shall be great, and shall be called the Son of the Highest: and the Lord God shall give unto him the throne of his father David: And he shall reign over the house of Jacob for ever; and of his kingdom there shall be no end.

Perfect Authority Promised

KEY TERM

Jacob: *son of Isaac, son of Abraham, forefather of the nation Israel*

FURTHER STUDY

Revelation 2:27
(rod of iron)

Jesus will reign over the house of **Jacob** (the Jews) and the entire world from the throne of David in Jerusalem. His rule will be with a <u>rod of iron</u>. This means that injustice, unfairness, maltreatment, and sinful activity of any kind will not be tolerated. Such acts will be broken instantly, and the perpetrator brought to perfect justice.

Jesus' government will be an absolute dictatorship, but it will not be a dictatorship like those of present-day earth. It will be a rule based upon the pure love of God, who gave his only Son for the people he will now be ruling over.

What Others are Saying:

Tim LaHaye: Mary's son, Jesus the Messiah, will reign over Israel forever. Since His ascension Christ reigns in heaven, but He will not reign over Israel until He sets up the Millennial Kingdom after His second coming. Secondly, Jesus will reign over His people Israel forever (2 Sam. 7:16).[2]

MILLENNIUM DEFINED

KEY TERMS

writer: *John*

Apocalypse: *another name for the Book of Revelation*

FURTHER STUDY

Revelation 20:2–7
(six times)

Six times the **writer** of the **Apocalypse** confirms that the kingdom of God on earth will last for a thousand years. (The Greek *chiliai etos* is translated *mille annum* in Latin. Our English translations correctly render *chiliai etos*, "a thousand years.")

We come by our theological use of the modern word "millennium" by combining the Latin *"mille,"* meaning "thousand," and *"annum,"* meaning "year." This awesome word does not mean just any thousand-year period of time but rather the kingdom of God on this earth when wars will be over and blessed peace shall prevail all over the earth. There will be no more genocide, violence, holocaust, robbery, rape, abuse, murder, or terrorism. Jesus will reign as king. There will be no more politics or elections, for earth will have a just government, a benevolent theocracy administered by our sovereign Christ.

Isaiah 65:22–25 They shall not build, and another inhabit; they shall not plant, and another eat: for as the days of a tree are the days of my people, and mine elect shall long enjoy the work of their hands. They shall not labour in vain, nor bring forth trouble; for they are the seed of the blessed of the Lord, and their offspring with them. And it shall come to pass, that before they call, I will answer, and while they are yet speaking, I will hear. The wolf and the lamb shall feed together, and the lion shall eat straw like the bullock: and the dust shall be the serpent's meat. They shall not hurt nor destroy in all my holy mountain, saith the Lord.

Differing Millennial Concepts

There was a time when the academic meaning of the word "millennium" equated to the Christian's definition of the word. Webster's original dictionary, published in 1828, defined it this way: "a thousand years; a word used to denote the thousand years mentioned in Revelation 20 during which period Satan shall be bound and restrained from seducing men to sin, and Christ shall reign on earth with his saints."[3]

For the Bible-believing Christian, the word "millennium" is filled with hope, which engenders anticipation of a glorious future for the born-again church and redeemed Israel. Isaiah paints a wonderful picture of a wondrous messianic age.

Millennium Trivialized

Now, however, we can no longer use the exquisite term "millennium" in its Christian context without qualifying it by adding the word "biblical." For example, we say, "The only place where the biblical Millennium is referenced in Scripture as a thousand-year period of time is in Revelation 20."

Since the advent of the year 2000 and the turn of a century, the word has inundated the world via advertising hype. To celebrate the turn of the millennium, the number 2000 and the word "millennium" were used to promote the sale of automobiles, Spaghetti-Os, Spam, soap, gambling schemes, video games, underwear, and countless collector items and memorabilia.

The word "millennium" falls too easily from lips that don't know how to speak of godly things. The Millennium has been trivialized and rendered meaningless, in any theological sense, to all but born-again people.

THE APOCALYPSE

KEY POINT

Hollywood and the news media portray the apocalypse erroneously.

Today, Hollywood scriptwriters and the news media equate the apocalypse with doomsday, the end of civilization, the destruction of all things. Many times the scripts and plots of fiction portray someone who does or tries to do something to prevent the apocalypse from happening. This is compounded error for three reasons!

First, the word "revelation," the title of the last book of the New Testament, does not refer primarily to destruction; rather, it literally means "an unveiling" or "a revelation."

Second, no person is capable of stopping the apocalypse.

Third, secular thinking about the matter leaves our Lord Jesus Christ out of the equation when, in fact, he is at the center of the matter. For example, two passages in Revelation emphasize Christ's focal role:

- *Revelation 1:1–2:* This is the proper title of the last book of the Bible: "The Revelation of Jesus Christ, which God gave unto him, to shew unto his servants things which must shortly come to pass; and he sent and signified it by his angel unto his servant John: Who bare record of the word of God, and of the testimony of Jesus Christ, and of all things that he saw."
- *Revelation 19:10:* "And I fell at his [the angel's] feet to worship him. And he said unto me, See thou do it not: I am thy fellowservant, and of thy brethren that have the testimony of Jesus: worship God: for the testimony of Jesus is the spirit of prophecy."

REMEMBER THIS

"Apocalypse," in the biblical sense, is derived from the Greek *apokalupsis*, which is translated "revelation" in the last book of the Bible. That is why the Book of Revelation is sometimes called the Book of the Apocalypse. *Apokalupsis* appears eighteen times in the New Testament text and is variously translated in the King James Version as follows:

- "revelation"—twelve times
- "to be revealed"—two times
- "to lighten"—one time
- "manifestation"—one time
- "coming"—one time
- "appearing"—one time

BEYOND IMAGINATION

The magnificence of the Millennium far exceeds anything we can imagine. Scripture gives us descriptive glimpses but does not answer all of our questions. We know many things with certainty though we do not know them completely. People will live long, healthy lives throughout the Millennium. Scripture seems to imply that the only people who <u>do not live</u> the full one thousand years are those who commit sin and do not seek forgiveness.

FURTHER STUDY
Isaiah 65:20 (do not live)

We do know Christ's kingdom will come and his purpose will be done on earth as it is in heaven.

The words of the hymnist will be fully realized:

> The sands of time are sinking,
> The dawn of heaven breaks;
> The summer morn I've sighed for,
> The fair sweet morn awakes.
> Dark, dark, has been the midnight,
> But dayspring is at hand,
> And glory, glory dwelleth
> In Immanuel's land![4]

Foreign & Commonwealth Office of the British Government

Foreign Policy: Global: International Organisations page
Taken from Internet Monday, April 22, 2002
Millennium Summit

HEADLINE HIGHLIGHT

The Millennium Summit in New York on 6-8 September was the largest ever gathering of heads of state/ government. It was a unique opportunity for leaders to push forward the UN agenda on topics such as poverty eradication, peacekeeping reform and Africa.

The UK was represented by the Prime Minister, Tony Blair, whose speech concentrated on two key themes; reform of peacekeeping operations and the way forward for Africa. On peacekeeping reform, he highlighted the need for the UN to 'alter radically its planning, intelligence and analysis, and develop a far more substantial professional military staff.' . . .

He concluded by reiterating the call to renew the UN, stressing that the UN is a force for good. 'If it did not exist, we would need to invent it.' . . .

In his closing address, UN Secretary-General, Kofi Annan, said he had been struck by the convergence of views from leaders at the Summit. He went on to say that the UN's first priority had to be the eradication of extreme poverty. He also highlighted the importance of a fairer world economy in an era of globalisation; called for support of the Brahimi Report on reforming UN peacekeeping; . . . and referred to the leaders' insistence on the need for continued reform of the UN. He noted that, although leaders had sketched

out clear directions for adapting the UN to its new
role in the new century, they themselves were the
UN and they therefore shared in the responsibility
to reach the goals that had been set.

The Millennium Declaration on the future role of
the UN was adopted on 8 September. The Declaration
spells out values and principles, as well as goals
in the key priority areas of peace, development,
the environment, human rights, protecting the
vulnerable, the special needs of Africa, and
strengthening the UN.

PROPHETIC IMPACT

Aspiring to better humankind's plight upon earth is a noble gesture. The trouble comes when the fallen human mind comes into the picture.

Promises of making earth a utopia have been around since Babel when Nimrod and the tower builders determined to bring together the whole world in an effort to take charge of their collective destiny (Genesis 11:1–9). The problem was they left God out of the equation, and God judged them for it.

The Millennium Summits of our day exhibit the same fatal flaw. They can never succeed, no matter how noble their intentions. The true Millennium Summit will be when Jesus Christ sits on the throne of David atop the millennial temple in millennial Jerusalem for one thousand years (Revelation 20:4).

CHAPTER WRAP-UP

- The Millennium is an expression of God's kingdom on earth as foretold in Revelation 20. It is one thousand years in duration. It comes to earth upon Christ's return at the end of the Tribulation.

- This promised kingdom will feature peace and perfect justice. It is the precursor to eternity.

- The term "millennium" used to mean the thousand-year reign of Christ on earth, but now the word has lost its biblical meaning.

- Since the year 2000, the term "millennium" has been used for promoting everything from products and causes to TV shows. The world system and its people don't understand the word's spiritual and literal significance.

- The word "apocalypse" is also misunderstood and misrepresented by Hollywood and the news media.

- The Millennium will be a time of unimaginable peace, health, and goodwill.

The Eternal Earth

BY JACK VAN IMPE

Let's Get Started

I am often asked if there are terms or concepts in the Word of God that might be synonymous with the Millennium, the thousand-year reign of Christ when the earth is blanketed with universal peace and serenity. Throughout the Bible numerous terms describe this period of tranquility to be administered under righteous governance.

NEW TESTAMENT ON THE MILLENNIUM

The New Testament uses many words to describe the Millennium. Some of those words are as follows:

- *Kingdom of Heaven:* "Blessed are they which are persecuted for righteousness' sake: for theirs is the kingdom of heaven" (Matthew 5:10).
- *Regeneration:* "And Jesus said unto them, 'Verily I say unto you, That ye which have followed me, in the regeneration when the Son of man shall sit in the throne of his glory, ye also shall sit upon twelve thrones, judging the twelve tribes of Israel'" (Matthew 19:28).

- *Last Day:* "And this is the will of him that sent me, that every one which seeth the Son, and believeth on him, may have everlasting life: and I will raise him up at the last day" (John 6:40).
- *Times of Refreshing:* "Repent ye therefore, and be converted, that your sins may be blotted out, when the times of refreshing shall come from the presence of the Lord" (Acts 3:19).
- *Times of Restitution:* "Whom the heaven must receive until the times of restitution of all things, which God hath spoken by the mouth of all his holy prophets since the world began" (Acts 3:21).
- *Day of Our Lord:* "Who shall also confirm you unto the end, that ye may be blameless in the day of our Lord Jesus Christ" (1 Corinthians 1:8).

See also Philippians 4:5; 2 Thessalonians 2:7–10; Hebrews 9:28; 1 Peter 4:13; and Revelation 1:7.

SUPREME HONEYMOON!

KEY POINT

The Millennium will give the earth long-lasting refreshment.

KEY TERMS

regeneration: *renewed to original status*
restitution: *restoration*
day of our Lord: *when Christ reigns and rules on earth*

FURTHER STUDY
Genesis 3 (Adam's fall)

If you have never thought of the Millennium in its overarching biblical context, realize that the thousand-year reign of Christ will be much more than simply ten centuries of divine rule. It will be the rule of Christ and his bride who descend from heaven to complete the **regeneration** of our planet. After so many centuries of experiencing earth's endless wars, illness, animosity, and strife, the Millennium will bring times of refreshing. This won't be the fleeting "pause that refreshes," to which recent generations have become accustomed; rather, it will be the kind of long-lasting, spiritual refreshment that only God can provide for his people.

Ultimately, there will be a **restitution** of all things—when all will be made new and when an original, pristine, Garden of Eden environment will again be the order of the day, because it will be the **day of our Lord** Jesus Christ. This restitution will take place under a government of righteousness and holiness such as the world has never experienced since Adam's fall.

A THEOCRACY

The great Bible prophecy scholar J. Dwight Pentecost has said that there are many views on the Millennium and all it will entail. Therefore, there is confusion. He says we must **inductively** study God's Word to understand it.

To Pentecost's conclusion, I can only say, "Stop, look, and listen!" As we do, we cannot help but conclude that the millennial government will be an earthly kingdom—a **theocracy**—the rule of God on earth, thereby distinguishing it from a strictly "spiritual reign" that may have occurred in the hearts of humankind through the many centuries of human history. Christ's rule will be real. People will know, firsthand, of God's enormous, divine power.

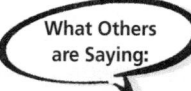

J. Dwight Pentecost: Through this maze of interpretations it is almost impossible to make one's way. The truths related to the kingdom will not be derived by an examination of the writings of men, but rather only by an inductive study of the teaching of the Word of God on this great subject.[1]

Literal Rule

What will the millennial government look like? First, Scripture counsels us to recognize the validity of more than one aspect of the kingdom.

Christ's millennial rule is literal, not figurative. This millennial kingdom must be regarded as the zenith of the prophetic program of God as it relates to the theocratic kingdom or Christ's rule of the earth. To some degree, this program

- began in the creation of earth's first man, Adam, in the Garden of Eden;
- continued through eons of every conceivable form of human government;
- was demonstrated repeatedly in the kingly line that ruled Israel; and
- has its culmination in the millennial kingdom, which in turn is superseded by the timeless eternity that follows.

I know that is a mouthful, but that has been the progression of events from the Garden of Eden to the present.

Though there is, to some degree, a rule of God in the age in which you and I now live that could be described by the word "kingdom," this rule does not yet fulfill those prophecies that speak directly to the millennial reign of Christ upon the earth. No matter how good earth has become by the close of the Millennium, at the Lord's Second Coming, planet Earth will be in terrible shape.

Earth in a Mess

The earth will be in such economic, political, and environmental shambles when the Lord returns that it will take every bit of Christ's rule of iron to make things happen. We cannot be specific about how earth will look during that period, but we can surmise the degree of degradation and decomposition by what we see on earth now.

Let me give you a few examples of where we are today. I'll simply ask you to let your imagination soar as you think of how planet Earth might look during the early years of the Millennium.

1 *The AIDS Problem:* Today, despite worldwide education and awareness programs, the medical authorities of the world said recently that almost 33 million people on earth are infected with HIV, two-thirds of them in sub-Saharan Africa.

If that is not enough bad news, Reuters reports new research that indicates one out of every 1,000 Americans could be infected with HIV without even knowing it. A new study in "low-risk" people revealed this disturbing news in light of a new urine test that has detected the AIDS virus in people who showed no signs of infection in their blood. Researchers said that this could explain why people mysteriously die of AIDS without having signs of HIV infection. They also said this fact could possibly help determine why some people resist infection.

2 *New Untreatable Form of Tuberculosis:* The British Broadcasting Corporation recently reported that because of Russia's overcrowded prison system, another deadly disease is

on the march. The report noted that prisoners have a new untreatable form of tuberculosis (TB) that is spreading with terrifying speed. Ten percent of Russia's 1 million prisoners suffer from TB and 20 percent of them are thought to have the drug-resistant strain—which means 20,000 face certain death. Once TB-infected prisoners step outside the prison gates, there is nothing to stop them from spreading the disease onto the streets of Russian cities and beyond. No one is immune, and new cases of tuberculosis are occurring all the time.

3 *Turmoil and Conflicts:* God's Word says this about where we are and where we are heading: "For nation shall rise against nation, and kingdom against kingdom: and there shall be famines, and pestilences, and earthquakes, in divers places. All these are the beginning of sorrows" (Matthew 24:7–8). These predictions are coming true.

CURRENT WORLD EVENTS

World Jewish leaders have reported an alarming rise in the number of attacks against Jews in Europe, saying anti-Semitism is at its worst level since World War II. Avi Beker, secretary-general of the World Jewish Congress, said there were 360 anti-Semitic incidents in France in the last two weeks of April 2002. A synagogue in Marseilles was burned to the ground. Jews are afraid to go to their synagogues, community centers, and schools for fear of violence against them.

Anti-Semitic violence in Europe has increased as Israel has retaliated against Palestinian terrorist attacks in Israel. The World Jewish Congress, an organization that represents Jewish groups from eighty countries, held a two-day emergency conference to discuss the recent violence. Belgium, where a half dozen attacks on Jewish institutions, including the burning of a bookstore and a shooting at a synagogue, was also mentioned as a trouble spot.

"There are Holocaust survivors who are telling their children: 'Look, this is exactly how it happened in the 1930s,'" Beker said, when anti-Semitism led to Hitler's reign and the mass slaughter of Jews.[2]

4 *Earth's Environmental Turbulence:* One of Russia's largest bodies of freshwater has already become a dead sea. The daily burning of huge areas of the Amazon rain forest destroys the lungs of the planet that produce the oxygen for the world. Increasingly poor weather and erosion rapidly expand the deserts of the Sahara, devastating northern Africa. "Deforestation" is the technical word; to the people who live there, the word is "hopelessness."

PROPHECY TO
WATCH FOR

Our world and its people have suffered for thousands of years because of the curse of selfishness and sin. Today, whose lungs do not feel the effects of debilitating smog from automobiles and industrial pollution? Millions have died or have been reduced to a life of pain because of air pollution. Even though it is bad now, imagine the ravages of the wars that will occur during the Great Tribulation and how they will further devastate our planet's delicate ecological systems. It will make the burning oil fields of Kuwait during the Gulf War look like a traditional Fourth of July barbecue.

Christ's Healing Hand

Praise God that Christ will heal the planet's wounds when he establishes his millennial kingdom. While there will be a massive rebuilding program, however, it will not be presto, *poof*—all is now well! It will not be that easy, and it will take years of harsh, righteous, dictatorial rule to set things straight.

JUDGE OF THE NATIONS

So how will Christ revive, revitalize, and restore the earth? What will be his divine strategy, and what will he use to return earth to its original status? The greatest restoration program in history is called "the times of refreshing" (Acts 3:19), "the time of restitution" (Acts 3:21), and "the regeneration" (Matthew 19:28).

Matthew 25:31–34, 41 When the Son of man shall come in his glory, and all the holy angels with him, then shall he sit upon the throne of his glory: And before him shall be gathered all nations; and he shall separate them one from another, as a shepherd divideth his sheep from the goats: And he shall set the sheep on his right hand, but the goats on the left. Then shall the King say unto them on his right hand, Come, ye blessed of my Father, inherit the kingdom prepared for you from the foundation of the world: . . . Then shall he say also unto them on the left hand, Depart from me, ye cursed, into everlasting fire, prepared for the devil and his angels.

Fit Subjects or Not

The times of refreshing and restitution may take years to complete; however, another occurrence will take only days and is virtually necessary to have a kingdom of peace and righteousness. It will begin as Christ judges the nations to determine whether they are fit subjects for the kingdom as Matthew described.

> **FURTHER STUDY**
> Isaiah 2:4
>   (judges the nations)
> Romans 2:5
>   (hardness of heart)
> Psalm 2:9, Revelation 19:15
>   (rod of iron)

Here the righteous rule of Christ will be administered with integrity and justice. Because of humankind's hardness of heart, however, Christ will have to break stubborn wills among the redeemed with a rod of iron.

THINK ABOUT IT

Jesus won't be a wimp when he rules as the King of kings. Multitudes of leaders will be under his governance—under his thumb—whether they like it or not. These leaders may think they control their nation's affairs, running their traditional, status quo programs, when, in reality, they will be servants doing our Lord's bidding.

> **Zechariah 14:9** The Lord shall be king over all the earth: in that day shall there be one Lord, and his name one.

Righteousness and Peace

What will be the result of this religious and political authority that Jesus Christ commands over the earth? Righteousness and peace. Isaiah 2:1–5 tells us that a millennial Temple will be built atop the Temple Mount in Jerusalem for Christ's thousand-year reign. The entire topography of Jerusalem and the region round about will be radically changed. The Temple will be raised high above the surrounding landscape.

All nations of earth will come to worship the King of kings and Lord of lords, Jesus Christ. People will, with great enthusiasm, greet each other with the words: "Let us go up to the mountain of the Lord, the God of Israel" (Isaiah 2:3).

Jesus will teach the people of all nations his truth and will judge in righteousness. He will enforce peace, which will bless all people for the first time since the fall in the Garden of Eden. Israel will, finally and forever, live in absolute peace with its neighbors.

Finally, the promise of the great spiritual "I ain't gonna study war no more" will become a reality. The mere physical presence of our great God and Savior Jesus Christ, ruling and reigning, will bring universal peace to earth.

FROM HOLLOW SLOGANS TO GOD'S PROMISES

Today, with nations continuing to arm themselves to the hilt, the only way to meet this world's crisis is for our Lord to intervene in the physical affairs of humans and set things straight.

With false doctrines spreading through ecclesiastical circles like wildfire; shallow, uninformed New Age thinking on the increase; and blasphemy against the name of Jesus as commonplace as breathing; only the personal presence of the King can set things right. It will take the return of Christ to this earth to deal with the challenges of the insane and dangerous international situation in which the world finds itself today.

THINK ABOUT IT

For centuries, men and women have promised peace to humankind. Politicians have guaranteed a "chicken in every pot." Every conceivable system of government has come and gone—all promising some degree of utopia. "The next election will make all things right," one promises. "Vote for me. I am the one who can turn the tables right side up. Put me in office and things will be different," says another. How foolish for us to believe a word of these hollow promises. It simply never happens.

PROPHECY TO WATCH FOR

When the blessed time of the Millennium comes, Romans 11:26 says Israel will be saved and living in her own unhindered land. In addition, at the beginning of the Millennium, Revelation 20:3 says Satan will be sent to writhe in the bottomless pit for one thousand years.

Zechariah 14:16 And it shall come to pass, that every one that is left of all the nations which came against Jerusalem shall even go up from year to year to worship the King . . .

Worship in Jerusalem

> **KEY TERM**
>
> **Feast of Tabernacles:** week long festival to commemorate Israel's forty years in the desert before entering the Promised Land
>
> **FURTHER STUDY**
>
> Matthew 25:34 (entered)
> Zechariah 16:16–19 (appear)
> Leviticus 23:33–43 (Feast of Tabernacles)

God will rule not only the nations, but also the hearts of humankind as well. However, there is one other matter to consider. Zechariah indicates that multitudes of unsaved people will also come into existence as they are born to the righteous believers who will have <u>entered</u> the kingdom at Christ's invitation. Because they will be born with the old nature, multitudes of unsaved people will replenish the earth right down to the Millennium's final hour.

Zechariah speaks of people from the Gentile nations who must <u>appear</u> in Jerusalem once a year to worship the King and to keep the **Feast of Tabernacles**. For those who fail to comply, there will be punishment.

One would think that the theocracy (God's government upon earth) would see all humanity enamored and totally dedicated to Christ. Not so! That's why the children born to believers during the thousand years reject Jesus and rebel against his reign at the conclusion of the one thousand years after being in his presence for thirty to forty generations. Revelation 20:7–9 depicts God's judgment upon earth's final revolutionaries. Sad, isn't it? But let's move ahead and dwell rather upon the great things that happen during this Millennium.

Isaiah 35:5–6 Then the eyes of the blind shall be opened, and the ears of the deaf shall be un-stopped. Then shall the lame man leap as an **hart**, and the tongue of the dumb sing . . .

TRUE PEACE AT LAST!

There will be nonstop, universal peace for one thousand years. Law and order will prevail. Righteousness shall cover the earth. Pollution will be no more. Wheelchairs, walkers, and canes will be thrown aside because of the healing. The universal curse placed by God upon the vegetable kingdom because of Adam's sin will have been removed. Farmland once useless will be fertile and productive. Isaiah 35:1–2 says, "The wilderness and the solitary place shall be glad for them; and the desert shall rejoice, and blossom as the rose. It shall blossom abundantly, and rejoice even with joy and singing."

Amos echoes the words of Isaiah: "Behold, the days come, saith the Lord, that the plowman shall overtake the reaper, and the treader of grapes him that soweth seed; and the mountains shall drop sweet wine, and all the hills shall melt" (9:13).

Can you imagine what life in the Millennium will be like? A pure river will flow from beneath the threshold of the throne of God. On either side of the river will grow the tree of life. Imagine! The leaves of this tree will not wither and will be used for medicinal purposes. The tree will produce a new crop of twelve different fruits each month.

KEY TERM

hart: *male deer*

FURTHER STUDY

Revelation 22:2 (healing)

Genesis 3:17–19 (curse)

Revelation 22:1 (pure river)

Revelation 22:2
(twelve different fruits)

But there's even more! The universal curse of the survival of the fittest will be removed from the animal kingdom. "The wolf also shall dwell with the lamb, and the leopard shall lie down with the kid; and the calf and the young lion and the fatling together; and a little child shall lead them. And the cow and the bear shall feed; their young ones shall lie down together: and the lion shall eat straw like the ox. And the suckling child shall play on the hole of the asp, and the weaned child shall put his hand on the cockatrice' den. They shall not hurt nor destroy in all my holy mountain (Isaiah 11:6–9a).

There will even be a shift in the operation of the celestial bodies, possibly even a dramatic shifting of the poles of the earth, resulting in a <u>universal climate</u> that will eliminate the extremes of cold and heat we experience today.

The physical health of humankind will so improve that today's "fitness craze" will go the way of unused treadmills and exercise bikes. If a person dies at the <u>age</u> of one hundred, his neighbors will shake their heads in despair, lamenting that their friend died in mere infancy.

Such will be the golden age of the earth ushered in at the Second Advent of the Lord of glory and governed righteously by our precious Lord Jesus.

FURTHER STUDY

Isaiah 30:26
   (universal climate)
Isaiah 65:20 (age)

KEY POINT

Living conditions will be ideal for health, comfort, and peace.

HEADLINE
  HIGHLIGHT

Near-Earth Object News & Updates

©1999 – 2002 SPACE.com, Inc.

Space-Based Missile Defense Needed to Thwart Asteroid Attacks

By Robert Roy Britt, Senior Science Writer
posted: 11:37 am ET
February 14, 2002

Earth is little more than a sitting duck in a cosmic shooting gallery, the scientists tell us. But that doesn't mean we can't shoot back. If an asteroid is ever found to have our planet in its sights, a carefully aimed missile can simply knock the rock off course. . . .

Some 587 large, potentially threatening asteroids have been found near Earth. All are bigger than 1 kilometer (0.6 miles), the threshold for what most researchers agree could cause global catastrophe. . . .

The weapons of choice [to deflect a killer asteroid headed for Earth] would be nuclear, however, and [Claudio Maccone at the Center for Astrodynamics in Turin, Italy] worries in his journal article that there would be significant political hurdles to getting any plan approved. . . .

"Many people's minds are still too much in the Cold War attitude," Maccone writes. "Since nuclear weapons in space are forbidden by international treatises [sic], a proposal to locate missiles with possible nuclear warheads at [strategic points in space] would immediately be perceived as an attempt to revive the Cold War."

Maccone thinks a new collective human conscience will need to emerge before much will be done to face the threat of asteroids.

"Only when humans will stop planning and conducting big wars among themselves, will the governments have more time to think about the new danger coming from space," he said. . . .

PROPHETIC IMPACT

Most people, even Christians who are truly close to the Lord, believe Bible prophecy is gloom and doom. News and entertainment media feed the worry that the apocalypse is beyond anyone's control—that what will be, will be, that the future offers nothing but dark, foreboding prospects.

Recently, we were told that an asteroid, which could have wiped out a large city, or caused even greater damage to earth, had come from space at such an angle that those who look for such things didn't see it until the danger was passed. The asteroid passed between earth and the moon, we were told.

God's prophetic Word foretells in Revelation 8:8–11 that two gigantic objects from space will hit the planet during the Tribulation. Although damaged and having suffered great loss of life, earth will continue to rotate and revolve as always.

Prophecy from the Bible is not a warning that earth will be destroyed. Bible prophecy promises that it is a "world without end"! (Isaiah 45:17; Ephesians 3:21).

God, who cannot lie, declares through his prophetic Word that someday he will make this sin-plagued planet into a "new earth," just as he will make "new heavens" (Isaiah 65:17; Isaiah 66:22; 2 Peter 3:13).

CHAPTER WRAP-UP

- Christ and his bride will descend from heaven to rule for one thousand years and complete the regeneration of planet Earth.

- There are several views of the Millennium, and a correct understanding will be gotten only through inductive study of the Word of God.

- Christ will return planet Earth to its pristine status from the shambles of today's world. The greatest restoration program in history is called "the times of refreshing," "the time of restitution," and "the regeneration."

- Christ will judge the nations and bring righteousness and peace.

- Christ's peace will bring vast change: Nature will be transformed, vegetation will no longer be cursed, and animals and people will live together in harmony.

- Following the thousand-year reign of Christ, the planet will be remade by God's holy fire. There is no end to planet Earth, only to the sin that is now so devastating to the world.

Conclusion: Planetary Impact!

BY WILLIAM T. JAMES

Let's Get Started

Throughout history humankind has struggled between hope for utopia on earth and despair over endless disasters, conflicts, and wars. Humankind has felt a collective ecstasy and pride over such events as the landing on the moon, the building of skyscrapers, and the rapid advance of technology. It has also felt defeat over the terror attacks in America, the lack of peace in the Middle East, the foreboding possibility of nuclear war.

Bible prophecy tells us this dichotomy of feeling will continue to the end of this age. Humankind will continue to attempt to control its destiny and that of the world. Satan's last-days missiles of hatred will continue to be aimed at the Jews. Yet God's judgments against the unbelievers during the Tribulation will cause a greater planetary impact than any act of racism, terrorism, or nuclear war.

At the same time God judges the unbelievers, he will provide a way of escape and ultimate utopian existence for his church and the remnant of those he will rescue during the tribulation period.

EYES TURNED UPWARD

Astronaut Neil Armstrong hopped from the bottom rung of the lunar lander's ladder and softly touched down on the powdery soil. His words upon contacting the moon's surface that day in 1969 have become a part of Americana like no other declaration. People of the world heard him say, "That's one small step for . . . man, one giant leap for mankind."

The singular tiny word lost in the transmission, because the static caused the words to break up as they traversed the black void, helped Armstrong capture the moment more profoundly than did the statement he actually made. He, in fact, said, "That's one small step for a man, one giant leap for mankind."

When he stepped from the ladder, Armstrong carried with him the aspirations of humankind since the time of the **antediluvians**. Humans' yearning to reach into the heavens has continued unabated since the days of the tower of <u>Babel</u>.

Apollo 11 represented not simply great achievement for the United States of America but for all humankind throughout the ages. The drive toward the stars seems partly God-engendered and partly Lucifer-engineered. This possibility is not so paradoxical as it might appear.

God, the Scriptures tell us, <u>created</u> the heavens. Jesus <u>ascended</u> into the clouds sometime after his resurrection. The **new Jerusalem** will <u>descend</u> from heaven to hover above planet Earth. We are told to "look up, and lift up your heads, for your redemption draweth nigh" (Luke 21:28). All eyes will be turned upward when the King of kings and Lord of lords returns to put an end to humankind's most catastrophic war, Armageddon.

> ### KEY TERMS
>
> **antediluvians:** *people living before the Flood in Noah's day*
>
> **new Jerusalem:** *heavenly city that will come to earth*
>
> ### FURTHER STUDY
>
> Genesis 11:1–9 (Babel)
>
> Genesis 1:1 (created)
>
> Mark 16:19 (ascended)
>
> Revelation 21:10–11 (descend)

THINK ABOUT IT

When contemplating God or when faced with powerful forces in nature, humans instinctively turn their eyes upward to the stars. This is undoubtedly because the Creator has put it in us to do so. Heaven is, after all, where he abides eternally.

Spiritual Insanity

Lucifer, the fallen angel now called Satan, tempts the creatures called humans, who also are fallen since the time of Eden. He whispers seductively into their ears that they are God and that they deserve to sit in the heavenlies, controlling their own destinies by doing what is right in their own eyes.

Humans' powerful drive to control their collective destiny in the heavens as well as on earth is spiritual insanity caused by the fallen state. Humans suffer from a sort of dementia because of sin. Their treachery and constant and willful desire to overrule the Creator God who made them is proof of their madness.

Even the name of the project that put humans on the moon shows the rebelliousness and pride in their hearts. In its sophistication and pride, modern humankind chose this name of Apollo for its reach for the stars. The ancient Greeks considered Apollo to be one of their greatest gods, the most magnificent in beauty and power.

Evils of Imagination

Am I saying the space program is sinful or insane? Of course not. God created us in his own image. Our ambitions, when they are of the right kind, are given by the Creator. This generation has lived during an era of near-miraculous achievements thanks to the imaginations of the most intellectually gifted and talented among us. Many, if not most, of those achievements, however, have been turned to evil use rather than to good. The reason this is true is told in God's Word.

- "There is none righteous, no, not one" (Romans 3:10).
- "The heart is deceitful above all things, and desperately wicked: who can know it?" (Jeremiah 17:9).

Upside-Down Thinking

> **KEY TERM**
>
> *reprobate:* sinful

Sadly, **reprobate** thinking more and more often rules the mind of humankind today. The same minds that have the highest regard for environmental concerns and for animal life think aborting a human child is no more to be concerned about than throwing a dirty diaper in the trash. In fact, throwing a dirty diaper in the trash is punishable by law if not done so in the environmentally safe way.

When one expresses disagreement with this low view of human life, one must be politically correct and always pause to qualify one's arguments so as not to be criticized for being insensitive. I have respect for the environment, for whales, eagles, and all other wildlife. I just believe human life deserves even higher respect and positive attention because humankind was created in God's own image.

Since reprobate reasoning, that is, upside-down thinking, often rules the minds of humankind, the successful Apollo project must be considered in less flattering terms than "one giant leap for mankind." The ultimate outcome of the feat for the improvement or the harm of humanity is yet to be determined.

When we think about what humans have done with the tiny atom, so far as thermonuclear weaponry is concerned, we can understand the need for caution in being overly optimistic about such a spectacular accomplishment as putting men on the moon.

HUMANISM'S PROBE

The United Nations envisions great things for the peoples of the world. Their brainstorming, however, centers around a strange dichotomy for thinkers of such good intentions.

The global elite want what is best for their constituencies (the peoples of the many sovereign nations who in most every case have not solicited their governance). These new world builders ignore national desires for independence and scheme for a single set of constitutional rules for all. These self-appointed leaders of planet Earth want everyone to live in equal environments, wealth, and health.

There is one major stipulation they find necessary to impose upon the rest of us. Some of us have to go; that is, some people will have to depart the planet they love so that this utopian existence can be achieved for those who are left.

Earth's Social Architects

The elitist planners will always **parse** their seemingly harsh pronouncements of population control with the thought that it will be accomplished through **attrition**. They call for increasingly stringent birth controls. Naturally, they will be the judges of who is to use these birth controls, who is to go from this life, and who is to stay. As difficult as it is to understand, the one-world planners are shooting for zero population growth and that policy is their officially sanctioned cornerstone.

> **KEY TERMS**
>
> **parse:** *critically examine*
> **attrition:** *normal deaths*
> **draconian:** *cruel*

Since the utopians proclaim they want only the best for all peoples of the world, it is confusing to try to understand how they intend to somehow rid the earth of massive numbers.

Abortion is one major ingredient of their zero growth strategy. The incessant call for toleration of the homosexual lifestyle, as part of the unity and inclusiveness agenda, appears to be another ingredient. Certainly, both abortion and homosexuality, in conjunction with **draconian** birth control implementation, are well underway. All are very effective at ridding the world of human beings.

Adolf Hitler had a somewhat similar agenda, didn't he? His agenda did not include encouraging homosexuality, of course. Quite the contrary, he included those people in his genocidal rampages. However, he threw in one ingredient the one-worlders have not yet added to their drive to reduce the unwanteds: eugenics—selective breeding. Astounding advances in genetics, DNA, genome research, and the practice of cloning, as humankind goes deeper into the new millennium, will make possible Hitler-like ventures into eugenics. Dare we think some future fuhrer will not make use of such perverted science?

Humanism's Deadly Pride

The twentieth century promised great things for the human race as that generation left the 1800s. The promises were fantastically exceeded in every respect.

Electricity, discovered for practical use by Edison, was captured by Westinghouse and others in spectacular technological break-throughs, dynamically changing the order of human life. Transportation advances exploded upon the scene, particularly in America, with Henry Ford, the Wright brothers, and others who created technologies that thrust humankind into a world full of thrilling possibilities. The Curies, Jonas Salk, and scientific pioneers pushed hard on the cutting edge of medical frontiers, expanding human longevity.

Probing by humanism's champions of self-sufficiency continue to impel us at a sometimes alarming rate from exciting possibilities toward the fearful future probabilities.

God's prophetic Word tells us that humanism will lead ultimately to the point that all people on earth will die unless Jesus Christ does not intervene and return to planet Earth: "And except those days should be shortened, there should no flesh be saved: but for the elect's sake those days shall be shortened" (Matthew 24:22). If God allowed humans to continue without his oversight and intervention, they would destroy themselves despite their every effort to do otherwise.

A GENERATION AT GROUND ZERO

Our generation stands at Ground Zero so far as Bible prophecy is concerned. Prophetic signals continue to burst from today's news, from conflicts in the Middle East to Islam's violent rumblings to globalists' influence of public policy to economic trends and technological advances. Even a cursory examination of modern Israel and its ongoing drama is proof of where this generation stands on God's timeline. This generation might well be the one that sees the coming of the Antichrist.

Christ's shout, "Come up hither!" (Revelation 4:1), will first issue forth, calling Christians into the clouds to be forever with him. It could happen at any moment.

"For when they shall say, Peace and safety; then sudden destruction cometh upon them" (1 Thessalonians 5:3).

Note the use of the pronoun "them." God's Word refers here to those who are not his children, the unsaved of the world. They have nothing to look forward to but God's wrath. Believers, on the other hand, have God's promise: "For God hath not appointed us to wrath, but to obtain salvation by our Lord Jesus Christ"(1 Thessalonians 5:9). Those who reject Christ and fall for the phony peace offered by the Antichrist will receive the Almighty's holy, righteous wrath.

REMEMBER THIS

Nowhere in Scripture is the believer of the church age instructed or commanded to look for the Antichrist or for the wrath of God. Rather, we are to look for the blessed hope, Jesus Christ. We are told to "look up, and lift up your heads, for your redemption draweth nigh" (Luke 21:28).

When Christ Speaks

Christ will at one stupendous moment in time shout with the voice of the archangel and the trump of God the words "Come up hither!" For God's child, that future moment promises not fear but prospects too wonderful to fathom!

Christians—all people of the church age, both living and those who have died since Pentecost—will supernaturally rocket from the planet in that moment, "in the twinkling of an eye" (1 Corinthians 15:52). That launch will require no help from NASA or anyone else. God's **omnipotence** will power that greatest of all explorations into the heavenlies. Truly, that will be a giant leap for humankind!

> **KEY TERM**
>
> **omnipotence:** *unlimited power*

THINK ABOUT IT

What do you need to be a part of this truly giant leap for humankind? "Believe on the Lord Jesus Christ, and thou shalt be saved" (Acts 16:31). Even so, come, Lord Jesus!

Experts Quoted

Nick Begich is the coauthor of *Earth Rising: The Revolution*.

George W. Braswell Jr., is the author of *Islam: Its Prophet, Peoples, Politics and Power*.

Dave Breese, see *Contributors*.

General Wesley Clark was NATO Supreme Allied Commander in Europe from 1997–2000.

Joan Collins is a Florida businesswoman and Christian life advocate who has extensively researched the Constitutional Convention.

Timothy Demy is a prophecy scholar and author of numerous books and journal articles on social issues, ethics, and theology.

Dr. James Dobson is a best-selling author of numerous books and founder of Focus on the Family.

Daymond R. Duck, see *Contributors*.

Oriana Fallaci is an Italian journalist, war correspondent, and novelist.

Mike Frost is a former Canadian intelligence officer.

Billy Graham is the most recognized Christian evangelist of our time.

Dr. Oliver B. Greene is founder of the Gospel Hour and author of more than one hundred books explaining the Bible.

Hank Hanegraaff, president of Christian Research Institute, is host of *Bible Answer Man* radio program.

Kenneth Hill is a broadcaster and author.

Dr. Arthur Kac, a Hebrew Christian, is a lifelong student of the Hebrew Bible, biblical literature, and biblical and universal history.

Gary Kah, Christian speaker and author of *En Route to Global Occupation*, is the founder and executive director of Hope for the World, a Christian apologetics organization.

Tim LaHaye is a prophecy scholar and coauthor of the *Left Behind* series as well as author of numerous books related to biblical prophecy, the end times, and Christian living.

Peter LaLonde is a Christian filmmaker, broadcaster, and author of many books concerning the end times.

Hal Lindsey is a prophecy scholar and author of numerous books, including *The Late Great Planet Earth.*

Dr. J. Vernon McGee is the late host of Thru the Bible Radio program.

Golda Meir was a Russian-born American-Israeli prime minister.

Stanley Monteith is a radio broadcaster, writer, and lecturer on geopolitics and AIDS issues.

Martin Niemoller was a German Lutheran pastor in Germany during the 1930s and 1940s.

J. Dwight Pentecost is a seminary professor and author of *Things to Come.*

Dennis Prager is an author, lecturer, teacher, and theologian with a nationally syndicated radio talk show.

Robert J. Pranger is a scholar and writer.

Randall Price, president of World of the Bible Ministries, has lived in Jerusalem and done graduate studies at the Hebrew University of Jerusalem. He lectures worldwide about Bible prophecy and directs tours in the Bible lands.

Renauld Showers, professor for the Institute of Biblical Studies, is the author of *Maranatha, Our Lord Come.*

Charles Stanley is a pastor, author, and founder of In Touch Ministries.

Jessica Sterns is the author of *The Ultimate Terrorists.*

John Walvoord, see *Contributors.*

Tertullian was an early church father and theologian.

Ravi Zacharias is a Christian philosopher, theologian, writer, and speaker.

Dr. Spiro Zodhiates is a recognized authority on the Greek New Testament and president of Advancing the Ministries of the Gospel, formerly known as American Mission to the Greeks.

Endnotes

CHAPTER 1 — WILLIAM T. JAMES

1. Gary Kah, interviewed on *Point of View* radio program with host Marlin Maddoux, week of August 21, 2000.
2. Ibid.
3. Joel Skousen's World Affairs Brief, November 30, 2001, <www.joelskousen.com> (November 30, 2001).

CHAPTER 2 — ZOLA LEVITT

1. Dennis Prager, "Is It 1938 Again for the Jews?" *WorldNetDaily.com,* April 9, 2002, <http://www.worldnetdaily.com/news/article.asp?ARTICLE_ID=27146> (July 1, 2002).
2. Ibid.
3. Sarah Hall, "Death to Jewish Settlers, Says Anti-Zionist Poet," *The Guardian* (April 13, 2002).
4. Associated Press, "Anti-Jewish Attacks in France Up," April 17, 2002.
5. Tony Czuczka, Associated Press, "Germany Takes Sharp Tone on Israel," April 15, 2002.
6. Oriana Fallaci, "On Jew-Hatred in Europe," *Israel Insider,* April 17, 2002.
7. David Naveh, "Inciting and Educating Children Towards Hate, Anti-Semitism and Violence in the Palestinian Authority," Government of Israel Publications, March 2002.
8. Donna Abu-Nasr, "Saudi Telethon Raises $55 Million for Palestinians," Associated Press, April 12, 2002.
9. "15 Girls Die as Zealots Drive Them into Blaze," *The Daily Telegraph* (London), March 15, 2002.

CHAPTER 3 — PHILLIP GOODMAN

1. "Putin's True Colors," *Newsweek*, Special Edition, Dec. 2000–Feb. 2001, 30.
2. Owen Matthews, "The Putin Crackdown," *Newsweek*, June 26, 2000, 17–19.
3. Mortimer B. Zuckerman, "A Great Step Backward," *U.S. News and World Report*, October 9, 2000, 76.
4. Sarah Karush, "Putin Wants to Reign in Regions," *USA Today*, May 30, 2000.

5. Sarah Karush, "Free Press Struggles in Russia," *USA Today*, August 14, 2000.

6. Andrea Eger, "Hoping for a Better Life," *Tulsa World*, April 3, 2000, A-13.

7. Beverly Nickles, "Will Putin Protect Religious Liberty," *Christianity Today*, August 7, 2000, 31.

8. Andrew Kramer, "Russia's Military to Make Deep Cuts," *Tulsa World*, September 9, 2000, A-7.

9. As reported on *60 Minutes*, August 27, 2000.

10. "Periscope: Clinton—Back to Moscow to Start START III," *Newsweek*, April 24, 2000, 5.

11. William L. Krewson, "Russia Eyes the Middle East," *Israel My Glory*, October-November 1999, 19–21; Center for Defense Information: Current World Nuclear Arsenals, Russian Nuclear Arsenal, Strategic Delivery Systems <http://www.cdi.org/issues/nukef&f/database/nukestab.html#Russia> (April 30, 2002).

12. CIA World Factbook, <http://www.odci.gov/cia/publications/factbook/index.html Israel/Military> (April 29, 2002).

13. Associated Press, "Proposal Would Give Jerusalem to God," *Tulsa World*, August 8, 2000, A-5.

14. I am indebted to geographer Ralph G. Chappell for his insights regarding the possible invasion routes, as well as the strategic considerations required by the geographic template of the land.

15. Russia's allies in the invasion—Iran, Turkey, and Libya—also have air force potential, according to the CIA World Factbook 1999, <http://www.odci.gov/cia/publications/factbook/index.html Iran/Turkey/Libya/Military> (April 29, 2002).

16. I am deeply indebted to Dian and Dr. Charles L. Pack, my coworkers at Thy Kingdom Come Ministries for the enormous amount of research they have done on prophecy and current events over a fifty-five-year ministry, and for providing me access to their extensive file collection.

CHAPTER 4 — LARRY SPARGIMINO

1. James A. Beverly, "Islam a Religion of Peace?" *Christianity Today*, January 17, 2002, 32.

2. Ibid.

3. Ibid.

4. Ibid.

5. George W. Braswell Jr., *Islam: Its Prophet, Peoples, Politics and Power* (Nashville, TN: Broadman and Holman, 1996), 15.

6. Silas, "Muhammad, Islam and Terrorism," Answering-Islam.org, <www.answering-islam.org/Silas/terrorism.htm> (May 23, 2002).

7. David Van Biema, "Why the Bombers Keep Coming," *Time*, December 17, 2001, 53.

8. Caesar E. Farah, "Political Islam Is a Threat to the West" in *Islam:*

Opposing Viewpoints, ed. David Bender and Bruno Leone (San Diego: Greenhaven Press, 1995), 191.

9. Ravi Zacharias, *Jesus Among Other Gods* (Nashville, TN: Word, 2000), 159.

10. Evan Thomas, "The Road to September 11," *U.S. News and World Report,* October 1, 2001, 40.

11. Jessica Sterns, *The Ultimate Terrorists* (Cambridge, MA: Harvard University Press, 1999), 6–9.

12. Dr. Israr Ahmed, address before the convention of the Islamic Society of North America, Columbus, Ohio, September 11, 1995.

13. Eric Pooley, "Recipe for More Terror," *Time.com,* December 17, 2001, <www.time.com>.

14. Shlomo Mordechai, "America's Double Standard," *Israel Today,* January 2001, 14.

15. Tim McGirk, "In the Crosshairs," *Time.com,* December 13, 2001, <www.time.com>.

16. Scott Macleod, "Relief or Aiding Terrorists?" *Time.com,* December 17, 2001, <www.time.com>.

17. See the discussion of this Hadith in Norma Archbold, *The Mountains of Israel: The Bible and the West Bank* (Jerusalem: Phoebe's Song, 1993), 84ff.

18. Taken from Victor Mordecai, *Is Fanatic Islam Global Threat?* 4th ed. (Springfield, MO: privately published, 1995), 7.

CHAPTER 8 — J. R. CHURCH

1. "6 Billion . . . and Counting," *Time,* October 18, 1999, 61.

2. Dr. Paul Ehrlich, *The Population Bomb* (New York: Ballantine, 1968), 84.

3. Ibid., 86.

4. Ibid., 86–87.

5. Ibid., 91–93.

6. Ibid., foreword.

7. Mihajlo Mesarqvic and Eduard Pestel, *Mankind at the Turning Point: The Second Report to the Club of Rome* (New York: Dutton, 1974), preface.

8. Ibid., 3.

9. Ibid., 17.

CHAPTER 9 — DAYMOND R. DUCK

1. Associated Press, "Zimbabwe to Seize 69% of White Farmers' Land," *The Commercial Appeal* (Memphis, Tennessee), August 2, 2000, A7.

2. Robert J. Pranger, The World Book Encyclopedia, vol. 21, 1990, 26.

3. Oliver B. Greene, *The Gospel According to Matthew,* vol. 1 (Greenville, SC: Gospel Hour, 1971), 318.

4. Billy Graham, *Storm Warning* (Dallas, TX: Word, 1992), 9, 197.

CHAPTER 10 — LARRY SPARGIMINO

1. Barbara Palmer, "Science Notebook," *The Daily Oklahoman,* July 11, 2000, 1-B.
2. Samuel Widner, "Digital Angel," *Forbes*, January 4, 2000, 42.
3. Jack Rowlett, "Visions 21: Our Work, Our World," *Time,* May 22, 2000, 62.
4. Timothy Demy, "Technology and Theology," *Issues 2000* (Grand Rapids, MI: Kregel, 1999), 37.
5. Ibid., 41.
6. Gary DeMar, *Last Days Madness* (Atlanta: American Vision, 1997), 425–426.
7. Ibid., 426.
8. Ibid., 427.
9. *Dictionary of New Testament Theology*, vol. 2 (Grand Rapids, MI: Zondervan, 1975), 573.
10. Richard Abanes, *End-Time Visions: The Road to Armageddon?* (Nashville, TN: Broadman and Holman, 1998), 278.
11. Ray Summers, *Worthy Is the Lamb* (Nashville, TN: Broadman, 1951), 33.
12. D. Ian Hopper, "Carnivore: Hungry for Your Rights," *Washingtonpost.com* (May 23, 2000), 18.
13. Ibid.
14. Carole Fernhold, "Visions 21: How Will We Live?" *Time,* February 21, 2000, 21.
15. Kenneth Hill and Joan Collins, *Constitution in Crisis* (Oklahoma City, OK: Hearthstone, 1994), 52.
16. Anthony Novak, "A Great Vacuum Cleaner in the Sky," *Time*, April 14, 2000, 8.
17. Ibid.
18. Jerry Guiltner, Southwest Radio Church Ministries, *Bible in the News*, aired March 29, 2000.
19. Ray Kurzweil, *The Age of Spiritual Machines* (New York: Viking, 1999); quoted in *Forbes,* November 30, 1998.
20. Jerry Builtner, Southwest Radio Church Ministries, *Bible in the News*, aired December 22, 1998.
21. Nick Begich and James Roderick, *Earth Rising: The Revolution* (Anchorage, AK: Earthpulse, 2000), 109–110.
22. Ibid., 15–16.
23. Ibid., 21.
24. Ibid., 56.
25. Stanley Monteith, "The Population Control Agenda," Radio Liberty, P.O. Box 13, Santa Cruz, CA 95063.
26. Ibid.
27. Ibid.
28. Begich and Roderick, *Earth Rising,* 94.
29. Ibid., 62.

CHAPTER 11 — J. MICHAEL HILE

1. Thomas Ice and Timothy Demy, eds., *When the Trumpet Sounds* (Eugene, OR: Harvest House, 1995), 443.
2. Chart adapted from Donald Wesley Patten, *The Biblical Flood and the Ice Epoch: A Study in Scientific History* (Pacific Meridian Publishing Company, 1966).
3. U.S. Department of Health and Human Services National Center for Health Statistics.
4. U.S. Census Bureau, International Data Base.
5. Hal Lindsey with C. C. Carlson, *The Terminal Generation* (Grand Rapids, MI: Fleming H. Revell, 1976), 173.
6. James C. Dobson with Richard Swenson, "Oblivious to the End," audiotape CT352/26199, Focus on the Family, 2001.
7. Billy Graham, *Approaching Hoofbeats* (Waco, TX: Word, 1983), 209–211.

CHAPTER 12 — WILLIAM T. JAMES

This chapter is adapted and reprinted from William T. James, "Suddenly Gone" in *Raging into Apocalypse* (Green Forest, AR: New Leaf Press, 1995).

1. Hal Lindsey, "The Rapture Factor," audio/video, Hal Lindsey Ministries.
2. Mal Couch, ed., *Dictionary of Premillennial Theology* (Grand Rapids, MI: Kregel, 1996), 258.
3. Peter LaLonde, "The John Ankerberg Show," audio/video, 1995.
4. John Walvoord, "The John Ankerberg Show," audio/video, 1995.
5. Charles Stanley, "Message on the Rapture," audio/video, In Touch Ministries, March 1995.
6. J. Dwight Pentecost, *Things to Come: A Study in Biblical Eschatology* (Grand Rapids, MI: Academie Books, 1964), 203–204.
7. Renauld Showers, "The John Ankerberg Show," audio/video, 1995.
8. J. Vernon McGee, Thru the Bible with J. Vernon McGee, audiotape, vol. 3 (Pasadena, CA: Thru the Bible Radio, 1983).
9. Thomas Ice, "Examining an Ancient Pre-Trib Rapture Statement," *RaptureReady.com*, June 8, 2002, <raptureme.com/featured/tt14.html> (June 26, 2002).
10. J. Vernon McGee, Thru the Bible with J. Vernon McGee, audiotape, vol. 5 (Pasadena, CA: Thru the Bible Radio, 1983).
11. Dave Breese, *John Ankerberg Show*, Dallas, TX, March 1995.
12. Hal Lindsey, "The Rapture Factor," audio/video, Hal Lindsey Ministries.

CHAPTER 13 — AGUSTA HARTING

1. Bruce McConkie, *Mormon Doctrine* (Salt Lake City: Bookcraft, 1966), 295. Quoting Teachings, 345–347.

2. John Ankerberg, *The Facts on Channeling* (Eugene, OR: Harvest House, 1988), 16. Quoting the spirit who wrote through medium Helen Schuckman in *A Course in Miracles*, 1977.
3. Hank Hanegraaff, "Reincarnation and Resurrection Are Mutually Exclusive," *CRI Journal* 22, no. 4 (2000): 62.

CHAPTER 14 — ARNOLD G. FRUCHTENBAUM

1. A more detailed study on the Campaign of Armageddon and other prophetic issues may be found in *The Footsteps of the Messiah* by Arnold G. Fruchtenbaum, published by Ariel Ministries.
2. Arthur W. Kac, *The Rebirth of the State of Israel: Is It of God or of Men?* (Grand Rapids, MI: Baker Book House, 1976), 337.
3. Randall Price, *Jerusalem in Prophecy* (Eugene, OR: Harvest House, 1998), 189.

CHAPTER 15 — JOHN WALVOORD

1. Tim LaHaye, ed., *Prophecy Study Bible King James Version* (Chattanooga, TN: AMG Publishers, 2000), 1287.
2. Spiros Zodhiates, ed., *The Complete Word Study New Testament* (Chattanooga, TN: AMG Publishers, 1991), 676.

CHAPTER 16 — DAVID ALLEN LEWIS

1. Daymond R. Duck, *Prophecies of the Bible: God's Word for the Biblically-Inept* (Lancaster, PA: Starburst Publishers, 2000), 125.
2. Tim LaHaye, *Prophecy Study Bible* (Chattanooga, TN: AMG Publishers, 2000), 1082.
3. Noah Webster, *Noah Webster's First Edition of an American Dictionary of the English Language,* vol. 2 (San Francisco: G & C Merriam Co., 1828).
4. Thomas Ice and Timothy Demy, *The Truth about the Millennium* (Eugene, OR: Harvest House, 1996), 44–45.

CHAPTER 17 — JACK VAN IMPE

1. J. Dwight Pentecost, *Things to Come: A Study in Biblical Eschatology* (Grand Rapids, MI: Zondervan, 1958), 427–428.
2. Raf Casert, "Jewish Chiefs: Anti-Semitism Grows" *Miami.com*, April 23, 2002, <http://www.miami.com/mld/miami/news/world/3118232.htm> (July 1, 2002).

Contributors

Dave Breese

Dave Breese was a well-known author, lecturer, and radio and television broadcaster. He was committed to the advancement of Christianity through evangelistic crusades, the distribution of literature, and the broadcast media. His radio broadcasts, *Dave Breese Reports* and *Dave Breese Reporting*, as well as *The King Is Coming* telecast, touched the world with the message of the gospel.

The ministries of which he was president, Christian Destiny in Hillsboro, Kansas, and World Prophetic Ministry in Colton, California, continue to build upon the firm foundation he laid.

Among his most popular books are *Satan's Ten Most Believable Lies*, *The Marks of a Cult*, *Living for Eternity*, *Discover Your Destiny*, and *Seven Men Who Rule the World from the Grave*.

Joseph R. Chambers

Joseph R. Chambers, senior minister of Paw Creek Church of God at Charlotte, North Carolina, is president of Paw Creek Christian Academy, which he founded in 1974. He is radio host of a weekly two-hour program, *Open Bible Dialogue*, and has been involved in broadcast and writing ministries on the evangelical-political scene for more than twenty-five years. His published works include *The Challenge of the Ministry; Miracles: My Father's Delight;* and *A Palace for the Antichrist*. In addition, he has written many articles for various publications.

J. R. Church

J. R. Church is author of numerous books about Bible prophecy, including *Hidden Prophecies in the Song of Moses*, *Hidden Prophecies in the Psalms*, and *Guardians of the Grail*. He has also written *They Pierced the Veil*, a commentary on the minor prophets, and *The Mystery of the Menorah*. Church developed the ministry, Prophecy in the News, which publishes a monthly newspaper on prophetic research. He also presents a syndicated television broadcast by the same name and frequently speaks on matters pertaining to Bible prophecy at national and international prophecy conferences and seminars.

Daymond R. Duck

Daymond R. Duck is a best-selling author of a shelf full of books, including *On the Brink: Easy-to-Understand End-Time Bible Prophecy*; *Revelation: God's Word for the Biblically-Inept*; *Daniel: God's Word for the Biblically-Inept* and *Prophecies of the Bible: God's Word for the Biblically-Inept*. His book on Revelation has been so successful that it has been adapted and published in a second version called *Revelation for Teens*. He is currently working with Joan Hake Robie on a book called *End-Time Survival Handbook*. He has been interviewed on numerous Christian radio programs, speaks at prophecy conferences, and preaches at revivals.

Arno Froese

Arno Froese is executive editor of the English edition of *Midnight Call* magazine. He is also the writer and speaker for the Message of the Month Club and the host of a unique bimonthly Video Club. Froese has written hundreds of magazine articles and tape features, and has contributed articles and chapters to various books about Bible prophecy. Additionally, he has sponsored more than fifty national and international prophecy conferences and has led numerous study tours through the Holy Land. He has written many books, including *How Democracy Will Elect the Antichrist* and *The Great Mystery of the Rapture*.

Arnold G. Fruchtenbaum

Arnold G. Fruchtenbaum is the director of Ariel Ministries, which offers intensive biblical and theological training of Jewish believers. He has written seven books, including *Israelology: The Missing Link in Systematic Theology*; *The Footsteps of the Messiah: A Study of the Sequence of Prophetic Events*; *Jesus Was a Jew*; *Hebrew Christianity: Its Theology, History, and Philosophy*; *Biblical Lovemaking: A Study of The Song of Solomon*; *A Passover Haggadah for Jewish Believers*; and *Messianic Christology*. Fruchtenbaum is a frequent contributor to compiled books and often speaks and teaches at conferences.

Phillip Goodman

Phillip Goodman is the founder and former president of The Spiritual Armour Project, Inc. He formed a partnership with Dr. Charles L. Pack of Thy Kingdom Come ministries in 2000, where he now serves as vice president. Together they host the weekly *Prophecy Watch* telecast and produce a series of Prophecy Watch Web Casts at Prophecywatch.com. They also conduct the annual Tulsa Prophecy Conference, publish the *Spirit of Prophecy Newsletter*, and conduct prophecy retreats utilizing PowerPoint presentations. He and his wife, Mary, a native of Bethlehem, Israel, have four sons: Christopher, Seth, Andrew, and Sean.

Agusta Harting

Agusta Harting and her husband, Dan, were proselytized by Mormon missionaries in 1966 and joined the Church of Jesus Christ of Latter-Day Saints (the Mormons) the same year. They held various positions of leadership in the LDS church for fifteen years. In 1981, they came to faith in the real Jesus Christ and the following year founded Families Against Cults of Indiana, Inc. They have been in full-time ministry ever since. Experts on the cults, the Hartings have spoken in hundreds of churches. They publish a monthly newsletter about cults and host a weekly thirty-minute program on Christian radio.

J. Michael Hile

J. Michael (Mike) Hile is president of Signs of Our Times, a biblically based research ministry. He is author of *Timeline 2000*, a study of three 400- and 430-year time cycles between 2000 B.C. and A.D. 2000. Hile was also a contributor to *Piercing the Future* by William T. James, in which he discussed Russia's and China's roles in Bible prophecy. He served as a writer for a weekly Christian publication for several years and has been active as a teacher and speaker. He and his wife, Joyce, have four children: Monica, Kristel, Brent, and Jordan; and two grandchildren: Jacob and Luke.

William T. James

William T. (Terry) James has written, compiled, or edited nine previous books: *Storming Toward Armageddon*; *The Triumphant Return of Christ*; *Earth's Final Days*; *Raging into Apocalypse*; *Foreshocks of Antichrist*; *Forewarning: Approaching the Final Battle Between Heaven and Hell*; *Foreshadows of Wrath and Redemption,* and *Piercing the Future*. Additionally, he wrote a novel, *Jacob's Trouble 666*. He has also contributed articles to Tim LaHaye's *Prophecy Study Bible* as well as other books and publications.

Totally blind since 1993, Terry says he is "thankful to my Lord for helping me better focus on the things he truly wants me to research, see, and report through my writing." He has been a frequent speaker and guest of prophecy conferences and radio programs.

Zola Levitt

Zola Levitt is a Jewish believer educated in the synagogues and brought to the Messiah in 1971. He is best known as the host of the national weekly television program *Zola Levitt Presents*. Levitt is also a widely published author of more than forty books in several languages. Zola Levitt Ministries, Inc., a teaching and evangelistic association, is guided by the standard of Romans 1:16: "To the Jew first and also to the Gentile."

David Allen Lewis

David Allen Lewis is a clergyman and author of thirty-seven books. He also serves as a lecturer, Bible teacher, evangelist, researcher, and publisher. Lewis is active in national and international circles in promoting the welfare of the church, Israel, and the Jewish people. Ordained with the Assemblies of God, he works widely throughout the scope of the churches. He and his wife, Ramona, live in Springfield, Missouri. They have two daughters, Rebecca and Cassandra, who with their families live and work in Jerusalem.

Larry Spargimino

Larry Spargimino is currently associate pastor and editor with Southwest Radio Church Ministry in Oklahoma City, and also the editor of the monthly *Bible in the News* magazine. His two latest books are *The Anti-Prophets* and *Religion of Peace or Refuge for Terror*. Having an earned Ph.D. from Southwestern Baptist Theological Seminary in Fort Worth, Texas, Dr. Spargimino has pastored several local churches and is currently teaching at the American College and Seminary in Oklahoma City.

Jack Van Impe

Bible scholar Jack Van Impe is founder and president of Jack Van Impe Ministries International. With thirty-five books to his credit, he also presents a television show distributed to 116 nations, does international radio programs, speaks at mass crusades across the United States and Canada, and operates a web site that reports more than two million visits each year. Van Impe and his wife, Rexella, live in Troy, Michigan.

John F. Walvoord

John F. Walvoord, theologian, pastor, and author, is described in the *Twentieth Century Dictionary of Christian Biography* as "one of the most influential dispensational theologians." Walvoord has been prominent in prophetic conferences advocating a pretribulational Rapture, a literal one-thousand-year Millennium, and distinction between Israel and the church. He has written thirty books, including *The Rapture Question, The Millennial Kingdom*, and *The Prophecy Knowledge Handbook*, as well as a number of commentaries. Walvoord became president of Dallas Theological Seminary in 1953 and chancellor upon his retirement in 1986.

BOOKS BY DAVE BREESE

SEVEN MEN WHO RULE THE WORLD FROM THE GRAVE

This book is widely used in high schools and colleges as part of their curriculum.

In reviewing this book, **Christian Literature World** said: *"This is an excellent book, well written, clearly understandable, and unashamed in upholding the teaching of Scripture as the only antidote to the current malevolent influences that threaten both our personal freedom and even perhaps the very existence of the world as we know it."*

Suggested Contribution: $15

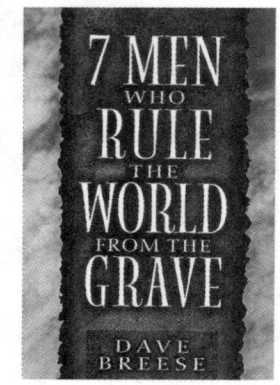

THE MARKS OF A CULT
The Warning Signs of False Teachings

This new expanded book gives you the information you need to recognize false teachings and religions. Discover solid helps for countering the growing influence of these counterfeit gospels.

Suggested Contribution: $15

SATAN'S TEN MOST BELIEVABLE LIES

This book was written out of increased concern that we, the Christians of our time, be not ignorant of his devices and describes ten of the enemy's false doctrines. Each chapter defines a satanic lie and compares it to the truth found in Scripture.

Suggested Contribution: $15

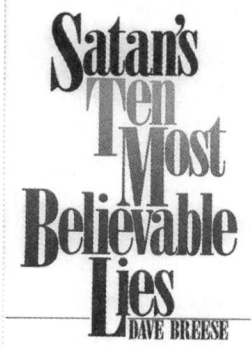

There are many other titles available in booklet, audio or video. *Write or call:*
CHRISTIAN DESTINY, INC.
P. O. Box 7
Hillsboro, KS 67063-0007
website: www.christiandestiny.org Phone: 1-800-777-8806 e-mail: dbreese@southwind.net

To write to William T. James please use the following address:

William T. James
P.O. Box 1108
Benton, Arkansas 72018

Look for William T. James's exciting new book, coming soon from Starburst Publishers!

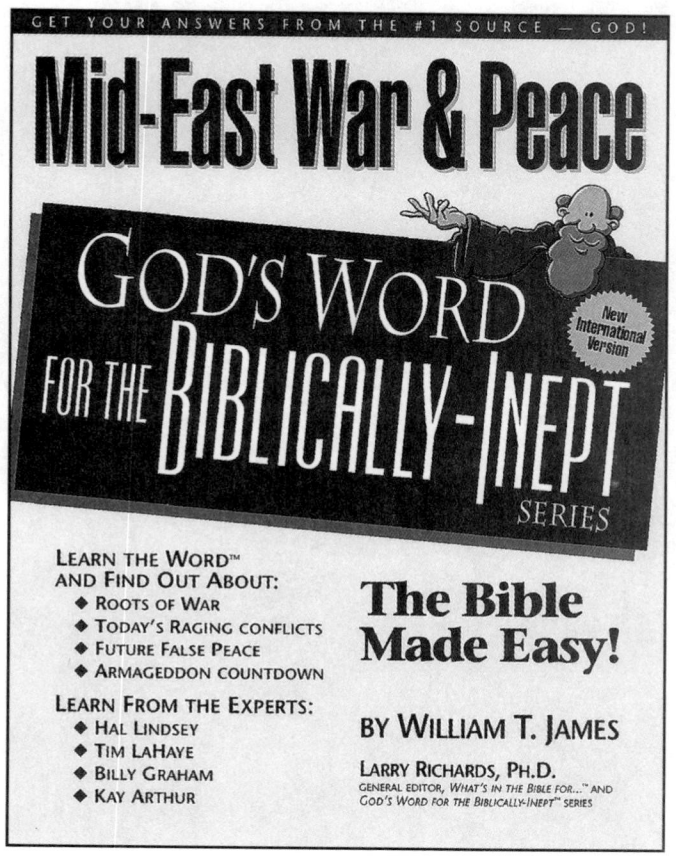

Families Against Cults

OF INDIANA

"Ye should earnestly contend for the faith, which was once delivered to the Saints." — JUDE 3

● Who are Dan & Agusta Harting?

Dan & Agusta were in the cult of Mormonism for fifteen years and worked in that organization in numerous capacities. Dan held the highest priesthood of Mormonism and served on the "bishopric" for years. Agusta held many positions in the Mormon Church, always in the area of teaching. The Hartings participated in the secret temple rituals.

Since the Lord brought them out of Mormonism in 1981, they have been involved in Christian outreach to those perishing in the cults and the occult.

They have spoken in hundreds of churches of many denominations and have been guests on many TV and radio talk shows, both Christian and secular, in the United States and overseas. The Hartings have counseled hundreds of people and distraught family members involved in the cults and the occult. Dan and Agusta host their own radio show "From Fables to Faith, and have written articles for Christian Advocate newspaper and "Love-Trax" Christian magazine. Agusta was a contributor to the book, *Contend for the Faith*, published by EMNR.

For further information or to have them as guest speakers, call

317-844-8055

Or write to

Families Against Cults

PO Box 491
Carmel, IN 46082-0491

Dr. Charles L. Pack   Thy Kingdom Come, Inc.   Phillip Goodman

7301 E. 14th St., Tulsa, OK 74112 (918)-835-6978
tkc@prophecywatch.com

We believe the prophetic signs of our day indicate that the time of Great Tribulation followed by the Second Coming of Jesus Christ to the earth to set up His Kingdom is near. We believe that prior to those events our Lord will come without warning to take all true believers to Heaven in an event called the Rapture.

It is our goal to reach people worldwide with the Gospel of Salvation in Jesus Christ through the teaching of Bible Prophecy. It is our ministry to alert the Body of Christ to the imminent fulfillment of Bible Prophecy, underscoring the urgency to live "by every word that proceedeth out of the mouth of God. " (Matthew 4:4).

Here are the seven arms of our ministry through which we perform our mission at Thy Kingdom Come, Inc., (a 501-C3 ministry).

1. The Annual Tulsa International Prophecy Conference— where each year five of the best prophecy speakers in the world join Dr. Charles L. Pack and Phillip Goodman of Thy Kingdom Come at the Sheraton Tulsa the first week of April to conduct Mid America's largest and longest running conference on Bible Prophecy.

2. The Spirit of Prophecy Newsletter— is an 8 page, 4-color bi-monthly publication featuring the latest news in light of the prophecies of the Bible (not the other way around). The first 6-months subscription is free.

3. The Email Prophecy Update— provides monthly highlights of world events which are particularly relevant when cast in the light of Bible Prophecy, each item referenced to a pertinent prophetic passage. Sign on at *thykingdomcometulsa.com*

4. The Prophecy Watch Television Program— is a half hour weekly telecast featuring Dr. Charles L. Pack and Phillip Goodman which focuses on what the Bible has to say regarding the events of our day and the coming days, and is seen nationally on the Sky Angel satellite system, as well as locally in some areas.

5. Web Page— at *thykingdomcometulsa.com* is updated monthly with Bible Prophecy information, including a Learning Page, an Emerging World of Bible Prophecy Page, a library of prophecy archives, and ministry information.

6. Web Casts— at *prophecywatch.com* include more than two-dozen twenty-minute full-color "prophecy-in-pictures" programs accessed over the Internet from our Web Page. The current format is Real Player, soon to be converted to Power Point.

7. Prophecy Retreats— are monthly Power Point "prophecy-in-pictures" presentations held in Tulsa as well as by invitation to other church locations. Biblically-based Be In Health Retreats are also held monthly.

ZOLA LEVITT PRESENTS

Television:
Zola Levitt Presents airs on ABC-FAM at midnight each Sunday (that's 1:00 AM Monday morning on both coasts and either 11:00 PM or 2:00 AM Mountain Time).

TBN broadcasts Zola's program on Monday mornings at 8:00 ET, 7:00 CT, 6:00 MT and 5:00 PT. Please see our airing schedule at www.levitt.com.

Free Newsletter:
The *Levitt Letter* features solid Bible teaching, Hebrew lessons, prophecy updates plus much more

Israel Tours:
Zola's Israel Tours, Mediterranean Cruises & Kibbutz Tours – each April, June, September and December

Teaching Materials:
For info on Zola's books, music, videos with teaching in Israel, Hebrew-Christian correspondence course, etc., please contact:

Web Site:
www.levitt.com
1-800-WONDERS
(966-3377)
(214) 696-8844
Box 12268, Dallas, TX 75225

JUST FOR TEENS!

PRESENTING

The God's Word for the Biblically-Inept™ Series

The God's Word for the Biblically-Inept™ series is a best-seller with over 300,000 books sold! This series of user-friendly commentaries is designed to make reading the Bible easy, educational, and fun! Including verse-by-verse Bible studies, topical studies, and overviews, these books mix information from experts with icons, illustrations, and timelines.

Acts by Robert C. Girard	ISBN 189201646X	$17.99
The Bible by Larry Richards	ISBN 0914984551	$16.95
Daniel by Daymond R. Duck	ISBN 0914984489	$16.95
Genesis by Joyce L. Gibson	ISBN 1892016125	$16.95
Health & Nutrition by Kathleen O'Bannon Baldinger	ISBN 0914984055	$16.95
John by Lin Johnson	ISBN 1892016435	$16.95
Life of Christ, Volume 1 by Robert C. Girard	ISBN 1892016230	$16.95
Life of Christ, Volume 2 by Robert C. Girard	ISBN 1892016397	$16.95
Luke by Joyce L. Gibson	ISBN 1892016478	$17.99
Mark by Scott Pinzon	ISBN 1892016362	$17.99
Matthew by Dewey and Rebecca Bertolini	ISBN 1892016486	$17.99
Men of the Bible by D. Larry Miller	ISBN 1892016079	$16.95
Prophecies of the Bible by Daymond R. Duck	ISBN 1892016222	$16.95
Revelation by Daymond R. Duck	ISBN 0914984985	$16.95
Romans by Gib Martin	ISBN 1892016273	$16.95
Women of the Bible by Kathy Collard Miller	ISBN 0914984063	$16.95

The End-Times Survival Handbook: What to Expect Before the Rapture and What to Do about It Now

By Joan Hake Robie and Daymond R. Duck

We are living in perilous times. This practical, easy-to-understand prophecy handbook tells us *what* the Bible says we should expect and *how* to prepare for it. Includes tips on waging spiritual warfare, praying for friends and family, avoiding fear, preparing for persecution, and protecting physical, financial, and spiritual health for self, church and community.

(trade paper)   ISBN 1892016729 $13.99

Announcing Our New Series!!!

What's in the Bible for . . .™

From the creators of the **God's Word for the Biblically-Inept™** series comes the innovative **What's in the Bible for . . .™** series. Scripture has certain things to say to certain people, but without a guide, hunting down *all* of what the Bible has to say to you can be overwhelming. Borrowing the user-friendly format of the **God's Word for the Biblically-Inept™** series, this new series spotlights those passages and themes of Scripture that are relevant to particular groups of people. Whether you're young or old, married or single, male or female, this series will simplify the very important process of applying the Bible to your life.

 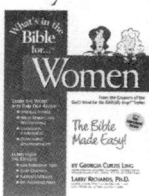  

What's in the Bible for . . .™ Couples *Kathy Collard Miller and D. Larry Miller*
(trade paper)   ISBN 1892016028 $16.95

What's in the Bible for . . .™ Women *Georgia Curtis Ling*
(trade paper)   ISBN 1892016109 $16.95

What's in the Bible for . . .™ Mothers *Judy Bodmer*
(trade paper)   ISBN 1892016265 $17.99

What's in the Bible for . . .™ Teens *Mark Littleton and Jeanette Gardner Littleton*
(trade paper)   ISBN 1892016052 $16.95

•   **Learn more at www.biblicallyinept.com**   •

Purchasing Information
www.starburstpublishers.com

Books are available from your favorite bookstore, either from current stock or special order. To assist bookstores in locating your selection, be sure to give title, author, and ISBN. If unable to purchase from a bookstore, you may order direct from STARBURST PUBLISHERS®. When ordering please enclose full payment plus shipping and handling as follows:

Post Office	**United Parcel Service (UPS)**	**Canada and Overseas**
$4.00 with a purchase of up to $20.00	$5.00 (up to $20.00)	Determined by destination
$5.00 ($20.01–$50.00)	$7.00 ($20.01–$50.00)	
9% of purchase price for purchases of $50.01 and up	12% ($50.01 and up)	

Payment in U.S. funds only. Please allow two to four weeks minimum for delivery by USPS (longer for overseas and Canada). Allow two to seven working days for delivery by UPS. Make checks payable to and mail to: **Starburst Publishers®**, P.O. Box 4123, Lancaster, PA 17604. Credit card orders may be placed by calling 1-800-441-1456, Mon–Fri, 8:30 A.M. to 5:30 P.M. Eastern Standard Time. Prices are subject to change without notice. For a catalog send a 9 x 12 self-addressed envelope with four first-class stamps.